TROPHIES AND TRIBULATIONS

Forty Years of Kent Cricket

TROPHIES AND TRIBULATIONS

CLIVE ELLIS AND MARK PENNELL

Greenwich Publishing

First published in the United Kingdom in 2010 by Greenwich Publishing,
2 Arlington Place, London SE10 8NR

British Library Cataloguing in Publication Data
A catalogue record for this book is available from the British Library.

ISBN 978-0-9564081-0-5

Main front cover photograph: Kent celebrate their Benson and Hedges Cup triumph in
1973. Courtesy of Press Association.

Inset photograph: Former Kent seamer David Masters dismisses Rob Key in the Friends
Provident Trophy final in 2008. Courtesy of Getty Images.

Cover design, typesetting and origination by
Graham Hales (www.grahamhales.co.uk)

Printed and bound in Great Britain by
Cromwell Press Group, Trowbridge, Wiltshire.

Contents

Acknowledgements

The authors would like to thank all the players (individually listed under Notes and Sources) whose reminiscences have helped to make this book what we believe is a valuable account of an extraordinary era for Kent cricket. Both the authors and publishers are grateful to Ron Green and Barry Hollis (former managing editor and current picture services editor of the Kent Messenger Group) for making available an extensive archive of photographs. Thanks also go to the KMG photographers whose pictures feature in the book, to Ady Kerry, a regular freelance presence at the county's home matches, and Graham Morris. Finally, the authors would like to acknowledge the help and advice of Kent's honorary statistician, Howard Milton, honorary curator David Robertson and ever cheerful scorer Jack Foley.

Mark Pennell writes: A project which I envisaged might take two months ultimately extended into five. So, with humble apologies for my short fuse, inattentive behaviour and general lack of understanding while engrossed in the writing of my first book, I would like to thank the following: my beautiful wife and most ardent supporter, Annabelle; our children, Oliver and Chloe; and my parents-in-law, Mick and Christine Turner, for allowing the use of their 'quiet room' and colossal dining table. I am also indebted to the players, relatives, friends and colleagues, whose interest in this 'labour of love' helped spur me on when I needed it most. Finally, my deepest gratitude goes to my co-author, Clive Ellis. Thanks for conceiving the idea, having faith in me to produce and for showing patience way beyond the norm.

The publishers would like to thank the following: Graham Hales (a tower of strength in the design and typesetting department), Alison Cooper (for her varied design input), Anton Rippon (for recommending Graham Hales), Mark Baldwin and Bruce Talbot (creative feedback).

INTRODUCTION

Kent Cricket: The Origins

THERE IS documentary evidence of cricket being played in Kent as far back as the first half of the 17th century, when it was regarded as a heathen abomination by the puritan establishment. In 1652 a group were convicted at Maidstone Assizes for playing "a certain unlawful game called Crickett". As the pastime evolved into an organised sport, Kent became the first cricketing stronghold. According to *The English Game of Cricket,* a Kent side confronted All England in 1711 and by the 1730s winners-take-all games, in which the prize was a formidable £1,000, were being sponsored by the aristocracy; even the Prince of Wales pitched in.

The earliest first-class match for which the full scorecard has been preserved was between All England and Kent at the Artillery Ground, London on 18 June 1744. Kent prevailed by one wicket in a low-scoring thriller (40 and 70 lost to 53 and 58 for nine) and were such a force that they won 16 out of 28 matches against England between 1839 and 1849.

The first, tentative attempt at forming a county club had been made in 1787, but it was not until 1870, at a meeting in the Bull Hotel, Rochester, that Kent County Cricket Club, in its modern form at least, was born. The County Championship was officially constituted three years later though, according to the respected statistician Peter Wynne-Thomas, Kent were the leading county for six seasons out of seven between 1837 and 1843 and again in 1847 and 1849.

The giants of Kent's first golden age were Alfred Mynn and Fuller Pilch. In his history of Kent cricket, R. L. Arrowsmith described Mynn as "the greatest match-winner that the game produced before W. G. [Grace]". He was a genuine all-rounder – a punishing batsman and brilliant slip fielder – but it was as a fast bowler that he excelled, generating extraordinary pace from a run-up of only six steps. In an era of rampant inaccuracy as bowlers struggled to master round-arm (soon flouting the Laws of the game by raising their arm above the shoulder), Mynn was in a class of his own. Arrowsmith wrote: "What made Alfred Mynn so formidable was that he combined great pace with great accuracy in a degree that no other contemporary could approach." Although he hit and hurt batsman who wore very little protection, Mynn attracted nothing but admiration from his contemporaries. The pain resulted from the bowler's skill rather than any malign intent.

Mynn was a man of simple pleasures and habits: he described his training regimen as "beef and beer" and if pressed for elaboration offered "beer and beef" as an alternative; he took a tankard of light bitter and the family prayer-book to bed with him each night. He made very little out of the game, but it was a mark of the greedy hold which gambling had on cricket that even someone as popular and respected as Mynn could be jeered in Maidstone from the heedless suspicion that he had sold a match between Kent and England.

Pilch was the 19th century equivalent of the overseas player. He was in his early thirties and already recognised as one of the finest batsmen in the country

– his innovative front-foot technique was known as the 'Pilch poke' – when the offer of £100 a year persuaded him to move from his native Norfolk in 1835. He became groundsman at Town Malling, then the main venue for Kent's most important matches; a population of 1,500, some of whom were still convinced that attending cricket matches was akin to devil worship, made the relocation to Canterbury inevitable. Pilch

Lord Harris, a hugely influential figure in the development of Kent cricket
Picture: Kent Messenger, PD1673800

moved too and was groundsman at the St Lawrence Ground for 21 years after its opening in 1847. In an early example of the multi-tasking which Lord Harris and Les Ames later brought to the county he also managed the Kent side off the field, as well as captaining them occasionally on it.

Canterbury Week's distinctive blend of sport, light culture and sociability had been launched at the Beverley Club ground in 1842. The daytime cut and thrust merged into the evening entertainment laid on at the New Theatre in Orange Street by cricket-loving actors, the Old Stagers. The week was already established as a highlight of Kent's social calendar when St Lawrence assumed centre stage five years later. The match between Kent and England on 2-4 August also marked what is thought to be the first use of a scorebox, putting the scorers "out of reach of pestering".

Kent were fortunate to have in Felix, aka Nicholas Felix aka Nicholas Wanostrocht, someone who linked cricket with the arts, not to mention various other fields. Felix was a schoolmaster of Belgian extraction who fully merited his place in the Kent team as a talented left-handed batsman. He was also a gifted musician – Pilch said "he could make music on anything from a church organ to a pair of tongs" – and conducted the band which backed up the Old Stagers at the inaugural Canterbury Week. He was an artist and wrote with whimsical good humour. His best-known work, *Felix on the Bat*, even included a diagram of his ingenious invention, the Catapulta, a forerunner of the bowling machine, which employed the same principle as ancient siege weapons. Felix also designed batting gloves and pads.

The reliable splendour of Canterbury Week was no longer matched by the standard of the Kent team in the 1850s, and another 50 years would pass before the county held sway. Kent could not call on a reliable nucleus of professionals, and the amateurs were an unpredictable breed. The kudos attached to playing for the county soon evaporated and it was only thanks to the dedication and energy of the most influential personality in Kent's history, Lord Harris, that respectability was maintained.

George Robert Canning Harris made his first-class debut for Kent in 1870 and finally bowed out at the age of 60, scoring 36 against the touring Indians in 1911. Although he played very little after 1889 he had already established himself as one of Kent's most reliable batsmen in an era of modest achievement. He was a cunning, if occasional lob bowler who was quite prepared to deliver a few 'sneaks' along the ground if the scoring rate needed slowing.

He led England in four Tests against Australia and assumed the role of Kent's benign dictator in 1875. He combined the roles of captain and secretary for 15 years and also served as club president at the start of his reign. Despite the off-field distractions he topped the national batting averages that summer and continued to captain Kent until 1889. Politics then made a rival claim on Lord Harris's time – he was Governor of Bombay from 1890 to 1895 and later Under-Secretary for War – but Kent and MCC still benefited from his wise counsel and he oversaw the purchase of St Lawrence for £4,500 in 1896. His philosophy was summed up by a letter he wrote to *The Times* in 1931, a year before his death. Colin Cowdrey chose it to preface his autobiography. Cricket, Lord Harris wrote, "is more free from anything sordid, anything dishonourable, than any game in the world. To play it keenly, honourably, generously, self-sacrificingly, is a moral lesson in itself, and the classroom is God's air and sunshine."

Lord Harris's voice was the loudest and most consistent in opposition to the plague of throwing which infiltrated the game in the late 19th century. In 1885 he insisted on Kent forfeiting a match against Lancashire when their committee refused to omit bowlers with suspect actions and demonstrated the consistency of his stand by barring Christopher Collins and Walter Hedley from playing for Kent. Finally, in 1900, the county captains drew up a list of blacklisted bowlers.

Twenty years earlier he had breathed new life into the Band of Brothers, "a bunch of guys getting together to play some one-day cricket" according to one modern-day member, Nick Kemp, but a group who, until recent times anyway, have exerted real influence on Kent cricket. BB, as they are commonly abbreviated, were founded in 1858, but between 1867 and 1879 members did little more than sport club colours and pitch their tent for Canterbury Week. Lord Harris turned the Band of Brothers into a well-heeled pressure group. As Arrowsmith put it: "For over 50 years he was the dominant force in the club and he played for it constantly. On the death of the last of the founders in 1919 he became its first Chief and continued in office until his death in 1932. It was entirely thanks to him that it became a great and valuable force behind the scenes in Kent cricket."

Even Lord Harris was incapable of conjuring up quality players from thin air. Kent still lacked a base of able professionals, though as the 19th century expired there were promising signs in the emergence of Fred Huish, the first in Kent's production line of excellent wicketkeepers. Huish, unlucky never to play for England, was a fixture from 1895 to 1914, claiming a county record of 1,253 victims.

Even a scene-setting canter through more than three centuries of cricket in Kent would be incomplete without mention of Gerry Weigall, a minor player

(6,866 runs at 19.39) but major character. He was charmingly described by E. W. 'Jim' Swanton as always having "a few pet bees buzzing around in his bonnet". He was unfailingly opinionated and dogmatic, even in the company of Lord Harris, and frequently wrong. Weigall used an umbrella to illustrate his trenchant views about batsmanship, whether in the hubbub of Piccadilly Circus or on a crowded bus. His quirky dictums were dutifully passed down from generation to generation, including 'never eat pie at a cricket match', 'never run to cover' (advice he was apt to ignore himself) and 'never hook till you've made 84'. In 1912 he succeeded the inspirational Capt William McCanlis as head of the Tonbridge Nursery, which had moved to Canterbury. Weigall was persuaded, reluctantly, to resign in 1929, on the grounds that he had been "unable to devote as much time to coaching the young players at the nets as the committee required".

McCanlis, a modest bat for Kent in the 1860s, played a huge part in the emergence of their first great side of the County Championship era. The Tonbridge Nursery, which had opened in 1897, was an earlier and more localised version of the Association of Kent Cricket Clubs which bore spectacular fruit in the 1960s. Colin Blythe, Jim Seymour, Wally Hardinge, Arthur Fielder, Frank Woolley and Tich Freeman all came through the disarmingly simple system. At the same time Kent were able to call on amateurs of the ability of Jack Mason, who though not always available was an excellent all-

The Kent side who broke new ground for the county by winning the championship in 1906

Picture: Kent Messenger, PD1673753

rounder in the period leading up to the First World War. In 1901 he became the first Kent player to do the double.

Two more amateurs, Cuthbert 'Pinky' Burnup and Kenneth Hutchings, were the batting mainstays in Kent's push for their first championship in 1906. Burnup, though he played in only 12 of Kent's 22 matches, averaged 67 to top the national batting averages. Hutchings played with such elegant ease that he was acclaimed by *Wisden*, in naming him as one of their cricketers of the year, as "the sensation of the season, the English Trumper".

Kent relied heavily on the pace of Fielder, who was another of *Wisden*'s chosen five on the strength of 172 championship wickets, and the guile of Blythe. The slow left-armer had taken a wicket with his first ball in first-class cricket, in 1899, and was soon to be recognised as one of the great all-time exponents of the spinner's art. For accuracy and flight he could not be bettered. Arrowsmith wrote: "In style he was the perfect bowler, the few dancing steps, the long last stride, the left arm flung behind his back, the right thrown forward to balance it, the long sensitive musician's fingers (he was a devoted and accomplished violinist) wrapped round the ball and every inch of his height used as his arm came over."

Blythe had also played talent-spotter in identifying Woolley as a cricketer of exceptional gifts. Kent's trials log called him "a fair bat", but the county soon discovered that they had three players in one. Initially he was the 19-year-old tyro in Kent's championship-winning side in 1906, a triumph only made possible by Yorkshire's unexpected one-wicket defeat by Gloucestershire at the end of August.

Kent travelled to Bournemouth needing only a draw, but Burnup cemented his place at the top of the averages with a dominant 179. An innings victory over Hampshire prompted *The Daily Telegraph* to report: "Beyond all question they have proved themselves the best team of the year and, leaving aside all partisan feeling, everyone will be glad to see them at the top of the table."

Newspapers also saw more than symbolic significance in the county's charity match against the Rest of England at the Oval the following week. The *Telegraph* reported: "The fact of Kent once more playing England on even terms is, perhaps, the most interesting thing that has happened in purely English cricket for many a day. When Lord Harris set to work more than thirty years ago to revive Kent cricket he could hardly have thought that such a match would be played in his lifetime."

It was characteristic of Kent's batting in their period of dominance that they scored their runs at breakneck pace and even when the foundations were shakier the cavalier approach persisted. The individual highlight of a disappointing 1907 season in which Kent could only finish eighth was Blythe's record-breaking feat of taking 17 for 48 in a single day against Northamptonshire. According to *The Daily Telegraph*, Blythe's figures could have been even better. "Northamptonshire gave a deplorable display. So helpless were the batsmen against the bowling of Blythe that the first seven wickets fell for four runs – two of them extras. The eighth should have gone down at the same total, but Vials was missed by Blythe." He still recorded figures of 10 for 30, the best by a Kent bowler, and followed up with seven for 18 as Northamptonshire were shot out for 60 and 39. Incredibly, this was not even the low point for hapless Northamptonshire in 1907: two weeks later they were bowled out for 12, the equal lowest first-class score, by Gloucestershire.

Blythe's nervous disposition – he suffered from epilepsy – was certainly a significant factor in his career. He was more acutely affected when he played for England, though 100 wickets in 19 Tests at an average of less than 19 hardly suggested that he was in a constant state of anxiety.

In the nine seasons leading up to the First World War, Kent were never lower than third. Even with a tail which began at No 7, the emphasis was on all-out attack and Kent's bowling was so strong that small totals rarely led to defeat. They were a distant second to Yorkshire in 1908 but clearly the stand-out side in 1909, when Blythe finished with 215 wickets at 14 apiece, and even more so the following summer: the title was wrapped up by 12 August. Blythe and Woolley combined to lethal effect as Warwickshire were bowled out for 16 at Tonbridge in 1913, *en route* to Kent's fourth title in eight glorious years

Blythe, who had already announced his retirement in 1914 and was due to be taking up a coaching appointment at Eton, was killed in 1917, a year after the conflict had claimed Hutchings' life. The spinner's mantle passed to Alfred Percy 'Tich' Freeman, in his way an even more remarkable master of the craft. Freeman played a handful of games for Kent in 1914, and though he was highly successful by ordinary standards his unparalleled orgy of wicket-taking only began when he turned 40 in 1928.

Kent were agonisingly close to another championship triumph in 1919, denied only by the resistance of Middlesex's tail in the final game, but their longer-term prospects were damaged by the absence of a fast-bowling successor to Fielder. Freeman was forced to shoulder an ever greater burden as Woolley's bowling powers waned; as a batsman the decline was barely detectable until he had passed his 50th birthday. Although the bare statistics of Woolley's career – 58,959 runs, 2,066 wickets and an unsurpassed 1,018 catches – are remarkable enough, admirers who saw him in action insisted that the figures only hinted at his true greatness.

Two of the greats: all-rounder supreme Frank Woolley and leg-spinner Tich Freeman

Jim Swanton, whose journalistic career was launched by an exclusive interview with the great man in 1926, wrote in an obituary notice for *The Daily Telegraph* that Woolley was "as graceful a batsman as ever played". He elaborated: "The modest self-effacing companion of the dressing room quickly became an utterly disdainful, aloof antagonist at the wicket."

Woolley himself insisted that Kent batsmen of his time were not allowed to play for their average. Reflecting on 30 years in the blissfully happy bosom of Kent's "well-ordered family", he wrote in *The King of Games*: "It is in no boasting spirit that I state my belief that we in Kent do play cricket in a spirit rather characteristically our own. To us a defeat is not a case of the skies falling and of the near end of the world, but rather of: 'Well done, ———-shire, good luck to you, you put us where you wanted us this time, next time we hope to return the compliment.'"

Freeman's achievement, in taking 2,090 wickets in eight seasons between 1928 and 1935, is perhaps the most startling example of drawn-out success in cricket history. It was as much a feat of stamina as one of pure bowling skill. Each year brought him more than 200 wickets; in 1928 he became the first bowler to take 300 wickets in a season. The 5,489 runs he conceded that summer will never be challenged; nor will the 2,033 overs, equivalent to 58 per match, which he delivered in 1933. Small wonder that he ground to a wearied halt in 1936, choosing retirement over what he saw as the demeaning option of periodic rests.

He was picked only 12 times for England, and never had the chance to pit his leg-spinning wits – the googly was always in the batsman's mind but rarely used – against Australia in England. Ironically, Freeman's Kent team-mate Percy Chapman, who also became his county captain in 1931, was the England captain who supported his omission both on the 1928-29 tour to Australia and for the home series in 1930.

As a batsman Chapman epitomised the flaky tendency in Kent's batting ranks between the wars. His innings of 260 against the then champions, Lancashire, at Maidstone in 1927 was a remarkable exhibition of controlled violence, but his lack of basic technique increasingly let him down. There was more substance in the batting of Bill Ashdown, whose 332 in Kent's total of 803 for four against Essex in 1934 (the whole innings lasted only seven hours) remains the highest score in the county's history.

Wally Hardinge, the second most prolific run-scorer for the county after Woolley, had almost matched him for longevity when he retired in 1933. Another notable link with the pre-war side had ended when Jim Seymour retired in 1926, though Seymour had a wider claim to fame which still earns him the odd mention in despatches. Reed v Seymour (1927) was the High Court test case, stoutly supported by Lord Harris, which established the right of sportsmen to avoid paying tax on their benefit. The official explanation given by Her Majesty's Customs and Revenue is that the case "established the principle that where a benefit match or benefit period is organised to demonstrate affection and regard for the personal qualities of the player, the proceeds are not earnings and not sourced in the employment". Unfortunately, Seymour died three years later, unable to make extended use of the farm which his benefit bought.

The high standard expected of Kent wicketkeepers was maintained first by Jack Hubble, then Les Ames, who made his debut in 1926. Hubble not only recognised Ames's potential as perhaps the finest of all wicketkeeper-batsmen, but also showed confidence in his business acumen by offering him a

Les Ames, who emerged as the first great wicketkeeper-batsman

partnership in his sports goods concern in Gillingham. The commercial good sense also served Ames well when he assumed control of Kent's finances in the 1950s. As a wicketkeeper he had neither the flamboyance of his successor, Godfrey Evans, nor the idiosyncrasies of Alan Knott. Even the apparent eccentricity of putting steak in his wicketkeeping gloves was a practical measure. The great fast bowler, Harold Larwood, explained to Chris Cowdrey in 1985 that it "softened up the gloves. It was all right in the morning but by three or four in the afternoon he was smelling a bit behind the stumps. And sometimes he used to put the steak in water overnight, keep it soft, for the next day as well." Ames remained, however, unfussily reliable, and was the main source of assists for Freeman. Ames claimed a record 128 dismissals in 1929 and another extraordinary best of 64 stumpings in 1932.

Howard 'Hopper' Levett was cast as Ames's eternal understudy. Levett, a chuckling bundle of energy, lost little in comparison with Ames as a wicket-keeper, but averaged only 12 with the bat. He and Ames were founder members just before the Second World War of the quaintly conceived Hoppers' tie club (so-named because of the tie's beer barrel and hops on a navy background rather than Levett's nickname). The club, which still flourishes, was a disgruntled response from professionals who were told that were not entitled to wear a newly launched members' tie.

Kent were reduced to mid-table anonymity in the last few years before the war, but at least the emergence of Doug Wright helped to soften the blow of Freeman's abrupt removal from the attack. Wright was, in Swanton's typically measured words, "on his best days a uniquely dangerous bowler of quick leg-breaks and googlies and on his not so good days a generous contributor to the general entertainment". The good days were highlighted by a record seven hat-tricks, but he failed to translate the threat on to the international stage and was also an unconvincing first professional captain for Kent after being catapulted into the job by Bill Murray-Wood's abrupt sacking in 1953.

The abiding memory of Kent between the wars was of a side who depended too heavily on one very tall man, the 6ft 3in Woolley, and one very short one, the 5ft 2in Freeman. The accent was on entertainment at all times and Kent batsmen were capable of great feats, even if they led too rarely to victories. In 1938 Arthur Fagg became the only player to score two double hundreds in a match when he made 244 and an unbeaten 202 in a tame draw against Essex at Colchester.

St Lawrence Ground suffered only superficial damage during the war, despite being the target for about 150 incendiary devices, but pilot Gerry Chalk, the captain in 1939, was shot down over France. His successor was Bryan Valentine, nicknamed Hetty the Hen because of his mannerisms at the crease. The crowds were excellent in 1946 and 1947, when 182,000 spectators watched Kent's home games, but two respectable seasons were followed in 1948 by a slump to 15th. Still the spectators flocked in: Kent's game against the touring Australians, despite finishing in a two-day defeat, attracted crowds loosely estimated at 19,000 and 25,000.

The club made renewed efforts to identify and nurture the best young players in the county by setting up an Association of Kent Cricket Clubs, but the fruits of the initiative were not really felt until the production line of talent led by Alan Knott and Derek Underwood came through the system in the early Sixties. There was no continuity on the captaincy side until Colin Cowdrey was given the job in 1957. Valentine was followed by David Clark, who was convinced that Ames should have been made captain instead, but Ames would not accept the proviso that he renounce his professional status. He played as a specialist batsman in his last few seasons, handing over the wicketkeeping

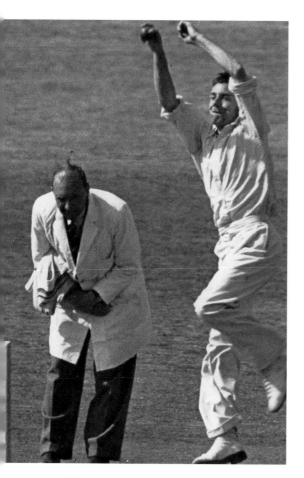

Doug Wright in leg-spinning action for Kent in 1947

gloves to the ebullient Evans. Ames was only a few months short of his 45th birthday when he made his hundredth hundred in 1950. Retirement should have quickly followed, but he was persuaded to turn out in early-season chill at Gillingham the following May. Alan Hill, in his biography of Ames, wrote: "Kent's old cricket warrior then stumbled in to bat, scarcely able to place one foot after another. 'I tried to hit a ball round to leg and collapsed in a heap.' "

Clark led Kent to a fresh championship low of 16th in 1951, prompting *Wisden* to describe Kent's campaign as "their worst since the turn of the century", but if Clark's playing credentials were questionable, there were no such doubts about his hapless successor, Murray-Wood. The tail started with him at No 7. He was asked to resign midway through 1953, his second season in charge, but refused. A full-scale player revolt was brewing when the committee finally sacked Murray-Wood, though the matter could clearly have been handled with more tact. Arrowsmith wrote: "Most unfortunately the news leaked out prematurely and was being shouted round the ground by the sellers of evening papers while Murray-Wood was in the field, and so an incident which everyone would have wished to pass with as little notice as possible received the maximum of publicity and created the maximum of feeling."

The committee now had little choice but to change tack. Wright was offered the job and remained in charge until the end of the 1956 season. He was popular and, unlike his immediate predecessors, could lead by example, but he was not a natural captain. The raw material at his disposal was far from outstanding, though Fred Ridgway was a hostile pace bowler so highly regarded by Brian Luckhurst that he included him in his best Kent XI since the war (despite the fact that he once withheld Luckhurst's 'gopher' payment of two shillings, claiming that the apprentice had failed to clean his bowling boots properly).

Although Kent's results continued to disappoint until well into the Sixties, 1956 can be regarded as a watershed season; they would have finished bottom in the championship if Leicestershire had managed to take the last Worcestershire wicket in their final game. Wright, handicapped by a persistent foot injury, was ineffective with the ball and weighed down by the strains of captaincy. It was no surprise when he announced that he would step down at the end of the season, allowing him to give full attention to his second benefit the following year. A win over Lancashire during Canterbury Week, when the two teams were bottom and top of the table, was described by *Wisden* as "the biggest surprise of the season". For much of the campaign Colin Cowdrey, who crafted an outstanding hundred against Lancashire, was a reluctant opener. Fortunately for Kent he was a less reluctant captain.

1957-66: Greatness in the Making

THERE WAS never any doubt that Colin Cowdrey would become Kent captain; it was just a question of when. He was young, at 24, to be taking charge, but expectations were so low and his credentials so outstanding that an open timetable lay in front of him. Cowdrey was eased into the job with a reassuring support network behind him.

David Clark was chairman of the cricket committee who hoped that by recruiting Les Ames as manager – a ground-breaking appointment – they would take some of the pressure off Cowdrey. He was already established as an England player, but still feared that the old lags might exploit his gentle nature. One of those senior pros, Godfrey Evans, assured him, "We're all behind you, master," but Cowdrey was still grateful for the buffer of experience and authority which Ames provided. "The fact that Les was around meant that they wouldn't take me to the cleaners," he admitted. As a no-nonsense disciplinarian Ames could dish out the stern rebuke when required; Cowdrey was left to hatch his tactical plans and, generally, to pick the side he wanted.

One of the first tasks facing Cowdrey and Ames was to rewrite the unwritten rules which still gave the enthusiastic amateur precedence over the more talented professional (the Gentlemen-Player distinction was officially abolished in 1962). Cowdrey remembered being presented with a book at the start of the season which listed the addresses and phone numbers of all the players, and detailed the amateurs' availability. On the strength of this information he was expected to promise them games in July and August.

He was also forced to confront the grim reality that until the county started producing a crop of good young players sustained success was just a distant dream. The formation of the Association of Kent Cricket Clubs seven years earlier was an important step in the right direction, but Cowdrey was determined to accelerate the development. "It meant searching behind every sightscreen and roller in Kent," he wrote in his autobiography. In the winter following his first season in charge he attended 164 social functions, ensuring that he listened as well as spoke.

Kent were also learning to balance the books and under the energetic chairmanship of Stuart Chiesman, Cowdrey's department-store-owning father-in-law, the county adopted a businesslike approach. Ames believed more in organisation than coaching and was instrumental in Claude Lewis, a capable slow left-armer for the county either side of the Second World War, being dispensed with as full-time club coach in 1958. The consolation prize for Lewis was a third innings: as first team scorer. Ames himself became even more powerful in 1960 when he combined the roles of secretary and manager. Within a year he had converted a deficit into a profit of £9,000.

On the field the green shoots of recovery were still hard to detect: Kent's best championship finish in the first seven seasons under Cowdrey was eighth in 1958. He was superficially as calm and diplomatic as ever, but 1960's annual report told a different story. "The cares and worries of the England captaincy with the inevitable publicity and criticism, usually unjustified, weighed heavily on his shoulders and the county and cricketing public seldom saw the Cowdrey we knew so well."

Colin Cowdrey in elegant action for Kent in 1962
Picture: Kent Messenger, PD1673755

The county's most remarkable game that season was a blink-and-you-missed-it affair with Worcestershire at Tunbridge Wells which remains the last championship match to finish in a single day. The relatively mundane part was Kent's innings of 187, which in itself spanned 80 overs and featured an enterprising innings of 73 from Peter Jones. Worcestershire began batting at 3.50pm, needing only 38 to avoid the follow-on; by 5.25pm, torn apart by the pace of Dave Halfyard and Alan Brown, they were dismissed for 25. The second innings began at 5.35pm and followed a depressingly similar pattern for Worcestershire. Cowdrey claimed the extra half hour and the game sped to its conclusion at 7.10pm; he admitted afterwards that the pitch had been "disgraceful".

Kent still lacked critically in all departments, though the natural successor to Blythe, Freeman and Wright finally appeared in the shape of Derek Underwood in 1963. The 18-year-old left-arm spinner became the youngest bowler to take a hundred wickets in his debut season. Although born in Bromley, Underwood's choice of Kent was far from automatic. He admits that prior to joining in April 1962 he had never seen the county play and could easily have ended up at the Oval instead. He had attended winter coaching sessions at Allders store in Croydon and made more impression on Surrey players Ken Barrington, John Edrich and Tony Lock as a promising batsman in the making than as a budding bowler. He also enjoyed watching a side who won an unparalleled seven successive championships between 1952 and 1958.

It might appear ironic that Lock, as a fellow slow left-armer, should be the man who recommended Underwood to Kent as a batsman, but Ames initially saw his cricketing potential in the same light. Kent's three wise men, Ames, Lewis and Colin Page, spotted something different when they saw Underwood bowling out in the open. Page's playing career – as an off-spinner with no batting pretensions – had hit the buffers in the late Fifties when Alan Dixon blossomed as an off-spinning all-rounder. He became, instead, a valuable lieutenant for Ames, taking charge of the 2nd XI and earning a reputation for a combustible temper and line-and-length good sense. Nick Kemp, a young player trying to establish himself when Page succeeded Ames in 1975, remembers: "He didn't really do any coaching. He was famous for phrases like 'hit fours and sixes and don't get out'. It's still used today...in a derogatory fashion."

The re-evaluation of Underwood was complete by the end of the 1963 season, though he himself expected more recognition for his achievement. He wrote in his autobiography, *Beating the Bat*: "Kent voted me a £50 bonus for taking 101 wickets, but I was looking for something else: not money, but my county cap. I was disappointed when it wasn't awarded to me. I don't think

Colin Cowdrey presents Derek Underwood with his Kent cap in 1964
Picture: Kent Messenger, PD1673756

many counties today would have held back if they had found an 18-year-old taking 100 wickets in his first season. But perhaps I expected too much."

The omission was repaired less than a year later when Underwood's schoolboy hero, Cowdrey, arranged for the presentation to take place during Kent's game against the touring Australians. Cowdrey had also tipped off Underwood's parents, who were among a capacity crowd at Canterbury. Cowdrey's generosity of spirit was again evident in 1966 when his wife, Penny, was primed to deliver a cake to Tunbridge Wells, where Underwood was playing on his 21st birthday. Bob Woolmer was another player to receive the cake treatment when he came of age in 1969.

Cowdrey was not a man given to brash predictions, but even the note of cautious optimism which he sounded at Kent's annual general meeting in 1963 could have been cynically received by members who saw the county win only five out of 28 championship matches that summer to finish a disappointing 13th. "We have now got a team of good cricketers," Cowdrey insisted. "My biggest problem is to lead them on to the field and convince them that they can actually win something. Mostly, they are young, immature and inexperienced, though we have a young Test cricketer or two on the horizon. But at least we stand a chance."

The chance of 'winning something' had improved for all 17 counties with the introduction of the Gillette Cup in 1963, but Kent, in common with most of the other sides, were slow to grasp the tactical demands of the original 65-over competition. Ted Dexter's fertile cricketing brain ensured that Sussex cottoned on quicker, winning the cup in both 1963 and 1964.

They pummelled Kent, and in particular a shellshocked Underwood, into submission in the first round in 1963. His figures of 11-0-87-0 were his worst in his entire one-day career, spanning 25 seasons. Curiously, an innings of 28 in the same game was also his highest score in the 438 limited-overs matches he played. It did not take long for Underwood to gain "ample revenge for the indignities I had suffered". His remarkable love affair with Hastings began with figures of nine for 28 in 1964 which were to remain as the best of his career.

The 1963 season also underlined the importance of Dixon to the side. Kent's stand-out seamer the previous summer, Halfyard, had overturned his three-wheel bubble car when two wickets away from his hundred for the season. A badly broken left leg prevented him from playing for almost two years and he took only one more championship wicket before being forced to retire. Amazingly, he revived his career with Nottinghamshire in 1968 and enjoyed three productive seasons for his new employers.

Dixon, already an indispensable member of the Kent side as an off-spinning all-rounder, now filled the Halfyard void as a new-ball bowler as well; not bad for someone who had walked away from cricket, utterly disillusioned, in the mid-Fifties. Dixon had become the county's second youngest debutant when he played his first championship game as a 16-year-old in 1950, but six years later he had still to command a regular place and decided to become a travelling salesman instead. "I'd become very frustrated by that point," he remembers. "I wasn't getting enough opportunities and I'd had enough. The following spring I drove past a cricket ground where the grass was being mown for the first time that season. I got out to make a phone call back to my headquarters and the smell of this lovely grass made me think, Alan, what are you doing? I got on the phone to Les Ames and said, 'I've made a mistake, can I come back?' Bless his heart, he said, 'You'd better come and see me.' I was told, 'Never do this again.' I was like a naughty boy. I was told, 'You're very fortunate to be taken back on.' I was made to eat a very large slice of humble pie. Something like that just wouldn't happen these days."

Dixon also recalls that he discovered his ability to bowl seam-up in unusual fashion in 1961. "We were playing against Yorkshire at Scarborough. I was there as a batter and, I thought, an off-spinner. Halfway through the match, Peter Richardson, who was captain, suddenly turned to me and said, 'Al, come and have a bowl.' I thought, 'Great, a few off-spinners,' though it struck me as a bit odd because it was a miserable, dark day. But Peter said to me, 'No, I don't want you to bowl spin, I want you to bowl seam-up.' I said, 'I don't really do that, Peter.' He said, 'Yes you do, I've seen you in the nets.' Anyway, the first ball to Brian Bolus whistled through cover for four. So I turned the ball round and bowled an inswinger. It swung and bowled him between bat and pad."

The other player to benefit from Halfyard's misfortune was Underwood who, despite his inexperience, found himself bowling the 1,000 plus overs which a fit Halfyard would have offered. After three successive seasons in which he topped 1,000 runs, Dixon's batting was on the wane, but he and Underwood both reached 100 wickets in 1964, the first time two Kent bowlers had achieved the feat since 1950. Despite his spectacular introduction to county cricket, Underwood found that he was bombarded by advice; very little of it made much sense to him.

"The best piece of advice I got in my whole career was from Claude Lewis," Underwood remembers. "He said on every wicket you play on there is a pace to bowl. So there are days when you need to fire it in on a slow wicket, offering slow turn. On a dusty one you might bowl a bit slower and use a bit more flight." No one quite worked out how to classify Underwood's style of bowling. Was he an orthodox spinner or a cutter? According to him he was neither, but if pressed for a description he would say 'slow to slow medium left-arm spinner'. Early in his career both Ames and Cowdrey urged him to bowl over the wicket, exploiting the left-armer's natural ability to angle the ball across the right-hander. He dutifully obeyed – "when Les Ames and Colin Cowdrey are suggesting something you don't say no" – but never felt comfortable. Even a day's experimentation in the Cowdreys' expansive garden at Bickley failed to produce a solution and a confused Underwood was less successful in 1965. The following summer he claimed 157 first-class wickets, a figure which has not been improved on since, but still decided to follow his best instincts by reverting to round the wicket, with the umpire up to the stumps.

The advice didn't stop coming, whether it be from journalist/broadcaster Jim Swanton, an influential voice behind the scenes at Canterbury, or various

England selectors. Swanton remained convinced that he bowled too quickly, though when challenged once by Ames after Underwood had taken seven wickets he conceded begrudgingly that his pace had suited the conditions that day. Kent team-mates and supporters were happy to accept Underwood as he was: a flat-footed phenomenon who switched uncomplainingly from county to country and back again and never seemed to tire of bowling. There were more subtle variations than he was given credit for and the less subtle device of his lethal quicker ball. It was variously known as the 'Keith ball', after the former Australia Test all-rounder Keith Miller had been pinned in a specially arranged net session at Beckenham, and the 'Exocet ball'. Brian Luckhurst reckoned it would have clocked in at around 80mph if given the speed-gun treatment.

The 1964 season was also notable for the first team debuts of Norman Graham and 18-year-old Alan Knott, who deposed Tony Catt as wicketkeeper and became a fixture in the side. Catt, incidentally, had gone down in history nine years earlier by conceding a championship record total of 48 byes in a game at Northampton. He was drafted into the side because Godfrey Evans was out with a broken finger and Derek Ufton on football duty with Charlton. *The Daily Telegraph* recorded that Catt "found difficulty in judging Wright's swiftly turning leg-breaks and googlies but he was also suffering considerably from a badly sunburned neck which handicapped his movements".

Knott, in common with Luckhurst and Underwood, soon amended his cricketing job description after joining the club. Even though his father was a capable club wicketkeeper (albeit one who believed that keepers had no need to show batting prowess as well), Knott was a budding pace bowler as a 10-year-old. As his schoolboy career evolved he both opened the batting and began switching from off-breaks to leg-breaks when his spinning finger became too sore. Ames saw him as an off-break bowler with reasonable prospects, but was also quick to spot his outstanding potential as a wicketkeeper when he kept for Kent's 2nd XI in 1963.

Even in his teens Knott was aware that he would have to work harder at maintaining fitness and flexibility than the average player. The stretching exercises which may have looked like nothing more than an extension of his fidgety demeanour were, in fact, born of physical necessity. Room-mates, at both county and international level, were accustomed to being woken at 5am to find Knott already putting himself through a punishing programme. He explained the background to the exercising in his autobiography, admitting: "In 1965 I was worried about how I would survive in the first-class game as a keeper."

After aggravating a groin injury Knott consulted an orthopaedic surgeon, Bill Tucker, who told him that he was 'more concerned about the lack of mobility, especially in my hip area'. Knott continued: "Before that injury in 1965 I had done a lot of stretching exercises and Bill Tucker emphasised that I must continue with them. He warned that if I didn't I would be very lucky to play after the age of 30 because generally mobility decreases and I would not be able to play sport at a high level. I went back to him annually for several years to be stretched under anaesthetic so that my limbs were totally relaxed for the mobility exercises."

Knott settled into a disciplined routine of at least half an hour's exercises each morning and, from the early Seventies onwards, expanded his on-field regimen as well. He took a mixture of kaolin and morphine to combat Test match nerves and was addicted to honey, preferably Romanian, which he would use to sweeten his lunchtime cup of tea. There were, too, a whole check list of idiosyncrasies and individual quirks which demonstrated an astonishing attention to detail. He wore a flannel to keep his back warm and soak up sweat; his shirt had to be oversized and long-sleeved to protect his elbows when diving; to prevent discomfort in the calf region he replaced the middle strap of his pads with a bandage; the trademark handkerchief which hung out of his left pocket was for ease of access rather than some arcane superstition.

And then, of course, there was the famous hat, added to Knott's accessories after he sustained a whiplash injury on England's tour of Australia in 1974-75. He was worried that the peak of his cap was hampering his vision when keeping wicket, and Fred Titmus, the Middlesex off-spinner, found the perfect solution with a floppy hat – complete with a rim which could be rolled up. If Knott was happy, the fashion police among Kent's members were not, complaining to the general committee that it was untidy. A new one did not meet Knott's exacting standards and a compromise was finally reached when he was allowed to wear a patched-up version of old faithful.

Kent were probably only an incisive pace bowler away from having an attack with championship-winning potential in the mid-Sixties. Before Graham's emergence, the seam attack rested largely on the shoulders of Brown, David Sayer and left-armer John Dye. Brown was sidelined by a cartilage operation in 1964, leaving Sayer and Dye to spearhead the attack, but he bounced back superbly in 1965 to take 104 wickets, earning a £30 bonus which raised his salary for the year to £700. According to Brian Luckhurst, the skiddy Sayer, one of few pace bowlers to wear glasses, challenged Frank Tyson for sheer speed but was too gentle in nature to be a great fast bowler.

By 1965, too, the top of the Kent order was graced by the opening pair who were to be the springboard for so many of the county's successes, Luckhurst and Denness. Luckhurst had been signed in 1954 as a 15-year-old (and paid a princely £4 10s a week) on the strength of his promise as a slow left-armer. He was still regarded primarily as a bowler when, playing in only his fourth championship match, he took what remained a career-best four for 32 against Somerset in 1962. By the end of the summer he was established as a batsman, and had been joined in the side by Denness.

The Scot's schoolboy dreams – his contemporaries at Ayr Academy included rugby union prop Ian McLauchlan and footballer Ian Ure – centred on playing rugby for his country. His promise as a batsman, however, alerted both Warwickshire and Kent, and Swanton's presence as guest of honour at Ayr Cricket Club's centenary dinner might have been expected to nudge Denness decisively towards Kent. In the event, Denness recalls, Swanton perversely suggested that Edgbaston, as a Test ground, would be a wiser choice than Canterbury. Fortunately, Denness followed his own instincts. "I looked at the Warwickshire lads who were around at the time and thought I stood a much better chance of getting in the Kent side." The other attraction was that Kent were able to find him off-season work in insurance, the alternative career he had been leaning towards in Scotland.

Denness soon discovered, in a roundabout way, that Ames had him pencilled in as a regular of the future. "He said to me, 'Mike, I don't know much about rugby, but I do read the local paper. In the Canterbury 1st XV team for Saturday there always seems to be an A. N. Other. What does that mean?' 'That means that they are not quite sure who's going to play.' " He was eventually forced to admit that, in this case, A. N. Other was none other than M. H. Denness, and was barred from playing (team-mates like Stuart Leary, who played another sport professionally, were exempt). Denness, who had hoped to turn out for London Scottish the following winter, recalls sadly: "I put the boots in the attic and never played rugby again."

Richardson was both first choice as opener in the early Sixties and Cowdrey's replacement as captain when England or injury demanded. Richardson was also one of the game's great practical jokers, continually risking the disapproval of the more staid members and officials. Denness said Richardson "was a tremendous humorist but there were times when his jokes did not go down too well with everyone concerned". In one Kent game which was being broadcast by the BBC, Richardson fed Brian Johnston the romantic-sounding but utterly false biographical information that Denness was the son of a sheep farmer from Banff.

Another broadcaster, Swanton, was the victim of a more elaborate jape hatched by Richardson and played out while he was batting against Hampshire at Canterbury in 1963. Opposing captain Colin Ingleby-McKenzie, Swanton's co-commentator, Peter West, and umpire Bill Copson were all in on the ruse, which began with West's waving of a white flag to indicate that Swanton was on commentary.

Richardson told David Rayvern Allen, Swanton's biographer, how the leg-pull unfolded. "Shack's bowling [Derek Shackleton] and so I stop the game and go up to Bill and say I can't concentrate, there's a booming noise coming from up there. Bill then starts to walk over to the commentary position and Jim's on air saying, 'There appears to be something going on down on the pitch. I can't quite make out what's happening.' By this time Bill's quite close and he calls out, 'The batsman's complaining about a booming noise, can you please stop?' Mystified, Swanton turns and whispers to West, 'What booming noise? I don't know what they mean.' 'It's you they're complaining about, Jim,' replies West, 'it's the sound of your voice.' "

Richardson's reward, even after scoring a match-saving 172, was a stern note from Swanton suggesting that if he concentrated more on batting and less on silly jokes he would be a better player. He was not just a very different personality from Cowdrey, but an off-the-cuff captain who was as decisive as Cowdrey was dithering. Richardson was highly regarded by the players – he was also capable of batting with quick-witted brilliance – even if they learned to be wary of a hyper-critical streak which was not reserved for the opposition. Dixon recalls: "He could be very amusing and quick-witted, but he wasn't everyone's cup of tea."

As captain Richardson was also capable of winding up opponents with a semi-serious objective in mind. A fiery spell from Somerset pace bowler Fred Rumsey had left Kent in a precarious position at the end of the penultimate day in their championship match at Taunton in 1964. Richardson's answer was to send out for champagne and invite his opposing captain, Bill Alley, to join the impromptu party in the Kent dressing room. A few glasses later Richardson had convinced Alley that if he opened up with Rumsey on the final morning Kent would simply block it out for a draw. They were confronted instead by spinners Brian Langford and Roy Kerslake and ended up winning a game in which they had been completely outplayed on the first two days. Denness recalls: "The Somerset players came up to Peter afterwards and congratulated him on captaining both sides."

Cowdrey was in a permanent state of mild anxiety about reports which might filter back about Richardson's abuse of power. After he had passed on

A Kent line-up from 1965. Back row (left to right): Alan Knott, Brian Luckhurst, John Dye, Les Ames (secretary/manager), John Prodger, David Nicholls, Mike Denness. Front: Derek Underwood, Alan Brown, Colin Cowdrey, Stuart Leary, David Sayer

the bogus information to a Nottinghamshire official that the Kent wicket-keeper, Catt, was actually called Souchak, and the scorer, Claude Lewis, was R. C. Frobisher-Smythe, Richardson was asked to explain himself to the Kent committee. Minutes for a meeting in June 1964 recorded: "The attention of the committee was drawn to a report in the national press that the acting captain, P. E. Richardson, had given fictitious names for inclusion on the score-cards at Trent Bridge and other grounds and this had caused considerable confusion and annoyance and on one ground the first issue of scorecards had to be destroyed. The committee considered that such publicity was undesirable and reflected adversely on the county club."

Richardson retired at the end of the 1965 season, when Kent finished fifth in the championship, their highest position since 1947. Cowdrey, though available for only half the games, averaged almost 65 for the county and topped the national averages. Kent's annual report chose to focus on the excessive caution of the batsmen and, more bizarrely, on their reluctance to go out to the middle. Dudley Moore, in his *History of Kent County Cricket Club*, wrote: "On many occasions it appeared that there was a considerable delay before the incoming batsman left the pavilion, and that contrasted sharply with the opposing batsmen, most of whom were crossing on the field. It was a matter which was receiving the attention of both the committee and the captain, the report added."

The upward curve was still evident the following summer when, despite a difficult Test baptism against the West Indies, Underwood led the national averages with 157 wickets at less than 14 apiece. His 144 wickets for Kent were the best return for the county since Tich Freeman in 1935, though he admits that he benefited from a curious innovation in the championship. In an effort to bring some of the Gillette Cup's urgency to the three-day format, first innings were restricted to 65 overs in almost half the games. Underwood's pace and accuracy made him a difficult bowler to attack and in one game, against Gloucestershire at Folkestone, he induced five batsmen to hole out in identical fashion to Alan Ealham at long off.

Underwood's best return of the summer, nine for 37, came in a game where the 65-over regulation was not operating, but no innings would have lasted that long anyway on a Westcliff pitch which Underwood described as the worst he had ever played on. He remains convinced that it would have finished on the opening day if Essex opener Gordon Barker had been caught off him early in Essex's second innings. As it was, Underwood had taken all seven wickets to fall before the close. He also claimed the eighth before Dixon dismissed Ray East; Barker was still there when Underwood finished off the innings and Kent were able to wrap up an eight-wicket victory before lunch on the second day.

There was an amusing aftermath when John Prodger, fresh from a duck in Kent's first innings, went out to re-examine the dusty, heavily cracked pitch. "Nice wicket that," he said to the groundsman. "Thank you," came the reply, oblivious to the heavy sarcasm in Prodger's voice. The defiant attitude was still apparent in the groundsman's retort to reporters who questioned the quality of the pitch. "Southend pier is just down the road," he said. "It is one-and-a-half miles long. And half these batsmen should be taken out and dropped off the end of it."

Dixon, who captained the side capably and cheerfully when Cowdrey was absent, again mixed seam and spin to telling effect in taking 115 wickets. In a difficult summer for batsmen the Luckhurst/Denness alliance once more impressed. Knott believed that the defensively suspect Denness's performance in making 97 and 87 against Somerset at Bath, a ground where spinners traditionally held sway, was the making of him. Kent's middle order never threatened to achieve the same measure of excellence.

Ealham raised Kent's already high fielding standards a further notch in his debut season, but did not even manage to reach 500 runs in 33 innings. Two early memories remain with him; of meeting Les Ames and being asked:

'What's your name, young man?' 'Ealham, sir.' 'I won't forget that' (Ames had been born in the identically pronounced Elham). The other is of a game against Lancashire and one of his boyhood heroes, Brian Statham. "I sliced him over gully and as I'm running down to his end he says, 'That's not in t'manual, young man.' "

Knott was, by now, reaching his peak years as a wicketkeeper – he reckoned that he was at his best behind the stumps between 1966 and 1972 – though he owns up to a hat-trick of bloopers during the championship game against Glamorgan at Gravesend in 1966: three dropped catches off successive balls, two from Brown and one from Dixon.

Despite the shortcomings of the batting and a seam attack which failed to match the wicket-taking exploits of Underwood and Dixon, Kent rose another place to fourth. Cowdrey's 1963 prediction that Kent were capable of winning titles and trophies suddenly looked less fanciful.

PART I
GLORY DAYS

By Clive Ellis

ONE

1967-71: Kipper's Dream

KENT WERE such a force in one-day cricket between the late Sixties and Seventies that their triumph in the 1967 Gillette Cup should have come as no surprise, but they had done nothing in the first four years of the competition to suggest that such a dramatic breakthrough was on the cards. They had not even managed to beat another first-class county in that time.

The traditionalist in Colin Cowdrey found it hard to embrace one-day cricket. All-rounder Graham Johnson, who made his first team debut in 1965, remembers: "Colin always used to play one-day cricket with a grin on his face, as though the game had moved on. I think he felt a little out of place in it. He was already a great player when one-day cricket wasn't around and coming towards the end of his cricket career when the John Player and Benson and Hedges Cup started. So it was almost like, 'How do I fit into this? Should I be handing it over to the younger guys who can hurtle around in the field ?' " Johnson finds no difficulty in answering the question. "Anyone who could take apart an attack the way he played was worth his weight in gold just wandering out with a bat."

Kent discovered almost by accident that a team who were naturally blessed with attack-minded batsmen and fielded brilliantly were ideally qualified to dominate the one-day game. "We were lucky in that respect," says Alan Ealham with modest understatement. "I think Brian Luckhurst, Mike Denness and myself helped to lift the fielding of the whole side. And if you had a bit of an off day with your throwing Knotty would still make it look good." Norman Graham, the least naturally athletic player in the side, says every player felt inspired by the excellence around them. "I wasn't one of the great fielders, but I must have been the hardest tryer. You couldn't not succeed in that team."

Ealham, who was apprenticed as a panel beater and welder when he left school, offers a down-to-earth explanation for his own brilliance as an outfielder. "My father had a newsagents so I did a newspaper round for him for about 10 years. We looked after a couple of big estates so I got used to rushing around and that helped me build up strength." He denies strenuously that he ever went as far as throwing papers through letter-boxes on the run. "I found that I was reasonably quick, even though I was quite a big lad. I was never short of mental drive and ambition and one of the things I did when I joined Ashford Cricket Club as a 13-year-old was to practise throwing at a stump from different angles." He had an uncanny knack for hitting the target and believes he would have got many more run-out verdicts if he had played in the era of third umpires and television replays.

Kent were not alone in taking advantage of the relaxation of rules regarding overseas players in the mid-Sixties, but they invested cleverly (and frugally). Cowdrey, Peter Richardson and Alan Knott were all in an International Cavaliers side, managed by Les Ames, who toured the West Indies in 1964-65. They came up against a Barbados team featuring two promising 21-year-old friends who were making their first-class debut. One was John Shepherd, the other Keith Boyce. Ames and Cowdrey soon discovered that Boyce had pledged his future to Essex, but the personal recommendation of the great West Indian batsman, Everton Weekes, helped convince them that Shepherd would be an equally good signing. Neither Kent nor Essex were to be disappointed. Both Shepherd and Boyce were forced to complete a two-year period of residential qualification before being eligible to play first team cricket, but the 2nd XI apprenticeship ensured that they were thoroughly acclimatised when they became available in 1967.

It was a mark of Kent's poverty or caution, or both, that they were happy to accept a £500 donation from a life member, Edward Wharton-Tigar, to "defray the cost" of Shepherd's "importation". Wharton-Tigar, incidentally, had been a spy and saboteur during the Second World War and was also recognised by the *Guinness Book of Records* for his collection of two million cigarette cards.

In his early days with Kent, Shepherd lodged with Denness and his wife Molly in Canterbury, and was responsible for baffling a telephone engineer one day. Denness was watching, out of sight, as the Candid Camera style confusion unfolded. "Shep used to wander around the house in his dressing gown, so when he came downstairs the engineer saw him, Molly and a very white baby in her pram. He shook his head and left the house in a state of complete bewilderment."

For Shepherd himself the culture shock was considerable. "For a youngster who had never travelled – the only place I'd ever been was to Jamaica with the Barbados schools side – it was quite strange to be thrust into something like that," he remembers. "I was 21 but I was quite naïve in many ways. When I came to England I knew nothing about county cricket. When I was starting out my whole idea was to play in the Lancashire Leagues, where the great West Indian players had been. I knew more about teams like Littleborough, Enfield and Nelson, just by hearing the names of the clubs and the professionals who were playing there, every Saturday night on the news at home. Suddenly I realised what county cricket was about and then it was quite a revelation. When Yorkshire walked out they looked like a Test team."

It was soon apparent to Kent supporters that the county had recruited well. Shepherd was a powerful striker of the ball and a skilful medium-fast bowler, effective with both the new and old ball. There was also an infectious sense of enjoyment in everything he did. He relished rather than resented the workload, and part of his after-dinner-speaking routine is to claim: "When I came to England I was 6ft 4in and white. I bowled so many damn overs that I was stunted and the hot sun turned me black."

In more serious vein he says: "It may have appeared to be hard work, especially for an all-rounder like myself, but it certainly didn't feel like it. In a naïve sort of way I was so privileged to be doing something like that. Every morning I couldn't wait to get to the ground to practise. I used to bowl about 1,000 overs a season. These guys now, they bowl 400 overs a year and they think they're hard-done-by. It's a joke."

The less expected plus for the county in 1967 was the emergence of Graham. Cowdrey had said at the end of the previous season that he wanted an opening bowler who was good for 100 wickets a season. Given that Graham had claimed only 44 victims in his first three seasons, it was doubtful that Cowdrey expected the 6ft 8in Northumbrian to answer his prayers, but he became a fearsome prospect on pitches with more than average or erratic bounce. Kent bowlers occupied first and third places in the national averages as Derek Underwood repeated his feat of the previous summer. Graham's 104 wickets cost less than 14 apiece and he was also fiendishly difficult to get away, conceding little more than one-and-a-half runs an over. "Mean, mean" is Graham's concise description of himself as a one-day bowler. Even allowing for the much lower rates of scoring in the early days of limited-overs cricket, an economy rate of just over three told its own impressive story. His method was simple but effective. "I suppose it's fair to say that I didn't do a lot with the ball," he admits, "but I was very accurate, hit the bat high, and hit the seam five balls out of six. If it was going to do anything it did it off the pitch."

Graham, then working for the General Post Office in London, had been recruited five years earlier after impressing in winter nets at Eltham. He began playing for Kent's 2nd XI in 1962, and though he faced a lengthy apprenticeship before breaking into the first team there were no complaints about his lot. There was also a healthy fellowship among the pace bowlers – Graham, John Dye, David Sayer and Alan Brown – who were in competition for places. "I got lucky in the end with a lot of determination and effort," he remembers. "It was bloody hard work but I loved it. We all got on so well, so although we were competing for places there was never anything personal about it. You just mature; you've struggled for three years in the second team and then it all comes together."

Graham is quick to acknowledge the part that Ames and Colin Page – "a perfect team" – played in his development. "Colin was a huge influence on me: he just made you want to succeed. He cut my run down and told me what to concentrate on. He could be a bit fierce sometimes, but players need that. You had to be good to get in that Kent side. There are players in the England side now who wouldn't have got past our second team." He believes that only injury deprived him of a Test debut against Pakistan in 1967. "I was very close to playing for England that summer. I was certainly picked in the side by all the press, but then I tore a shoulder muscle at Southampton and that was it."

For much of the season Kent seemed capable of winning both the championship and Gillette Cup. The dream was still a flickering possibility when they beat Somerset at Lord's on 2 September, but Yorkshire needed only to outscore Gloucestershire in the first innings of their final match at Harrogate to retain the title. In the event they won by an innings, leaving Kent to reflect that the real damage had been done in Canterbury Week, when only two points were picked up from a draw against Leicestershire and defeat by Yorkshire. The sense of expectation was shown by the 40,000 spectators who watched the six days' cricket and contributed £6,082 to the Kent coffers.

The game against Yorkshire was of huge significance in its own right, but the nostalgic sideshow was the appearance of 46-year-old Godfrey Evans, eight years after his retirement, to keep wicket in place of Knott, who was on England duty. A crowd of 10,250 paid homage on the opening day and witnessed high drama almost from the first ball. Fred Trueman, captaining Yorkshire in the absence of Brian Close, bowled with such short-pitched ferocity after losing the toss that he broke Luckhurst's hand and received an official warning.

Trueman was also at the heart of the action on the second day when Ealham pulled off one of the most extraordinary catches of his career to leave the Yorkshireman shaking his head in disbelief. Ealham, who was fielding substitute, recalls with typical modesty: "It was a strange one. I remember that David Nicholls was on the midwicket boundary. I just started off from long on and put my head down. I looked to see where David was because I didn't want to bump into him, saw that he'd stopped and suddenly the ball was there so I stuck my hand out. The umpires didn't know what was going on because the crowd were in the background. That learned me. After that I always threw the ball up to show I'd caught it."

Curiously, Ealham's catch came either side of glaring lapses by Kent in the field. First Bob Wilson dropped a skyer, dislocating a finger in the process, then the normally reliable Alan Dixon, Kent's stand-in captain, spilled a sitter at mid-on. It proved to be the difference between first-innings points for Kent and a two-run advantage for Yorkshire. Wilson, effectively batting one-handed, made a heroic 50 as Kent were bowled out for 100 in their second innings. They had dismissed Yorkshire for 40 on a rain-affected Bradford pitch earlier in the summer, Graham inflicting the only pair of his career on Geoff Boycott, but there was no likelihood of a repeat at Canterbury. Yorkshire eased home by seven wickets.

There was still mighty consolation for Kent in finishing second, their highest place in the championship since 1928, even if some of their 12 wins were secured on home pitches which kept MCC inspector Bert Lock on high alert. The Mote wicket at Maidstone, taken off the 1st XI roster in 2005 after Kent had eight points deducted, was regarded at the time as one of the county's more reliable surfaces, but Lock was duly summoned after Hampshire had been rolled over for 95 and 31.

Given that Kent and Leicestershire finished second and third in the championship, understandable cynicism greeted the news that they had earned the lowest marks in the pitches' merit table for 1967. The wickets prepared at Gillingham and Dover were said to be causing "grave concern" to the MCC's special committee, though Graham was hardly complaining after taking six wickets in each innings and recording match figures of 12 for 80 (also passing 100 wickets for the season) as Kent wound up their championship campaign with a nine-wicket victory over Essex at Dover's Crabble Athletic Ground. Cowdrey, speaking after the win but before the Gillette Cup final, told reporters: "You're seeing us at our worse now. We are a young side and we are going to get better. I hope that the next five years will be triumphant for Kent."

The innovation of Sunday cricket in the championship, even if a combination of religious sensitivity and ancient legislation meant that play could only begin at 2pm, re-designated Tuesdays as the county cricketer's day of rest. Despite the restriction the crowds were encouragingly high – Kent's total attendance almost doubled to 75,000 – and laid the foundations for the birth of the John Player Sunday League in 1969.

Kent also attracted ever larger crowds as their cup campaign gathered momentum in 1967. They began with a 42-run victory, completed in near darkness, over Essex at Brentwood. Graham's four for 19 in 12 overs ensured that a total of 239 was defended comfortably. In the third round Dixon set up a six-wicket win at the Oval by cutting through Surrey's powerful batting line-up to take seven for 15 bowling seam-up. The figures remained the best in the competition until Underwood's return of eight for 31 against Scotland in 1987, his final season.

Underwood thought very highly of Dixon as an off-spinner, but admits that he "never really rated him as a seamer". He adds: "He could have bowled with an orange that day." Dixon's response 20 years later, when asked if he had heard that Underwood had beaten his record, was: "Yes, but I'd still rather have my seven than Deadly's eight."

Players of the calibre of John Edrich, Ken Barrington, Micky Stewart and Graham Roope were his victims, though Dixon freely admits that Surrey's batsmen were gripped by a collective death wish. He also remembers having to employ unusual tactics to ensure that he completed his 12 overs. "I was at the end of my run-up and I think I'd taken about five for eight or something ridiculous at that stage. Colin Cowdrey used to have this lovely habit of throwing the ball in the air with one hand then catching it in the other and throwing it hard at his other hand again. 'Al,' he said, 'I'm thinking of taking you off and bringing you back for the tail.' He threw the ball in the air and I snatched it as it came down and said, 'This is the bloody tail,' and marched back to my mark."

The semi-final against Sussex at Canterbury attracted a crowd of 16,500, the biggest at St Lawrence in modern times. Ames was adamant that the ground was even more packed than it had been for Kent's game against the touring Australians in 1948. The early loss of Denness proved to be just a minor irritant as Luckhurst and Shepherd added 135 for the second wicket, then Cowdrey proved that orthodoxy and one-day cricket were not mutually exclusive with a glorious innings of 78. Even a fired-up John Snow was treated with contempt. A total of 293 was well outside Sussex's compass once they had slumped to 27 for three.

Cowdrey reckoned that most of his best innings were "the product of a highly tense state of mind at times when I have almost felt that I was fighting for my life". The knock against Sussex was a case in point. "That was one of the greatest innings I have ever played but rarely, if ever, have I been in worse shape. I was hiding a variety of aches and pains and felt under considerable pressure. That morning I would have given anything to have turned my back on the ground and gone away to play a relaxing game of golf. But suddenly, after two or three shots, the ball was bulleting off the middle of the bat and I was launched into as fine a piece of batting as I have ever been able to produce."

Denness recalls a strange prelude to the same innings, one which illustrates the lack of self-belief which plagued Cowdrey throughout his career. "Ken Suttle was bowling left-arm round from the Nackington Road end with five in the covers. Colin was padded up to go in at No 4, but he suddenly said to Alan Dixon, who was sitting beside him in the dressing room, 'Dicko, go and put your pads on.' 'Why Colin?' 'Someone's got to knock this lad off his length. You're the man to do it.' You just know that whatever's going through Colin's mind, Ken Suttle's thinking, 'How am I going to bowl to this lad?' Luckily Alan managed to persuade him to go in. The first ball he receives bisects the covers and he's off."

Not surprisingly, the man-of-the-match award went to Cowdrey, though Shepherd reckoned that he had a decent rival claim, arguing that he and Luckhurst had battled through when the going was tougher in the early stages of the Kent innings. Underwood agreed.

The final was an occasion beyond comparison with anything that the bulk of the Kent players had experienced. Cowdrey was the only seasoned international; of the others Underwood and Brown boasted six Test caps between them. "I believe we won the game against Somerset the night before," argues Denness. "We were all staying in the Clarendon Court. Some of us were having a drink at the bar with some of the Somerset lads and suddenly we say to them, 'See you later.' They reply, 'Where are you going?' 'Oh, we've got a team meeting.' 'You've got a what?' Nobody ever talked about team meetings before. 'What are you going to talk about?' 'See you tomorrow, lads.' They were still talking about it the following morning."

For the supporters who formed the bulk of the 20,000 crowd, undeterred by an unpopular rise in admission charge to 15s (75p), it was a battle between hop and cider. The hop county made merry after Cowdrey had won the toss, Denness playing with great fluency in an innings of 50 which won him the man-of-the-match award. Kent were ideally placed on 129 for one after 34 overs at lunch, but slumped as the flow of runs was reduced to a trickle.

Colin Cowdrey clutches the Gillette Cup, the first honour of many for an outstanding team, in 1967

Picture: Kent Messenger, PD1673771

A modest total of 193 should have been within Somerset's scope in 60 overs, but they ground to a halt as Brown and Dixon got through four successive maidens, then an eight-over spell in which Shepherd conceded only 10 runs effectively settled the issue. Shepherd's contribution was all the more laudable because he was struggling with a foot injury and, according to Jim Swanton, "scarcely able to put his front foot to the ground". Rigorously impartial in his verdict on the game, Swanton wrote in *The Daily Telegraph*: "I say that the glory was almost exactly shared, and perhaps the qualification might be dispensed with, for Kent had the good luck to win the toss."

Luckhurst, who had faced an anxious wait to see if a finger broken by Trueman three weeks earlier would heal in time, wrote in his memoirs *Boot Boy to President*: "Afterwards, there were some lovely moments as players mingled with a throng of Kent fans gathering outside the Grace Gates to greet those of us who had ventured out from the dressing-room celebrations. When we walked out of that great ground we had proved that we were winners. It was an incredible day, full of the excitement of realising that we could be taking part in a new, long overdue era of success for Kent cricket."

1968

The sense of optimism was heightened by the signing of Asif Iqbal as Kent's second overseas player. Less than a week before the Lord's final, Asif had played one of Test cricket's most extraordinary backs-against-the-wall innings. The outcome was still an easy victory for England over Pakistan at the Oval, but Asif was like a force of nature as he drove, hooked and scythed his way to 146. He revealed afterwards that he was "annoyed because I heard that a 20-over exhibition was being arranged to compensate the crowd for the early ending of the Test. Everyone seemed to accept that it was already over. I certainly didn't."

Although Asif was suddenly besieged by potential suitors – Middlesex and Warwickshire were among the counties interested in signing him – Kent were rewarded for their patient wooing. Asif had spoken to Les Ames when he managed an England Under 25 side, including Alan Knott and Derek Underwood, on their 1966-67 tour of Pakistan. "We didn't talk about the possibility of my joining Kent then," he recalls, "but when I came to England with the Pakistan team, Colin Cowdrey approached me verbally. 'Would you be interested?' And I said, 'Yes.' I went back to Pakistan and received a letter from Les Ames offering me a contract."

Asif's ability had first come to Kent's attention in 1963 when he was part of a Pakistan Eaglets side who beat the county by an innings at Dartford. He was and remained a genuine all-rounder, though recurring back trouble prevented him from playing a full part as a bowler after 1967. "It actually helped my batting a lot because I knew from then on that if I was to keep my place in the team I had to perform as a batsman, whereas when you're an all-rounder you can always make up for not scoring runs by taking wickets and vice versa."

He bowled a paltry 46 championship overs in his first season for Kent, only four more than he had delivered in England's first innings at the Oval the previous summer. Asif enjoyed a reasonably consistent year with the bat, though he failed to make a hundred, and there was a familiar dependence on the opening partnership of Brian Luckhurst and Mike Denness. Their chemistry on the field continued off it, with the families joining forces for off-season holidays.

The superstitious Luckhurst – Underwood recalls that if he scored a hundred he always wore the same clothes the following day – insisted on walking out on the right; while it was always Denness who took first ball. He remembers a period of adjustment in the partnership's early days. "Lucky was not the easiest to run with because of these little movements he had, but we worked out a system. We used to drive other teams mad, especially in one-day cricket: Lucky would just drop it in the block hole and run."

Kent looked rather less secure at No 3, further evidence of Colin Cowdrey's inability to see that the best solution to a problem might lie with him. Instead, Knott was asked to go in at three at the start of the season; David Nicholls, Asif and Graham Johnson all filled the role at various times. Bob Woolmer was blooded in 1968, adding to the already healthy complement of all-rounders on Kent's staff. Norman Graham was the one player who knew from game to game what his allotted place would be, though even No 11 seemed almost too good for someone who boasted a career batting average of 3.88.

Asif Iqbal, a hugely entertaining addition to the Kent side in 1968

Luckhurst described both 1968 and 1969 as "highly disappointing in their different ways", though the frustration in 1968 was a reflection of the new-found self-belief rather than sub-standard performances. They now believed that they were good enough to win the County Championship, but again finished second to Yorkshire. Kent won 12 matches, one more than the champions, and were beaten only because of their inability to exploit the bonus points system in place that year. Yorkshire's superior firepower understandably brought them 19 more bowling points, but they also outmanoeuvred Kent in the batting-points department. One was awarded for every 25 runs which a side scored above 150 in the first 85 overs.

Four of Asif's six championship wickets came in Kent's opening match, when they rolled over Lancashire for 69 to win by seven wickets. Underwood, who averaged an impressive 13.58 in taking 91 championship wickets, claimed match figures of 11 for 146 as they saw off Somerset as well. The one significant setback in the first month of the season was an early conclusion to Kent's Gillette Cup defence, though they almost conjured an extraordinary victory when seemingly down and out against Gloucestershire at Bristol. Kent made only 110 on a tricky rain-affected wicket, and Gloucestershire were 109 for four in reply before losing five wickets on the same score. The last pair saw them nervously over the line.

Underwood was such an awkward proposition on helpful pitches at Swansea and Gillingham, which was reported to Lord's for the second successive season, that back-to-back wins over Glamorgan and Hampshire brought him a combined haul of 22 wickets at a cost of just 126. A second innings victory over Glamorgan, this time in the final match of the season, ensured that Kent pipped the Welsh county for second place.

John Shepherd was even more successful than he had been in his first season and, despite missing three championship games through injury, was only four wickets short of becoming the first Kent player since Les Todd in 1936 to complete the double. A memorable run-a-minute innings of 170 against Northamptonshire would remain the highest score of his career. Kent could congratulate themselves on shrewd business: Shepherd's salary may have risen from £450 to £700 a year, but it was still only a tenth of the money which had enticed Gary Sobers to join Nottinghamshire in 1968. Cowdrey sounded more like a contented committee man than a captain when he observed that Shepherd and Asif were "both prepared to fall in with our existing scales of pay".

Shepherd suffered as much as anybody from the game of musical chairs which Kent's batting line-up often resembled, but he was appeased by Cowdrey's vision of the future. "Alan Dixon was coming towards the end of his career and Colin wanted me to take over the all-rounder's role. As a result he thought if I was going to be bowling more I'd need more time to recoup. They used to put me on at one end and forget, but I couldn't realistically be bowling 30 or 40 overs and then padded up to come in at three. If someone got out first ball I'd have been out in the middle again after 10 minutes off the field." His only complaint was that rain-affected pitches – a happy hunting ground for Underwood and Graham – were maddeningly elusive when Underwood was on England duty.

There could be no complaints about the commitment of either Shepherd or Asif, but Kent were not immune from the growing concern in the late Sixties that overseas players were depriving home-grown cricketers of county places. Even someone like Alan Ealham, who was to become such an integral part of the Kent team, felt the pressure. "I was in and out of the team quite a lot at that stage."

The sniff of sustained success was certainly helping the county's finances. Membership rose to 6,734 in 1968 and kept on climbing until it peaked at

8,300 in 1974. There was a crowd of 12,000 on the first day of Kent's match against Yorkshire at Canterbury, again a potential championship decider, but the match was wrecked by rain. A second-day wash-out coincided with the Duke and Duchess of Kent's first visit to the ground.

Three weeks later Kent supporters could be forgiven for paying only partial attention to an entertaining game against a Rest of the World XI as Underwood inspired one of the most exciting finishes in Test history. John Inverarity, later to be Kent coach, padded up inexplicably with six minutes' playing time remaining to become Underwood's seventh victim at the Oval. The hero of the hour was surprised to be reminded that he and Kent were collapsing against the pace of Middlesex's John Price at Lord's less than 24 hours later.

1969

Alan Dixon again led the side during Colin Cowdrey's frequent absences, but one of the more significant aspects of a distinctly disappointing 1969 for Kent was the emergence of Mike Denness as a potential successor to Cowdrey. They already knew that they would be without John Shepherd for the first half of season, deservedly chosen to play for a West Indies side in transition. In the event he barely played in the second half of the season either, laid low by a back injury which Kent, and Denness, in particular, regarded as the legacy of an over-punishing workload in the three-Test series.

The additional concern for Shepherd was that he might actually finish the season out of pocket. The salaries of Kent's senior players crept over the £1,000 mark in 1969, but Derek Underwood and Alan Knott both felt undervalued. The club's response, instead of changing the basic wage structure, was to give players £75 for each Test they played in. Shepherd, whose tour fee was £450, argued successfully that the same principle should apply to his international appearances.

He was to play only twice more for the West Indies, and though their increasing reliance on out-and-out pace in the Seventies was a partial explanation, he remains puzzled. "To this day I don't know why. I felt I was a reasonable cricketer but later, after I was dropped, I realised what I could have contributed to the team. I think when they got rid of me I was becoming a far better player. When I was starting out, everyone was saying, 'Oh he'll captain the West Indies.' Suddenly I went from being thought of as probably a captain at some time to not even being selected."

Shepherd, at that stage anyway, could feel perfectly secure about his job prospects with Kent. The same could not be said of the county's branch of the pacemen's union. David Sayer, Alan Brown, John Dye and Norman Graham were co-signatories of a letter in 1969 which, according to committee minutes, "concerned the possible loss of emoluments in the forthcoming season, due to the impracticality of playing all four in the county side". Their worries were far from groundless: Sayer, Brown and Dye had all been released by the end of the 1971 season.

The club were still coming to terms with the death in early March of their dynamic chairman, Stuart Chiesman, when his son-in-law suffered an injury which was to end his season almost before it had begun. Cowdrey snapped an Achilles tendon while batting against Glamorgan in a televised John Player Sunday League match at The Mote on 25 May. Kent still recorded a fourth successive win in the competition, which attracted excellent crowds in its first season, but their challenge soon fizzled out on all fronts.

Denness, who embraced one-day cricket much more readily than Cowdrey, had already taken charge of Kent's championship side when Dixon was suffering from flu. He had expected to rejoin the ranks when Dixon was fit again, but was told: "You're the future." Denness was given an early taste of the Kent players' capacity for enjoying themselves on the road while they were playing Nottinghamshire. "Police arrived at Newark wanting to see me because a bicycle was seen being hauled up to the second floor of a B & B we were in. It finished up in Stuart Leary's bedroom; Norman Graham was probably the culprit. The owners of that pub didn't want us back again for some reason."

The Scot had come perilously close to losing all future claims to the captaincy almost seven years earlier. Fresh from his first season in the Kent side he had fielded a question-and-answer session at a function in Dartford just before Christmas 1962. His recollection now is that when asked pointedly by a supporter if it was not possible for Kent to be both entertaining and successful, he responded that it was difficult when the best batsman, Cowdrey, was absent for so many games. No room for misinterpretation there perhaps, but the explanation in his autobiography that "to achieve unity in the side it was necessary to have the captain there the whole time" painted a more ambiguous picture.

He was contacted by a newspaper reporter a few days later and asked to elaborate. Was he not suggesting that Cowdrey should be sacked? Denness categorically denied that he was proposing anything of the kind, but was confronted the following day by a screaming headline in the *Daily Sketch*. It read: 'Sack Cowdrey from Kent captaincy – says Mike Denness'. The story was soon reverberating around the cricketing world, including Australia, where Cowdrey was on tour with England. A succinct telegram from Billy Griffith, the England manager, read: "Cowdrey perturbed. Explanation wanted."

Denness's defence was relayed to Les Ames after a quick dash to St Lawrence. Ames then attempted to douse the flames with appearances on the BBC and Southern Television and an interview for *The Daily Telegraph*. Denness remembers: "I received a nice letter from Stuart Chiesman, the chairman, saying that the club totally accepted that I had been misquoted and that nothing more would be said." Cowdrey himself was so mollified that, according to Denness, the matter was never raised again.

Kent's complement of England players increased when Denness was rewarded for a productive season with the bat by making his Test debut alongside Underwood and Knott against New Zealand. For the second successive year the Oval proved to be the happiest of hunting grounds for Underwood, who recorded outstanding match figures of 12 for 101. Denness helped clinch an eight-wicket win with an unbeaten 55. Brian Luckhurst enjoyed his best season to date, hitting four centuries, and found, much like New Zealander Glenn Turner, that one-day cricket had a liberating effect on his batting. Underwood, in his foreword to Luckhurst's memoirs, wrote: "For three years – 1969, 1970 and 1971 – Brian Luckhurst was, in my opinion, the premier batsman in England. Moreover, and this applies for the whole of his long and remarkable career, he was the gutsiest cricketer I ever came across."

Another of Kent's most loyal servants, Dixon, deserved better for his benefit match against Gloucestershire than the lifeless Canterbury pitch which, according to a committee report, produced an "appalling" game. The fall-out was so great that the head groundsman, Ed Baker, lost his job, leading to the appointment of the long-serving and highly respected Brian Fitch. The club were considering an eviction order when Baker finally moved out of the groundsman's cottage at St Lawrence the following year.

For all the mitigating factors, there was immense disappoint-

A great combination: Kent's openers for all seasons (left) Brian Luckhurst and Mike Denness

ment that a Kent side who had promised so much in finishing runners-up in the championship in the previous two seasons should regress to 10th in 1969. Two of their four wins were condensed into five days of low-scoring mayhem in May. One of Luckhurst's luckier hundreds (he was dropped four times) was followed by a feeble batting display by Middlesex. Underwood and Bob Woolmer took all 10 wickets between them in a first-innings total of 50. Kent's innings victory at Lord's was quickly followed by a seven-wicket win over Essex at Brentwood, where the conditions were so in favour of the bowlers that 27 wickets fell on the opening day. Kent trailed by 50 on first innings after being bowled out for 81, but the steep lift gained by Graham so discomfited a strong-looking Essex side that they were bowled out for 34, a total which remains their lowest since 1901. Graham returned career-best figures of eight for 20.

According to *Wisden*, the "real ray of sunshine" in a distinctly overcast summer for Kent was Graham Johnson, a player with considerable ability in all three cricketing disciplines. He had first played for Kent as an 18-year-old in 1965, but soon found himself mulling over various possible career paths. "I'd had an offer from Manchester University and also got the offer to sign forms for Kent," he recalls. "I thought I was god's gift to cricket and I'd be playing in the first team so I signed forms for Kent. I did play a little bit, but it was more a case of what was I going to do out of season that determined that I went to Les Ames and said, 'Look, I really want to play cricket, but there must be more to life than some of the things I'm doing out of season.' In the end I went to LSE [London School of Economics]. It was a bit ground-breaking because the county paid me half my salary to go to university provided that whenever I played cricket during the summer I was available for Kent."

1970

Colin Cowdrey described his attempt to turn Kent into a championship-winning side as a 15-year "crusade". Fulfilment finally arrived in the county's centenary year, though he admitted in his autobiography: "There were times in that summer of 1970 when life would have been infinitely preferable on the moon." Early that year Edward Heath, Kent native and leader of the Conservative opposition, had dared to indulge in some optimistic crystal-ball gazing at the club's centenary dinner. "I should have thought that until now 1906 was probably our most important year. It saw a change of government and it saw Kent win the County Championship for the first time. Now 1970...well, what could be more certain?"

Three months later Heath was duly installed as Prime Minister, but Kent were better bets to win the wooden spoon than the championship pennant. Heath despatched a telegram to Cowdrey saying, "I've achieved my ambition, but I'm a bit worried about yours." On 1 July, Kent were bottom of the championship table, 68 points adrift of Surrey. The morale of players and supporters slipped another notch a week later when the side slipped to a tame Gillette Cup defeat against Sussex.

The turning point was not on the field of play, but at a behind-closed-doors meeting on the eve of a championship match against Derbyshire at Maidstone. The under-performing side were subjected to a straight-talking tirade from Les Ames. Mike Denness remembers: "The plain fact was that we were playing badly. We were losing matches we shouldn't have lost and Les laid into us. It was the most critical I'd ever known him be. He made it very clear that it was just not good enough, and that members would leave if we carried on that way." Cowdrey insisted: "I may be overstating the case, but I shall always think that the spirit generated in that meeting provided the basis for our winning the championship."

Graham Johnson takes a more sober view of the part which the Maidstone summit played in Kent's revival: "I'm not sure it was very different from a couple of other meetings we had that summer. The thing which made it stand out was that the focus was on the fact that we were bottom of the championship. We were thinking: the only way from here is up. We had a pretty open and honest bunch of players who told it how it was in those days. We had an approach which carried through much of the Seventies which said, go in the dressing room, lock the door, say what you need to say in a constructive way, even if some of it is pretty hard. Once the door is open again you're out there as a bunch of players supporting each other. Whatever the magic was it achieved the result."

The specific, if rather obvious message, was that Kent's free-scoring batting line-up had to exploit the generous batting bonus point system more productively if they were to stand a chance of making up the leeway. For the third successive season a point was awarded for every 25 runs a team scored over 150 in the first 85 overs. Hampshire had shown just what could be achieved the previous summer by managing 11 in a single game. Cowdrey himself had utterly failed to lead by example at the start of the season, making only 152 runs in 13 innings, and though his form improved considerably Kent were forced to dig ever deeper into their reserve strength as Cowdrey, Denness, Luckhurst, Knott and Underwood were all picked by England for their fill-in series against the Rest of the World.

The player who exemplified Kent's surge of self-belief in the second half of the season was Asif Iqbal, not just for some scintillating innings, but through his cheery refusal to accept that anything was beyond them. "I've always had this optimistic outlook on life," he admits. "I believe that firstly you go out there to give your best and secondly you're an entertainer. And you can't entertain the people who are paying to watch you if you don't have a smile on your face." The welcome by-product of an increased scoring rate in the first innings – Kent upped their game so impressively that they claimed 24 batting points in their last four games alone – was that they gave themselves longer to force victories. They did not lose a single one of their last 13 matches.

Cowdrey was still convinced, after Kent had drawn a game with Middlesex at Canterbury at the start of August, that they had left the charge too late. He confessed as much to Asif: "What a tragedy this season isn't a week longer. We would win the title the way we are playing now." Asif responded: "No, no, skipper. You've got it wrong. We've got enough time. If it was any longer we would get stale. I've already told Mike Denness. We shall win it in our last match at the Oval."

The Kent players had to negotiate floods to reach Weston-super-Mare at 2.45am before the start of their game against Somerset. A lost toss and ominously solid start by the Somerset openers, Roy Virgin and Tony Clarkson, added to their under-prepared fatigue before Bob Woolmer swung the game Kent's way with inspired figures of six for 53. They went on to win by 10 wickets and Woolmer remembered it as a landmark game, the first time he had felt able to contribute significantly to a Kent victory in the championship. He was brought back down to earth when he returned home and discovered that Alan Brown, a practical joker of repute, had stuffed half-a-dozen beer glasses into various spare compartments in his suspiciously heavy travelling case.

The whole side started to believe Asif when they pulled off an improbable victory on a spinners' wicket at Cheltenham. Kent only avoided the follow-on by a single run, but a quick-footed hundred from Asif somehow enabled them to chase down a victory target of 340. He then pulled off, in Cowdrey's words, "as remarkable a catch as I have seen in cricket", running "about 200 yards" (Asif's semi-serious estimate) to intercept what seemed a certain six from Surrey's last man, Pat Pocock, in the penultimate over at Blackheath. A likely defeat, and probable end to the title challenge, became a 12-run win instead.

More heroics followed at Folkestone, where Gary Sobers put his Nottinghamshire side in a dominant position by making an unbeaten century. Kent were reeling on 27 for five after a three-wicket burst from their former seamer,

Dave Halfyard, but Brian Luckhurst came to the rescue with an unbeaten 156 which he described as his most important ever innings for Kent. Alan Ealham was capped after playing a key supporting role in the recovery.

Two years earlier Sobers had played what Derek Underwood described as "the most incredible innings I have seen" to bring Nottinghamshire an unlikely triumph over Kent at Trent Bridge. Alan Dixon had angered Sobers by delaying his declaration and watched, increasingly helpless, as the peerless left-hander made 108 out of 148 in 75 minutes to guide Nottinghamshire to a memorable victory with 20 minutes to spare.

Fortunately for Kent, Sobers was in a calmer frame of mind in 1970. As captain he could have slammed the door closed on a perfect pitch, but recognised that a title-hungry Kent side would chase just about anything. The eventual target was an exacting 282 in three hours, but Denness led the way with 90 and a flurry of boundaries from Alan Knott took Kent home with eight balls to spare. The *Times* described it as a "sensational" win.

Knott, then at the height of his powers as a wicketkeeper, was less certain about his role as a batsman. He later reflected: "It was an unusual county season for me, batting once at number three and for the rest of the campaign anywhere between six and ten. Twice I didn't get in when batting at ten and yet I had averaged 30 in five Tests against the Rest of the World, batting at seven."

The following day Norman Graham went into hospital for an operation to remove poisoned, ingrowing nails on both big toes and Kent began their penultimate match, against Leicestershire; they were by now so irrepressibly dominant that they claimed a then record 23 points to win by an innings. Johnson followed his 12-wicket haul in the win over Surrey with a brilliant century, completed with a mighty six off Peter Stringer in the final bonus-point over. At the start of the over Johnson and Shepherd had needed 18 runs to secure an eighth batting point, and a sequence of 4, 6, 1, 0, 6, 2 achieved the aim.

Jim Swanton was transported back to the inter-war era, declaring that Kent's batting "has been in the character of the great years, uplifting all hearts and illustrating in the most emphatic manner what the modern cricketer can do if he has the will, and is granted a good pitch". To Swanton, the quicksilver Asif was like the carefree amateur in a world of hard-nosed professionals, a modern incarnation of Percy Chapman. Swanton contrasted Asif the batsman with the Kent captain: "Cowdrey's inclinations lie in quieter waters, but he adapted himself to the needs of the moment rather like a benevolent uncle indulging the children." Asif himself is quick to deflect credit to Cowdrey: "He was quite influential in letting me play the way I was used to, without telling me to curb my instincts. He had great faith in me."

The sustained pressure on Kent had suddenly lifted, and they needed only a handful of bonus points from their final game at the Oval to end the 57-year wait for a fifth championship crown. To Luckhurst it was, simply, "the stuff of legend" and "must rank alongside any of the more remarkable stories which sport throws up with glorious regularity". Swanton reminded *Telegraph* readers that Cowdrey's two longstanding ambitions had been to lead England in Australia and carry off the County Championship. The first ambition remained unfulfilled, but the second was gloriously confirmed by a innings of high quality from Cowdrey. "The county of hops can drain its collective tankard," Swanton wrote.

Cowdrey had dissuaded the Kent committee from reducing the playing staff for 1970 – the previous summer's disappointing results had put the county back in the red – and though he felt vindicated the financial reality had not changed. "Thrilling and gratifying though it was," Cowdrey wrote in his autobi-ography, "it brought only temporary relief from the pressing problems of finance. To be honest, we could not afford the champagne we drank and shared with our friends that September evening in our dressing room at the Oval." Cowdrey had made no previous decision about the captaincy, but when questioned by the press about his future plans he announced that he would be stepping down at the end of the 1971 season. Edward Heath, who recalled how as a boy he had cycled the 18 miles from his Broadstairs home to watch Kent at Canterbury, joined in the champagne celebrations and later fulfilled his pre-season promise by inviting the players to a dinner at 10 Downing Street.

Despite the draining effect of making up so much lost ground in the champi-onship, Kent had also managed to sustain their challenge for the John Player League. They eventually finished five points behind Lancashire, the one side who would challenge Kent's one-day supremacy in the early Seventies, but at least had the satisfaction of inflicting one of only two defeats on the Red Rose side. There was a confused aftermath to the rain-affected game: Kent reached a 10-over target of 57 with an over to spare but Lancashire challenged the result on the grounds that Kent's innings had not lasted the minimum 10 overs required under the competition's regulations; Lord's upheld the result. Stuart Leary, who until 1966 had led a sporting double life as hard-hitting batsman and prolific striker for Charlton and Queens Park Rangers, topped the league's six-hitting table, while Woolmer was on course to becoming the first player to reach 50 wickets.

He was so highly regarded as a one-day bowler that he was picked to play in the Prudential series against Australia in 1972, three years before he was recognised at Test level. The need to maintain strict line and length, in a

Prime Minister Edward Heath plays host to Kent's championship-winning side in 1970

Picture: Kent Messenger, PD1673758

defensive context, helped Woolmer to develop as a bowler in all forms of the game. He found, however, that some of his new England colleagues were more cynical about one-day cricket. "It was as though they considered it not to be the real thing," he said. Kent, according to Woolmer, were one of the first counties to appreciate the value of the block-hole ball in restricting scoring opportunities. Even at a stage when his playing career had barely taken flight, Woolmer was a coach in the making. He assisted Colin Page with courses at Sevenoaks in 1967 and 1968 and soon afterwards launched the Bob Woolmer Coaching School at the Drill Hall in Tunbridge Wells ... before being ejected by the local council.

Although the achievement attracted few headlines, it was no less laudable that the 2nd XI managed to win their championship for the second successive season in 1970. Underwood, one of the players whose frequent England appearances left the back-up troops in a constant state of flux, feels that they showed immense patience. "It says a lot for the spirit of the side," wrote Underwood in 1975, "that these movements have taken place without a major row flaring up inside the camp." He also believes that players were subject to Cowdrey's whim on selection and batting order. "He tended to change the side around, feeling that some players were suited to certain conditions. That didn't go down too well with some."

A thoroughly decent man though Cowdrey was, part of him seemed to reside in a bygone world of polite propriety. He had an almost reverential regard for good manners and customs which, he believed, were too easily jettisoned in the name of progress. Winning the championship was not the only thing on his mind in 1970. He witnessed the kind of player behaviour which, to his mind, could lead to "awkward, unpleasant and unnecessary tensions" and was troubled by the experience. Significantly, the episode has not stuck in the minds of the players involved.

"An example occurred in 1970 when a number of Kent players appeared for breakfast in the dining room of the Grand Hotel, Leicester, wearing sweaters instead of jackets and ties. It was the last morning of the match and that evening we were driving off to another game. Sweaters were probably more suitable for the evening drive but the fact remained that this was breakfast and I had always requested my players at least to wear a blazer, if not actually a suit when they appeared officially for a Kent match. No one in the hotel complained but the fact remained that Kent County Cricket Club looked more like a coach party than a professional cricket team with a long tradition. I felt that we had a responsibility to the club and to cricket to look the part, both on and off the field. Twenty years earlier the captain would have informed the senior professional that he had better see to it swiftly that the players were properly dressed, a course of action which the players would have accepted without complaint. In 1970 [this was written in 1976] I played it quietly. I knew that if I created a scene I would probably have had to live with the resentment of the players for the next two matches and it was the cricket which was important."

It is easy to forget that Kent cricket was still a highly moveable feast at the start of the 1970s. The St Lawrence Ground, spruced up for the centenary with reconstructed pavilion and new dressing rooms, was just another port of call on the complicated itinerary. Prior to the redevelopment, wrote Cowdrey, the ground was like "a fourth division club" to the Oval's "Highbury". Players were still risking splinters on a dressing-room floor which had been "roughed up by the studs of Frank Woolley".

In 1970 Kent played one championship game at Dartford, Gravesend and Dover, two at Tunbridge Wells, Maidstone and Canterbury, then finished off the season with a single match at Blackheath and two at Folkestone. Cowdrey observed that the dressing room at the Bat and Ball Ground in Gravesend was so small that players had to take it in turns to change. Gillingham (downgraded in 1968), Blackheath and Tunbridge Wells all offered basic facilities and Cowdrey admitted: "Several of our players solemnly believed that Kent could never win a championship playing on nine different grounds with such variable conditions. It was as if we were playing away."

The winds of change were starting to blow, however. Blackheath and Gravesend both disappeared from the roster after the 1971 season and Dover lost its first-class status in 1976. James Graham-Brown, then restricted to 12th man duties with the first team, remembers an amusing prelude to the game against Derbyshire with which Kent concluded their championship business at Blackheath. "Colin Cowdrey was driving me to the game in his wonderful car with the registration plate MCC 307 [his highest score]. When we got through the Dartford tunnel we realised that we were going to be late so he stopped the car and phoned the ground. Ian Buxton, the Derbyshire captain, came on the line and Colin tossed the coin in the telephone box. 'Your call,' he said. 'Heads,' Ian replied. 'Heads it is. Bat or bowl?' "

Gravesend had been staging Kent matches since 1849, but there had been few more memorable personal confrontations than that between Warwickshire's Rohan Kanhai and Underwood in 1970. For Underwood there was the strange experience of taking 14 wickets in a match for the only time in his career and still finishing on the losing side. On a pitch which favoured the bowlers throughout, Kanhai set the mood by hitting his first ball from Underwood for a straight six and went on to make a brilliant 107. The bowler recalled that Kanhai's genius was in playing on a line with his stumps rather than instinctively following the turning ball.

Opposition batsmen viewed Kent's outgrounds with suspicion, convinced that they were prepared to suit 'Deadly' Derek Underwood. The bowler himself enlisted the help of BBC statistician Bill Frindall to investigate the claim and was delighted (as well as being a bit surprised) to discover that in the first seven years of his career his wickets-per-match ratio was actually higher outside the county (4.58) than in it (3.78). One undeniable fact was that there was no more feared bowler in the world on the rain-affected wickets which preceded the introduction of fully covered pitches in 1980 (an 'evil day' was Jim Swanton's verdict). Kent players would greet the arrival of threatening skies with a half-joking aside to Underwood, 'That's a five for 40 cloud up there, Deadly.'

Denness, one of the England and Wales Cricket Board's panel of pitch inspectors in recent seasons, insisted as captain that team-mates should accept things which they could not change. "I used to say to the Kent players, go out and have a look at the wicket, and then I don't want anyone to complain about it after that. I don't want people coming in and throwing their bat down in the dressing room and saying, 'That was a bloody awful wicket.' If you're good enough you'll win on any pitch which is produced. That's your job. So the only time players came in and threw their bat down was when they thought they'd got a bad decision."

1971

Mike Denness, who had been desperately disappointed to miss selection for England's tour of Australia – a trip on which Brian Luckhurst came of age as a Test player – again found himself captaining Kent for an extended period in 1971, when Colin Cowdrey went down with pneumonia. Part of the dressing-room furniture was missing that summer: Alan Dixon. The bespectacled all-rounder's popularity extended well beyond Kent's boundaries; to Derek Underwood he was the player who best illustrated that cricket was meant to be enjoyed rather than endured. Dixon himself reflects: "If you started in 1950, as I did, you saw the rock bottom of Kent and then by 1970 the highlights and everything in between. I saw some pretty awful times which probably made me more appreciative of the good times than most."

Dixon's final season encapsulated all the elements: his father died and he could only bowl in discomfort after wrenching his shoulder when he landed awkwardly trying to take a return catch. The injury, which ended his career, has troubled him ever since, though he went out on a personal high when he hit fellow off-spinner Fred Titmus for six at Canterbury. A month later he was sharing in the pride that enveloped the club after they had won the championship and went on to play a significant role in the development of the next generation of Kent players as coach at Tonbridge School.

Although Graham Johnson had stepped into Dixon's shoes, Underwood believed that his subsequent development as an off-spinning all-rounder was mismanaged. When Denness, as captain, started pushing himself down the order, Johnson was promoted to open, though Denness himself admitted: "I don't think Brian ever settled into having anyone else to open with him, but I was only looking at how the Kent side might be more successful."

Underwood was of the view that Johnson's bowling should have taken priority, but the player himself saw his role in a pragmatic light. "The more options you have the more chance you've got of being in the side, so I worked hard at all three aspects. In my benefit brochure I described my career in stages. The first bit was a bowler who batted, then it was a batsman who bowled, then reverting back to a bowler who batted and the last four years was confused. If I was being hard on myself, I could say I was jack of all trades but not quite master of enough to get to a higher level. If I'd been playing in a less talented side I'd probably have got more opportunity to bat and bowl, but I wouldn't have changed anything on the way. Let's face it: when you've got Deadly in the side you're not going to be getting on as the first spinner."

The disruption caused by England calls, illness and injury seriously undermined Kent's attempts to retain the championship in 1971. Asif Iqbal was vice-captain of the touring Pakistan side in the first half of the summer, and Denness himself, John Shepherd, Norman Graham and Bob Woolmer were all missing for extended periods. In the circumstances fourth place could be considered a reasonable outcome. Luckhurst played outstandingly, and Alan Knott enjoyed one of his best seasons with the bat, but Kent were over-dependent on the wickets of Underwood and Graham.

John Dye, who had never quite fulfilled his promise as a left-arm bowler, inevitably suffered the consequences of Kent's decision to sign Bernard Julien, another left-armer, as their third overseas player, and was released at the end of the 1971 season. Members inevitably concluded that Kent had never got the best out of Dye when he moved to Northamptonshire and took 79 wickets at 18 apiece in his debut season. Dye had a non-conformist streak which, for the most part, endeared him to team-mates but ruffled committees. His pointed response to being told, just before Kent's final championship game against Nottinghamshire, that he was being allowed to leave, was to take seven for 118, his best analysis for the county. Two days later he was lining up against Lancashire at Lord's.

Dye's capacity to infuriate was summed up for stand-in captain Dixon by an episode in Kent's championship game against Northamptonshire at Wellingborough in 1968. "John had been out with a pulled muscle and at tea on the first day I looked out of the pavilion window and there he was kicking a football around with some kids. I said, 'You can't do that, John, we've got a cricket match to win here.' Northants began their first innings after tea and John took the new ball with Norman Graham. He'd bowled all of four balls when he started his run-up, took about four paces, stopped, threw me the ball and said, 'Guess what?' We didn't get another ball out of him in that game." The ever dependable John Shepherd and Underwood still enabled Kent to sneak home by five runs.

Alan Ealham recalls another occasion when Dye was bemoaning his luck at Derby. "There was an edge to second slip which went down and John stood there, hands on hips and said: 'That's the 32nd catch I've had dropped off me this year.' Colin Cowdrey just said, 'Come on John. Get back and bowl.'"

Kent had to settle for mid-table anonymity in the John Player League, but their season was kept gloriously alive by a barely troubled passage to the

Poetry in motion: the rhythmical action which helped Derek Underwood to be Kent's greatest match-winner of the modern era

Gillette Cup final. Cowdrey fell only two runs short of his maiden one-day hundred against a first-class county as Kent beat Northamptonshire, then Julien took five for 25 to claim the man-of-the-match award against Yorkshire. Luckhurst scored heavily in both the quarter-final and semi-final. They should have gone into the final against Lancashire with confidence but, in contrast to 1967, there was an eve-of-match anxiety about Kent which did not bode well. Inevitably, the one player who exuded calm self-belief was Asif.

Luckhurst remembered: "Despite our previous success at Lord's something didn't seem quite right and Asif himself sensed it. He suddenly announced to everyone, 'There is no need to worry, lads, because we are going to win today and I am going to win the man-of-the-match award.' That immediately lifted the tension and I remember thinking how clever it was of Asif to do it that way."

Without 'That Darn Catch', to adapt the title of a 1960s Walt Disney film, Asif's prediction would probably have come stunningly true. He deservedly won the man-of-the-match award for a wonderful innings of 89 but, with Kent needing 28 at exactly a run a ball, Lancashire captain Jack Bond sabotaged their hopes with a once-in-a-lifetime catch as Asif made room to hit Jack Simmons through the off side. Asif wept in frustration when he returned to the dressing room; Kent's last three wickets followed in a panic-stricken rush and they lost by 24 runs.

Asif hesitates to call it the lowest point in his Kent career, but admits: "What made it particularly disappointing is that I believe we were the better side. We just didn't perform well as a team. I wouldn't say it was *the* most disappointing occasion, but it was certainly the one match which nobody ever let me forget, right through to my last day of playing for the county."

Woolmer described the game as "a personal disaster for me". On Cowdrey's recommendation he had spent the previous winter in South Africa – the start of a long and fruitful association – and described himself as "fit and raring to go". He felt that Alan Brown's retirement had, for the first time, made him a first-choice selection and was bursting with optimism when he dislocated a shoulder trying to scoop up a catch at short leg during the Canterbury Week championship match against Yorkshire. He was still suffering recurring pain from the injury when he retired 13 years later. He was included at Lord's, though still short of match fitness, and after being unusually expensive with the ball he was bowled trying to hit Peter Lever out of the ground.

Julien, who also perished tamely, had more natural ability than Shepherd, his fellow West Indian, but the latent promise was rarely translated into telling performances in his seven years with Kent. Underwood feels that he was never given the guidance he needed, and that the pattern was set from the very moment he arrived, as a slightly bewildered 20-year-old in the spring of 1970. There was no one to meet him at Heathrow Airport, so he had to take a taxi to Canterbury. He was unwisely installed at the city's Monument pub.

Both Underwood and Knott were playing against Julien when he scored a brilliant Test century at Lord's in 1973, and Knott was convinced that Kent could have got more out of the Trinidadian if he had gone in higher than his customary No 9, especially in one-day cricket. Knott described him as "potentially the best all-rounder" Kent had ever had. "He was a very formidable new-ball left-arm bowler, swinging the ball into the right-hander, with a great line and length; he had the ability also to bowl orthodox spin and wrist spin." Julien's party piece was to throw a cricket ball from the far side of the square at Canterbury over the Frank Woolley Stand.

He never became part of Kent's social fabric like Shepherd and Asif, who achieved a warm rapport with supporters. Mike Denness, in nostalgic mode, paints a picture of rarely achieved unity between sportsmen and the people who pay to watch them. "The Kent public wanted to see entertaining cricketers play entertaining cricket. In the Seventies, when John Shepherd used to field down by the old scorebox, it was extraordinary the number of supporters who used to congregate down there because they knew John would chat to them. Alan Ealham used to field down by the old lime tree; he dives on one occasion to stop the ball and rips his shirt and the next day they gave him a new shirt. There would be supporters standing outside the gate at the St Lawrence Ground at six o'clock in the morning before a big one-day match. That's what it's all about and they knew that the players were not going to be at arm's length. We wanted them to be part of it."

The affection was reciprocated by Shepherd, who remembers: "I loved the Kent supporters and I think they respected the fact that I always gave a hundred per cent. I always say to people that I knew half the supporters and the other half knew me. I had a great, great time."

Kent's players were aware by now that Cowdrey and Denness were very different, both as people and captains. Cowdrey may have earned the nickname 'Kipper' because of his tendency to drop off without warning, but he was regarded with exaggerated respect by many of his team-mates. To Luckhurst, he was simply 'The master'; he described him as "the nicest man I had the pleasure of playing cricket alongside". Derek Underwood was also in the reverential camp and remembers that as a teenager new to the Kent staff he always wanted to bowl in Cowdrey's net. The sense of awe in the great man's presence never quite left him and he did not even feel qualified to use his christian name. "Not long before he died he mentioned it to me at Arundel," Underwood recalls. "He said, 'You never called me Colin.' And I said, 'I couldn't.' For some reason, being my schoolboy hero, it wouldn't have seemed right."

Cowdrey's genuine interest in the welfare and well-being of his players earned him loyalty well beyond the norm. Both Shepherd and Woolmer regarded Cowdrey as a "mentor" and Ealham pays this tribute: "Colin Cowdrey was like a father figure. To all us youngsters he was like our dad and we were going to do what we were told. He helped you with your cricket but he helped you off the field as well, in your private life. If there was someone who felt left out because he hadn't got a bonus he'd raise it with the committee. He was always looking after the players."

Dixon adds: "The top and bottom of Colin was that if you'd just met him today and it came out in conversation that you'd got a child in hospital there was every chance that within 48 hours that child would have had a card and probably a Matchbox toy. That sums him up: an absolute gentleman."

There was, too, a deeply analytical side to Cowdrey, one which, according to Graham Johnson, extended into other fields of endeavour. "He was someone with a lot of theories and it wasn't just cricket. He was the same if he was talking about golf or squash." Woolmer, another keen theorist, wrote: "His ability to communicate his knowledge of the game, without a bat and from the driving seat of a car, was unbelievable." The by-product for Cowdrey himself was a neurotic obsession with style: a single ill-conceived shot could halt a fluent innings in its tracks. Knott wrote in It's Knott Cricket: "I always felt that he might have enjoyed it even more if he hadn't had the worries of captaincy."

Underwood, as someone who resented every run taken off his bowling, warmed to captains who set sympathetic fields. Although his speed through the air and accuracy made him a natural for one-day cricket, he found it hard to accept negative field placings. "My chief worry concerning limited over cricket," he wrote in Beating the Bat, "was that in order to save runs I had to give runs away. That may sound a little Irish, but it does sum up the situation." Underwood likened Cowdrey's fourth-innings tactics in the field to "a grand prix racing driver nursing his car round a twisting circuit in wet weather" but also felt that he could be indecisive when Kent were set a target, uncertain about whether to accept the challenge and unsure as to his own role in the chase.

According to Underwood, Denness was "too nice a man" to be ranked among the best of captains. He was not an instinctive communicator, especially when he was new to the job, and found his leadership under question almost from the word go, initially with Kent, then also when he took charge of the England team. This is his own analysis of the essential differences between him and Cowdrey: "Colin used to take a lot of consultation and liked advice. It seemed a long time before a decision was taken. I just used to discuss it with a couple of the senior lads, but I already had in my mind the decision to take. From a cricket point of view I never liked to wait for something to happen. I wanted to *make* something happen."

Denness also took the realistic view that the lack of a genuinely quick bowler, coupled with the inevitable England calls, made it hard for Kent to challenge for the championship on a consistent basis. He reflects: "If there had been an explosive individual in the side it would have been easier to keep the pressure on. I was attack-minded and always wanted to take the initiative, but we couldn't do anything about the Test calls, so when I took over as captain I believed that the only chance Kent would have, initially, was in the one-day competitions. If we won there it would also give confidence to the lads who came in and might then spill over into the championship as well."

TWO

1972-76: Denness's Downfall

ALTHOUGH MIKE Denness did not take it for granted that he would be asked to succeed Colin Cowdrey as captain, it became clear that he was strongly favoured when Les Ames sounded him out towards the end of the 1971 season. There was no further discussion until the appointment was confirmed during Folkestone Week, when Cowdrey finally rubber-stamped the decision he had made a year earlier.

Denness immediately targeted the John Player League as a competition which he felt Kent were capable of winning for the first time, though by now they were so well geared for one-day success that bookmakers had little hesitation in installing them as favourites for all three limited-overs competitions. The birth of the Benson and Hedges Cup, a marginally shorter version of the Gillette Cup, gave counties another chance for a day out at Lord's. Denness had enough faith in his side to predict at the club's annual meeting that they would win "at least one of the four major competitions in the next four years". The actual return was six trophies in five years, but even success on that scale could not keep him in the job.

He soon discovered that he could not rely on the same loyalty, blind or otherwise, which had characterised Cowdrey's captaincy. Norman Graham did not view Cowdrey as the strongest of captains, but found it hard to warm to Denness's more single-minded approach to the job. "Mike Denness became an individual on his own," he says. "Most of us felt he wasn't listening. I remember that we had a few run-ins, though there was nothing personal about it. It's just the way things were at the time. You can't be all things to all people."

John Shepherd, who himself was seen as a potential captain in the late Seventies, reflects on the make-up of the Kent side of 1971: "We were a very, very good unit by then. I think whoever had taken over we would have been successful. Mike had different ideas, but we all knew what we had to do. We had a team that was like a jigsaw puzzle: the pieces just fitted perfectly. I don't think it really mattered who was captain of that side."

The apparent underachievement in the championship during that period was the one blot on Denness's captaincy CV. He could offer a perfectly plausible explanation – the bowling, in particular, was short of match-winning potential when Derek Underwood was on Test duty – but purist members brought up on nothing but the County Championship still regarded one-day cricket as an ill-bred interloper.

Kent failed to get through the group stages in the Benson and Hedges Cup's first season, but gathered momentum in the remaining three competitions. Warwickshire were so dominant in the championship that long before the end of the season the other 16 teams were fighting it out for the runners-up spot. Given that only one other county, Sussex, finished with fewer bowling points, Kent did remarkably well to come second. Bob Woolmer's under-rated medium pace was to the fore in back-to-back wins in Canterbury Week – he took 19 wickets in three innings against Glamorgan and Sussex – and they pulled off a series of improbable run chases.

There were shades of 1970 in Kent's start to the season: they did not muster a win in the championship until the first week of July. Alan Ealham was the catalyst, making 89 in just over an hour as Kent raced to victory over Middlesex at Maidstone. Bernard Julien's innings of 90, then his best for Kent, was an equally exhilarating affair as Northamptonshire were beaten, and Denness led from the front with a brilliant 146 as they defeated Hampshire. Five victories in the last six games, capped with a thumping innings win over Yorkshire at Bradford, where Underwood returned season's best figures of eight for 70, gave the side renewed confidence in their ability to compete in the three-day format.

The 1972 season was also notable for Alan Knott's finest hour with the bat for Kent. Astonishingly, even allowing for his often lowly place in the batting order, he had taken five years to score his maiden first-class hundred in England. Knott felt at his most proficient as a batsman between 1974 and 1976, but in May 1972 he subdued a Surrey attack spearheaded by Geoff Arnold and Robin Jackman to make unbeaten hundreds in both innings. The venue, appropriately, was Maidstone, Knott's favourite Kent ground, but if the surroundings were familiar there were aspects to his performance which were far from business as usual.

He wrote in his autobiography: "In neither innings at Mote Park did I bat wearing a cap, which was my usual custom, and in the first innings I dropped another of my regular habits – touching the bails on arrival at the crease. It wasn't superstition, as many people thought – it was my way of saying to myself, 'You're out in the middle now,' to switch on the concentration."

The John Player League campaign started promisingly for Kent, with four wins in the first five games, but they somehow managed to throw away a crazy game against Middlesex at Folkestone. Needing only 128 to win, Kent were 109 for three at one point; they then lost their last four wickets on the same score to go down by a single run. Les Ames angrily tore up the winners' cheque which he had already made out to Kent.

Four defeats and a no result in their first 10 games left Kent with no further scope for error, and they showed enormous resolve to win their last six games. A five-run victory over leaders Leicestershire was critical, even more so when Leicestershire then lost to Yorkshire in their last game, giving Kent the chance to clinch the title by beating Worcestershire the following Sunday. They held their nerve magnificently in front of a crowd of 12,000 at St Lawrence; Brian Luckhurst capped an excellent one-day season with an authoritative innings of 67 as victory was clinched with two overs to spare.

Kent's form in the Gillette Cup was less impressive, but they still found themselves in a semi-final against Lancashire, the one side who could be relied upon to stand toe to toe with Denness's side. A fluent innings of 65 by Graham Johnson helped to set up a 33-run win over Gloucestershire in the second round; they then batted carelessly to be rolled over for 137 by Essex at Leyton

Denness on the mike: Kent's captain addresses supporters after the side's John Player League triumph in 1972

Picture: Kent Messenger, PD1673759

in the quarter-finals, only for Shepherd to respond with an outstanding spell of four for 23 which allowed Kent to sneak home by 10 runs.

Their cause was aided by the absence of Keith Fletcher, who four days earlier had been helping an Underwood-inspired England to beat Australia at Headingley on a pitch afflicted with fusarium fungus. Underwood recalls that his team-mate was not as delighted as he might have been that the match was finishing in three days. "Fletch came up to me and said, 'Steady on, Deadly, we don't want the match over today: Essex have got a Sunday League game at Scarborough tomorrow.' I said, 'Hard luck, mate. Kent haven't got a game.'"

Lancashire, especially at Old Trafford, considered themselves next to invincible in the Gillette Cup. They had also acquired a raucous, football-style following and a clear psychological edge over Kent. The tension extended into a second day because of rain, but the balance had tilted in Lancashire's favour with what turned out to be the last ball of the first day. Kent's third-wicket pair, Denness and Cowdrey, were making decent progress in dire light when Dickie Bird agonised before giving a leg-before verdict in Peter Lee's favour and against Cowdrey. Despite Denness's 65 and an entertaining innings of 35 from Julien, Kent fell eight runs short of their target and Lancashire went on to complete a hat-trick of Gillette Cup wins at Lord's. Lancashire, who had already beaten Kent in the championship and John Player League that season, drove the dagger ever deeper by defeating them in both the Fenner Trophy and the challenge match between the Gillette Cup and John Player League winners.

Norman Graham, the pace bowler described by Underwood as "one of the most nervous cricketers I have seen before a match starts", was inconsolable after the semi-final defeat. Luckhurst remembered him being "so distraught that he refused to speak on our return home from Old Trafford. As I was the only other one in the car, it made for a very long journey."

1973

Kent wasted no time in asserting their one-day superiority in 1973 and by mid-July they had the Benson and Hedges Cup safely tucked away; they were also runaway leaders in the John Player League and continued to compensate for a lack of victories in the championship with a torrent of batting bonus points. Assisted by an experimental extension to the already over-complicated system, counties could claim additional points if they reached 75 in 25 overs and 150 in 50. Kent exploited the possibilities so fully that in 20 matches they amassed 98 batting points, 14 more than unbeaten champions Hampshire. In 1974 the system was simplified and democratised so that the maximum bonus points available to sides was four for both batting and bowling.

The clue to Kent's impotence with the ball in the championship was Derek Underwood's moderate figures. For the first time in his career he failed even to reach 50 first-class wickets and that despite taking eight for nine (match figures 13 for 52) in the first match of the season at Hastings. Sussex, bowled out for 67 and 54, gained a measure of revenge two weeks later when they beat Kent in the group stages of the Benson and Hedges Cup then ended their interest in the Gillette Cup in the quarter-finals.

John Shepherd did his best to compensate for Underwood's lack of success, bowling magnificently throughout to take 92 wickets, but the pace department, too, was left depleted by Bernard Julien's absence on international duty in the first half of the season and the side won only four times in the championship. Kent's batsmen enjoyed themselves rather more, Mike Denness and Asif Iqbal hitting four centuries and five batsmen passing 1,000 runs. Alan Knott, although restricted to only 11 appearances for the county, averaged more than 60. They won three of their first five games, but only once thereafter and could consider fourth place a fair return for an indifferent season in the championship.

The highlight, in landmark terms anyway, was the 40-year-old Colin Cowdrey's hundredth hundred, 22 years after he had made his first, for Oxford University against Free Foresters. He had been stuck on 98 centuries for almost a year and was so far down the batting order that it should have been inconceivable for him to make two hundreds in four days, against first Somerset then Surrey. If there was something incongruous about Cowdrey coming in at No 6 and No 7 to complete the feat there was nothing inappropriate about the surroundings: the "glorious" Mote at Maidstone was one of his favourite grounds.

Cowdrey's version of events, still reasonably fresh in his mind when his autobiography was published in 1976, was: "The picture on the scoreboard showing 99 against my name in that last innings sent my heart beating faster than the medical profession would have liked. Asif and I met for a chat in the middle of the wicket. With a typical feel for the situation he said: 'Just keep your eye on the ball and push it anywhere and I will run.' There was no possible chance of a single, or so it seemed, when I pushed the ball straight to cover, but before I could make a decision Asif was almost arriving in my crease. All I had to do was scramble to the other end somehow. What a magnificent partner to have at that moment." The following day Cowdrey presented a bottle of wine to each member of the press box who had witnessed the innings.

He also batted at seven in the Benson and Hedges Cup final, making what he called a "cheeky" unbeaten 29. Cowdrey's late arrival was whimsically described by one writer as akin to [bandleader] "Victor Silvester dancing at a discotheque". Cowdrey may have seemed publicly relaxed about demotion as his career drew to a close, but it was undoubtedly a blow to his pride. Peter May, his great friend and fellow ex-England captain, was doing more than expressing his own opinion when he said in the foreword to *M.C.C* that he "just could not comprehend" how selectors were "for ever asking him to bat down the order after batsmen who weren't worthy of buckling his pads". The observation ostensibly referred to Cowdrey's England career, but was also a cryptic rejoinder to Kent.

The county were reasonably happy to make 225 in their 55 overs after stuttering to 34 for two in the first 20. Asif was a shoo-in for the gold award after following up an innings of 59 with his best one-day figures, four for 43. Kent were comfortable 39-run winners in the end, though there was just a flutter of concern as Basil D'Oliveira supervised a Worcestershire recovery from 98 for five. Denness was still sporting a plaster on his chin, the legacy of a top edge a few days earlier which required four stitches, when he received the trophy.

Kent, whose celebrations were restricted by an important Sunday League match at Brackley the following day – they duly thrashed Northamptonshire by 192 runs to strengthen their grip at the top – had reached Lord's via relatively low-scoring games against Hampshire and Essex. Bob Woolmer's dismissal of danger man Barry Richards was critical to a tense 11-run win at Southampton, and Woolmer also bowled superbly in the semi-final as Kent comfortably defended a seemingly inadequate total of 169 against Essex, watched by a crowd of 14,000 at St Lawrence.

In the context of his international ambitions, Denness was more available for Kent than he would have wished that summer. Despite playing in all eight winter Tests in 1972-73 he was overlooked for both three-match series against New Zealand and the West Indies. He admits that the sense of anti-climax affected his form with Kent, initially anyway, but the challenge for honours on various fronts soon sharpened his focus once more.

Kent had made an unspectacular start to the John Player League season, but discovered such a rich of vein form that they won 10 matches in succession. Brian Luckhurst and Denness added 179 in a thumping victory against Somerset, Shepherd supplying a violent flourish with four sixes off fellow Barbadian Hallam Moseley in the final over of the innings.

Kent's supremacy over the rest was so complete that they could have clinched the title on 5 August if rain had not wiped out their game against

Sussex; Lancashire's defeat by Essex a week later completed the job instead. Kent celebrated by beating Worcestershire and would have overhauled Lancashire's points record for the season, 53, if they had beaten them at Maidstone in their final game. Kent's attack was crucially weakened by the absence of Underwood and Woolmer and a crowd of 12,000 were denied the perfect end to an almost perfect season in the competition.

They were also fancied to win the Gillette Cup after an unbeaten century from Luckhurst had inspired a comfortable eight-wicket victory over Hampshire in the second round, but they reserved probably their worst performance of the whole season for the quarter-final against Sussex at Hove. Norman Graham was ruled out with flu and Kent's designs on a victory target of 264 quickly evaporated as they slumped to 66 for six.

Les Ames, the benign dictator who had pulled the strings on and off the field as secretary/manager, began a phased retirement by stepping down as secretary at the end of the 1973 season; he stayed on for one more year as manager and kept a detached eye on the side's development as president in

Repeat performance: Kent fans gather to celebrate the retention of the Sunday League title in 1973

1975. Underwood, one of the 'Ames boys', paid this tribute: "A successful club is a happy club and Les played his part there. He was very shrewd and sensitive in his dealings with people. Only 11 of us could play for Kent. He was keenly aware that those left out had to maintain their morale and he kept on top of the situation." Graham Johnson, another of the locals made good under Ames's tutelage, remembers: "Basically the club was run by Les, Bert Crowder [assistant secretary] and a couple of girls in the office. I had a lot of respect for him because he told it as it was." He adds: "With things like health and safety to worry about there's no way a club could be run like that any more."

The players also discovered that Ames had no interest in glamorising his playing days. Underwood says: "He was quite a difficult man to draw out and get him talking about cricket. He would be loathe to talk about when he played. I remember saying to him, 'Don Bradman must have been a great player, Les.' And he changed the subject completely. 'Never buys a pint though, does he?' That was a typical Les Ames way of dealing with a cricket question."

1974

The Kent players were determined to give Les Ames an appropriate send-off in 1974, and they duly obliged by winning the Gillette Cup, though there were none of the grand deeds which had distinguished previous games between the sides who collided so regularly in big one-day games in the Seventies, Kent and Lancashire. The weather was so bad that there was no play on the Saturday and, under the odd competition regulations which applied at the time, Kent were obliged to travel up to Worcester to play a Sunday League game before the Lord's final got under way on the Monday. Kent lost heavily at New Road, though Brian Luckhurst did have the personal satisfaction of becoming the first batsman to score 1,000 limited-overs runs in a season.

Mike Denness reflected: "We realised that if we played the same way again on Monday we could not possibly win the Gillette Cup. A defeat like that can often do more good than harm." Kent responded in the manner intended, though even Denness could not have predicted that the hero of the hour would be the little-known James Graham-Brown, who had only made his first team debut earlier that summer. Despite excellent figures of 5-3-4-3 in a John Player League game against Lancashire at Old Trafford a few days earlier, Graham-Brown himself was convinced that he would not play at Lord's. He was even more certain, after suffering at Glenn Turner's hands on the Sunday, that left-armer Richard Elms would be preferred.

"I was astonished when I discovered I had been selected," he admits. "It was never clear by what process they arrived at the decision to play me, though as it turned out conditions were more suited to medium-pace dobby seamers than they were for quick left-arm bowlers with a bit of a history for having radar problems. I came on just before lunch and ended up bowling my 12 overs straight through. The weather was dank and Septembery and the ball swung prodigiously."

Graham-Brown's figures of two for 15 in 12 overs were instrumental in Lancashire toiling to 118 in their full 60 overs and he remembers being padded up and extremely nervous as Kent slumped to 89 for six before Alan Knott and Bob Woolmer saw them home. A more romantically minded man-of-the-match adjudicator than Brian Close might have given the award to Graham-Brown, but Knott was chosen on the strength of two catches, a stumping and an unbeaten 18.

There were no complaints from Graham-Brown. "I have to admit my success was primarily due to the conditions and also to the fact that Alan Ealham ran out Clive Lloyd. Bowling outswingers to right-handers is one matter, but bowling inswingers to left-handers like Clive Lloyd is quite another. I also think one of the reasons Alan got the award was that he took a fantastic catch standing up to me, a very thick outside edge from Jack Simmons which would probably have gone to third slip. He also stumped Farokh, who was one hell of a player, off me."

Jim Swanton, again quietly proud to see Kent add another trophy to the sideboard, was less impressed by the crowd and, try as he might to distance himself from the observations, Swanton's own interpretation peered through the fog. "As to the noise there were contrasting views, ranging from those who thought that the red-necked cluster in front of the Tavern bar 'made the day' to certain crusty reactionaries more inclined to mutter about mindless oafs. Denness was roundly booed on arrival, the applause being all but drowned. But I was assured it was all friendly stuff. What the older generation chiefly resent, I think, is the unceasing assault on the ears."

Knott, curiously, had claimed his first ever man-of-the-match award in the semi-final win over Somerset (including the 18-year-old Ian Botham) with a similarly low-key contribution. Seasoned internationals like Knott and Derek Underwood could have been forgiven for suffering adrenaline deficit when they played for their county, but Underwood insists: "I was very professional on that score – I would never just go through the motions – and it was the same for Knotty: every day was like a Test match for him." He adds: "There's something very special about playing for your county in big games, especially

One that got away: A rare Kent lapse as the ball bisects Alan Knott and Graham Johnson in 1974

Lord's finals. It's a wonderful day for a club and its members and it's something you can't capture at international level." Underwood remembers the semi-final against Somerset as one of the most tense matches in his entire career and the anxiety also seems to have afflicted the crowd at St Lawrence: two spectators died of heart attacks that day.

Graham-Brown's Kent career fizzled out in 1976 and after two more low-key seasons with Derbyshire he retired to reflect on a first-class career which featured only 12 wickets. "It was wonderful to have that moment," he insists, "and to have the privilege of playing with people like the great M. C. Cowdrey." Graham-Brown's life since has been no anti-climax. He is headmaster at the Royal High School in Bath, writes plays under the pseudonym Dougie Blaxland and is in demand as an after-dinner speaker, featuring David Beckham as Macbeth and more respectful impressions of Mike Denness and Colin Cowdrey

The real Denness had captained England to a highly creditable drawn series against the West Indies early in 1974 and the same winter was critical to the future direction of Woolmer's career. He was growing increasingly concerned that his lowly position in the Kent batting order was hampering his development as a true all-rounder, and though he was adamant that he never actively wanted to leave the county he was open to inquiries. While playing for D. H. Robins' XI in South Africa he was approached by Leicestershire, Middlesex and Sussex, and Leicestershire followed up with a written offer. Woolmer was given the impression that he could open both the batting and bowling if he wanted.

He sounded out his mentor, Cowdrey, who saw Woolmer as a potential Kent captain. "He talked of the kudos in playing for Kent, the friendship and the good fellowship in the county and the fact that I might be able to go on and get a benefit with Kent." On the strength of discussions with Denness and Ames a compromise emerged: Woolmer would bat in the top five in all three-day matches and receive a pay rise of £150 a year.

Although it seemed like the happiest of solutions for Woolmer at the time, the promotion (confirmed by a written guarantee from Ames), and the seemingly Machiavellian way in which it was brokered, did not endear Woolmer to his team-mates at the start of the 1974 season. "I shall never forget the look on John Shepherd's face when he was told he was batting at No 10 in the first match against Worcestershire," Woolmer remembered.

A line-up of Luckhurst, Johnson, Denness, Asif Iqbal, Woolmer, Cowdrey, Ealham, Knott, Julien, Shepherd and Underwood just served to emphasise that Woolmer's place was by arrangement rather than on merit, but the whole impressive edifice crumbled as they were bowled out for 59 by Worcestershire in the second innings. Denness's unbeaten 35 averted even worse humiliation.

As Woolmer himself struggled to make runs in the succeeding weeks he felt the dressing-room atmosphere becoming "tense and unfriendly". When he made 24 in the first innings against Somerset at Taunton his run tally from six innings was 87; the whispers of disquiet could be contained no longer. "The ill-feeling around had to be discussed properly and there was a clear-the-air session in the Taunton dressing room. Home truths were pointed out on all sides and the reasons for my promotion, apparently misunderstood in some quarters, were explained. At no stage did I say to the county: 'Give me a prime batting slot or else.'" Woolmer chose an opportune moment to end a six-year wait for his maiden first-class hundred. An unbeaten 105 in his 159th innings could not prevent a Kent defeat, but he reached three figures twice more that summer, paving the way for his England Test debut in 1975.

England commitments were, by now, such a predictable feature of Knott and Underwood's summers that would-be replacements could pencil in probable appearances months in advance. Denness was still in favour with the national selectors, Asif Iqbal was on duty with Pakistan for the bulk of the season and the would-be spearhead of the Kent attack, Bernard Julien, played very little because of an ankle injury. As good a bowler as Shepherd was – he and Woolmer operated very effectively in tandem – he was not as comfortable when asked to open the attack. Elms failed to make the most of the opportunity presented by the absence of his fellow left-armer, Julien. Underwood took his wickets cheaply when he was available, but it was not nearly often enough for the liking of Kent supporters.

They were 10th in the championship, their lowest position since 1969, and even the vaunted batting looked comparatively frail. Kent lost four successive games early in the season and enjoyed only isolated successes thereafter. Underwood's match figures of 12 for 80 on a rain-affected Dover pitch set up an innings victory over Gloucestershire, but the stand-out game was a draw against Essex at Dartford. Kent, bowled out for 97 in their first innings, trailed by 198 before making 358 second time round. Woolmer then took five for 58 as Essex, needing a six off the last ball to win with their ninth-wicket pair at the crease, finished four short of the target.

There were shades of 1973 when Kent put together a run of seven successive wins in mid-season in the John Player League, and were seemingly on course for a hat-trick of titles in the competition, but this time their challenge evaporated and they had to settle for third. The defence of the Benson and Hedges Cup had started promisingly with a hundred per cent record in their four group games, but despite a resourceful hundred from Luckhurst they surprisingly lost to Leicestershire in a tight game at St Lawrence.

1975

When Mike Denness and Colin Cowdrey parted company at the end of the 1974 season the simple message from Cowdrey would have been, 'Good luck in Australia. See you next April.' Three months later, however, they were reunited in the attempt to resist one of the most fearsome fast-bowling combinations in the history of the game: Dennis Lillee and Jeff Thomson. Denness, though he had personally made the SOS call to Cowdrey, was reminded during the Christmas Test at Melbourne that their priorities as captains were sometimes poles apart. Denness remembers: "He came up to me and said, 'Have you thought what you're going to say at the press conference?' I could hardly believe it." Denness, at a low ebb when he dropped himself for the fourth Test at Sydney, battled back to make 188 in the final match in the series and another big hundred against New Zealand left him in better heart for the start of the 1975 season.

The lack of confidence in Denness as England captain was demonstrated when he was appointed solely for the first Test at Edgbaston. His decision to put Australia in backfired horribly, and he had already decided to resign when his sacking was confirmed. Denness's availability for Kent was offset by an England call for Bob Woolmer and at full strength the county could now put out a side featuring nine Test players: Luckhurst, Asif Iqbal, Woolmer, Denness, Julien, Cowdrey, Shepherd, Knott, Underwood. In mid-season, however, the first World Cup deprived the county of six of these players, and they were unable to sustain a challenge for any of the four competitions. Ultimately it was a season remembered more for outstanding individual performances than team successes.

John Shepherd, Kent's one player of international class who did not get the recognition he deserved, had been the county's heartbeat ever since making his debut in 1966. Surprisingly, though, he took 10 wickets in a match only twice, and obliterated his previous best with a one-man demolition of Sussex in 1975. His stamina, too, was exceptional as he bowled unchanged in both innings (a total of 61.5 overs) to take eight for 93 and seven for 54. His match figures of 15 for 147 were the best by a Kent bowler since Dave Halfyard in 1959.

A month earlier Shepherd had engineered an extraordinary Kent recovery in a Benson and Hedges Cup game at Lord's, scoring 96 out of an all-out total of 137 and monopolising the scoring in a stand of 81 with Derek Underwood which remains Kent's best for the ninth wicket in limited-overs games. Shepherd followed up with three for 21 and Kent squeezed home, improbably, by two runs.

They still failed to reach the knockout stages and were bundled out of the Gillette Cup in the second round by Nottinghamshire. For Denness, the game came too close on the heels of England's humiliation at Edgbaston. "I wanted another 24 hours to wash the whole thing out of my mind. I am not necessarily blaming myself completely for the failure of Kent in that cup tie, but I must take my fair share of the blame. The only consolation I had at Trent Bridge was the reception I received from the crowd."

Kent also flattered to deceive in the John Player League, winning their first four matches then floundering as the World Cup and a Test series against Australia depleted the team. The championship was still just about in reach until a narrow 18-run defeat by the eventual winners, Leicestershire, at the start of September. The match was, effectively, won and lost in a ninth-wicket stand of 136 between Norman McVicker and Graham McKenzie, which rescued Leicestershire from 115 for eight on the first day. Kent could do no better than fifth, but at least they could draw encouragement from the form of two home-grown bowlers. Kevin Jarvis, 22, looked distinctly sharp in his first season, taking 40 wickets, and Richard Hills also recorded respectable figures. "We used to call him the vicar because he only played on Sundays," remembers Graham Johnson, "but he was a vital cog in what the John Player side did."

Colin Cowdrey, in the midst of a largely modest final season, turned back the clock in a memorable unbeaten 151 which enabled Kent to chase down a victory target of 354 and beat the Australians for the first time since 1899. He remembered that there was little atmosphere at St Lawrence at the start of the final day and Kent began so poorly that Ian Chappell, the touring side's captain, told their coach driver to be ready for a teatime departure to Hampshire. Midnight was approaching when the touring side finally arrived in Southampton.

Cowdrey was reminded of the game's infinite capacity to humble when, captaining MCC against the Australians a week later, he made the fourth and final pair of his career. Sussex then dangled the tempting carrot of a three-year deal, but Cowdrey weighed the evidence with sober care before judging that the time was right to finish. He also rejected the chance to captain the 2nd XI but played a lone championship game for Kent in 1976 and was able to watch with pride as his eldest son, Chris, who had first played for the seconds as a 14-year-old in 1972, broke into the 1st XI in 1977.

Alan Dixon, who had played alongside Colin Cowdrey for 20 years, articulates the mixture of admiration and exasperation which team-mates felt. "If Colin had only recognised how good he was, how much better a player he would have been. It sounds silly because he was a magnificent player anyway, but he never had that confidence to push himself on and murder attacks. I remember there was a run chase on in one game. He said, 'I'd like you to go up the order.' I said, 'Hang on, Colin, you're our best player. You should be out there hammering this attack all over the place. We can win this.' He dropped himself down to five then six and finally he went in. He flung his bat at every ball he faced, made a few and then his castle went over. He came in, threw the bat down and said, 'I suppose you're all satisfied now.'"

The annual report's description of Kent's performance level in 1975 as "extremely disappointing" showed Denness that previous glories counted for little. It was a also a further reminder that judgments were shaped by the team's results in the County Championship rather than in any of the one-day competitions.

Denness was concerning himself with the image of the team off the field as well as their performances on it. In October 1975 he lodged a proposal, saying "it was strongly felt among the players that they would like the committee to consider changing the colour of the blazers to maroon". Jim Swanton was predictably vocal in his opposition to Denness's sartorial initiative and the general committee, equally predictably, decided to stick with navy blue blazers. "They were incapable of forward planning," says Denness, "and they always thought that decisions were for them to make rather than someone from outside the committee to suggest." By way of a subsidiary knockdown, it was also agreed that "players should only wear their track suits when in the dressing room or when engaged in some form of physical training".

Swanton, though *Daily Telegraph* readers would have been oblivious to any bias, was utterly dedicated to Kent cricket, but his pig-headed arrogance was a constant source of frustration to friends, players and club officials. Jim Woodhouse, who served on the Kent committee with Swanton, remembers: "The problem with Jim, although he was a great pal and I loved his company, was that he was a dictator. If he said the colour of the wicket should be straw-coloured, not green, he expected everybody to have wickets of straw colour. I remember at a committee meeting once I was starting to talk and he butted in and said, 'Oh chairman, obviously Jim thinks that he knows a great deal more than I do, so we better hear from him first.' And I said, 'Jim, it's not that at all. It's just that I've got an opinion and I think some of my opinions are as good as yours. You cannot just sit here and tell us that because they did it like this in 1923 we should do it in 1986.' He had this friendly, bullying attitude that if you didn't do it his way you were a fool; and if you were proved right he never said, 'Gosh that did work, didn't it?' He would just pick up that idea about four weeks later as his own. He was never, ever, ever wrong and that was why he was never president of the MCC. He should have been."

Chris Cowdrey, automatically regarded in an approving light by Swanton because of his father, says: "He could be very difficult. He had a brilliant cricket brain and his knowledge of the game was second to none. He was also very opinionated, and once he had an opinion that was it, you couldn't really change it. There were people who hated him with a passion because of his old-school approach to things."

1976

The sport, though memorable in its own right (Kent won both the Benson and Hedges Cup and John Player League), was submerged by the politics in 1976; it was a year which marked the start of a needlessly self-destructive phase for Kent. There were further successes to follow, but it was not until the late Eighties that the county's industrial relations were back on an even keel. Bob Woolmer joked that if he appeared on *Mastermind* he would nominate "sackings of successful Kent captains" as his special subject.

To those on the fringes of what was brewing, or supporters utterly oblivious to the in-fighting, Kent was still a club in its pomp. Championship consistency was the missing link and it was that single chink in the armour which stood between Mike Denness and complete acceptance as Kent's captain. In his autobiography, published the year after he left the county, he said: "Ever since I had taken over the captaincy in 1972, certain players had not been pleased with my appointment. I do not think it stopped there, for there were probably people on the committee who were also against me as captain. Whatever people were thinking, I had been having thoughts of my own in this direction."

The rumbles of disquiet had grown a little louder in 1975. "Obviously, some players were not happy," Denness admitted. "One of our problems had been that we had nothing to look back on or forward to. For the first time since 1972 we had not won anything. Consequently, at Swansea we held a special team meeting, revolving around disagreements, the different views of players, and so on. It was an opportunity for players to get everything off their chests. Invariably such meetings produce one target, which in this case was the captain. I thought we had cleared the air, however, and would be able to start the 1976 season on a different footing."

Graham Johnson, for one, believes there was nothing particularly unusual or ignoble in other players coveting the captain's job when Colin Cowdrey stepped down. "It's not too strange. If you were a betting man you'd have put money on Mike, but there were a lot of strong characters in that side, people who probably could have captained the team. There was always going to be a settling-in period, especially after someone had been in the job as long as Colin had. And when you've got 16 or 17 players who are all good enough to get in the team, someone's always going to be unhappy because you can't play 17 in a team. There were a lot of good, ambitious players who had a view on things, but that was one of the benefits of that side."

Johnson himself was very much in Denness's thoughts when he spoke informally to Colin Page, Les Ames's successor as manager, during a championship game against Surrey in mid-July. Denness was attracted by the prospect of a younger player – he specified Johnson – taking over while the county still enjoyed winning momentum. "Making the move then," he wrote, "instead of in two or three years' time, meant that the younger man would have the benefit of myself, as a kind of right-hand man, plus the experience of senior players like Knott, Underwood and Asif to call upon."

Page gave the impression that he was not keen on the idea, but two days later he asked Denness what the next course of action should be. Denness suggested a conversation with the chairman of the cricket committee, John Pocock, who also exerted considerable influence through the Mote Cricket Club. Jim Woodhouse, a later chairman of cricket, says mischievously of Pocock: "He thought he was god number two to Jim Swanton."

A month later Denness was still awaiting feedback, but out of the blue he was invited for drinks at Pocock's house and was astonished to hear that not only was the captaincy question to be discussed at a meeting in four days' time, but that there was a faction on the committee who were keen on a change of leader. Names of possible contenders were raised, but Denness was adamant that he would only agree to stand down if Johnson got the job.

He assumed that when possible resignation dates – 5 or 8 September – were raised, it was on the express understanding that his succession plan was acceptable. He was unable to get a clear picture of what had been discussed or decided at the cricket committee meeting and was still none the wiser when Pocock approached him on 9 September, the second day of Kent's final championship game against Sussex, to ask why he had not yet resigned. Denness again stressed that he would step down only if Johnson's appointment was approved. Pocock then spoke to Asif and Johnson, the committee's chosen captain and vice-captain.

Towards the end of the month Denness was sent a copy of a statement which the club intended to put out after the cricket committee had formalised the decision on the captaincy at a meeting on 30 September. It read: "Mike Denness has intimated to the Kent County Cricket Club committee that he would like to relinquish the captaincy of the county eleven. The committee have with much regret accepted this decision and have appointed Asif Iqbal to captain the side in the 1977 season, with Graham Johnson as vice-captain. The committee would like to place on record their appreciation of Mike's outstanding service to the club, both as captain and player, and are delighted that he has intimated his intention to continue as a player."

Denness, inevitably, refused to sanction the statement's release, though at the start of October newspaper reporters were told that he had resigned. A weary and confused Denness said at the time: "At the moment I feel I do not care if I pick up a bat again." The sorry episode dragged on until 22 November, when he met Walter Brice, the club chairman, for the first time. By now members were agitating for an official explanation and Denness found himself discovering one unsavoury fact after another. Even the statement released struck him as a "smokescreen". Senior players, some of whom now seemed happy to snipe anonymously at Denness in the press, had been canvassed about the captaincy; they had complained about him directly to the committee; the decision to replace him had been taken on 20 August, only one person out of 11 voting in his favour. According to Denness, Brice told him he was "aloof, stand-offish, non-communicative and not good with the young players". When pressed, Brice also admitted that the main source for this damning verdict – Denness pointed out that similar accusations had been made ever since he got the job in 1972 – was Page.

Throughout, Denness had the impression that he was up against an invisible enemy (he also believes that if Ames had still been manager he would have prevented the matter escalating). Even when he had the chance to speak directly to Brice he sensed that he was being patronised by an inadequately briefed mouthpiece. Reflecting on the cricket committee's original decision to change captain, he said: "This confirmed to me that no thought had been given to the resulting publicity at national and provincial level, and there had been no humane feeling displayed towards me, the person who would suffer most from such publicity."

It was significant that Denness, by way of mild protest at his treatment, should have asked Alan Knott to lead the Kent side out for the final session of the season against Sussex at St Lawrence. Knott confessed that he was "embarrassed" by the request, but Denness was adamant. He now reflects: "Knotty

will be the first to say to you that whenever he heard anybody, no matter who it was, suggesting that there should be a change he would either ask them to leave the dressing room or not talk on that subject again. He would say, we're having a great time the way we are at the moment. You can't ask for any more loyalty than someone who's in the dressing room all the time."

He was justified in regarding Knott as a trusted lieutenant, but may have overestimated his exposure to dressing-room gossip. Knott described the decision to get rid of Denness as "amazing", though his autobiography suggests that his finger was not as firmly on the pulse as Denness gives him credit for. "As is quite often the case, everybody in the Kent camp seemed to know before I did," he wrote. Knott said it was only when Denness asked him to lead the side out that he "realised something might be amiss".

The controversy obscured notable feats on the field: Knott's 70-minute hundred won him the Walter Lawrence Trophy for the fastest century of the season. An innings of 144 was also his best ever score in the championship, but a highly entertaining stand of 205 with Denness did little to lighten the captain's mood. He was left to wonder who else was batting for him when the pressure was on in 1976. There was even evidence that Colin Cowdrey, though now retired, no longer backed the man whose appointment he had cheerfully endorsed four years earlier. Interestingly, Cowdrey's name cropped up as a short-term damage-limiting replacement when Asif Iqbal was stripped of the captaincy 18 months later for his involvement with World Series Cricket.

Bob Woolmer was one colleague who openly admitted that he was in favour of the decision to replace Denness as captain, though he was no more enamoured of the tactless means to that end than anyone else. Woolmer wrote: "He was the best one-day captain I ever played under. He had immense discipline, did the simple things right, and also possessed the intangible quality of doing the right thing at the right time. But his ability as a leader did not come through as clearly in first-class cricket. He did not – who knows, perhaps, could not – communicate his thinking to the players. When he called on you to bowl, he seemed to have no clear idea of what he wanted from you or how long he wanted you to bowl."

The wounds have healed, and Denness was welcomed back into the Kent fold when his playing days finished, but he retains a firm sense that the drawn-out humiliation of 1976 could and should have been avoided. He was neither the first nor last Kent player to discover that Jim Swanton for ever lurked as a quietly dogmatic voice of influence, both singly and through the Band of Brothers. Denness recalls: "Swanton wrote me a letter suggesting that I should let bygones be bygones and carry on playing for the club. I said, 'You obviously don't know the full story, Jim.' It would have been better if we'd had a conversation face to face about it." He discovered soon after he had left Kent that his Band of Brothers' membership had been quietly withdrawn.

Jim Woodhouse, later chairman of cricket, certainly detected the hand of BB in Denness's sacking as captain. "The committee thought they'd flex their muscle and get rid of him," he suggests. "He probably got a bit big-headed and BB couldn't have that." Woodhouse also believes that that Band of Brothers could have exerted a more positive influence on the running of the club. "When I was a little boy [immediately after the war] and later started to play 2nd XI cricket the BB reckoned that they should run Kent cricket and therefore the committee was probably 50 per cent made up of members of the brethren; the president was almost always a member of the brethren. They lived in the shadow of Lord Harris and tried to carry on with the way he had run the club. They were lovely people. Some of them had the financial nous, but they didn't get involved in the running of the club."

Denness now describes his artless suggestion about Johnson as "an initial step which went haywire because they got it totally wrong. They took it, or chose to take it, that I was resigning full stop. The next step should have been for them to come back to me and say, 'The committee might have ideas about appointing someone else. What do you think of Joe Bloggs?' Why did they just accept that it was a good idea to get rid of Denness. He's made a suggestion that we don't agree to. That to me was very, very bad man management and I never wanted to be a part of something like that again."

Once Denness had resisted half-hearted attempts to persuade him to stay on as a player – he also turned down a "token of appreciation" for his years as captain – he threw himself into an exciting new venture: helping to build a title-winning dynasty at Essex. "It had always struck me when I played against Essex that they had so much talent in the side," he says. "I couldn't believe they hadn't won anything. It was a terrific challenge to help turn them into winners."

Denness played under Keith Fletcher from 1977 to 1980, and was part of the side who won both the County Championship and Benson and Hedges Cup in 1979. He also observed subtle differences in dressing-room life between Canterbury and Chelmsford. "At Kent certain players would always change together. That wasn't the case in the Essex dressing room. Brian Hardie and Stuart Turner were great friends, but they didn't necessarily change together. There was more of a mix in the dressing room. Maybe there was a little clique in the Kent side that I wasn't aware of."

There had already been a sense of something missing when Kent began the 1976 season without Colin Cowdrey and within six weeks supporters were also having to contemplate life without Brian Luckhurst. The ultra-dependable opener, who had passed 1,000 runs for the 14th successive season in 1975, broke a knuckle in his right hand playing against Northamptonshire. He missed the rest of the season and the opportunity to coach the 2nd XI, in succession to Colin Page, persuaded him that the time was right to retire.

"I would unhesitatingly say that I enjoyed my work with the second team far more than I did when I was involved for five subsequent seasons as first team manager," he wrote in his memoirs. "Colin was a different character to me, and his methods in and around the dressing room worked well for him. I realised, long before I even accepted the offer of the second team job, that I could not do it in a similar way – but Colin understood that as soon as I talked it over with him."

The abrasive Page was to be far less understanding after feeling that Luckhurst had stolen his job with the first team in 1981. Page sat out that season while recuperating from a heart attack, but both men expected normal service to be resumed the following year. In the event, Luckhurst was asked to remain with the 1st XI and Page reverted to the second team job. "I'm afraid the situation also put a big strain on my relationship with Colin Page," wrote Luckhurst. "Colin, of course, wanted to be top man. He had earned that position by right, after all, and now it was being taken away from him against his will. Yes, he had been told by the doctors to take things more steadily, but Colin could still not accept that he would not be in charge of the first eleven. I, of course, was caught in the middle and it was not pleasant." Page suffered a fatal heart attack three months after taking early retirement in 1990 (Les Ames, his predecessor as manager, died in February of the same year).

Unfortunately for Kent, and their championship prospects in particular, Luckhurst's injury was not an isolated piece of misfortune that summer. Resources were so stretched by illness, injury and Test calls that pace bowler David Sayer, who had last turned out for the county in 1968, came out of retirement for a lone appearance and Cowdrey also played in one game. If the quietly manipulative Swanton had got his way, supporters would have seen Cowdrey snr and jnr lining up alongside each other in 1976. Alan Ealham takes up the story: "Jim approached Mike Denness and said, 'Mike, do you think it would be a good idea to play Chris Cowdrey and Colin together in Canterbury Week?' Mike said, 'Yes Jim, it would be a good idea…if you can tell me how to do it. Just because it's a good idea doesn't mean I can upset the balance of the side.' Jim said, 'I'm sure Alan Ealham wouldn't mind standing down.' Mike relayed that to me a little later and I couldn't believe it: I was having a better season than anyone."

Kent's total of 57 bowling bonus points in 1976 was the lowest of any county and the batting generally misfired as well. They finished 14th, their lowest position in the championship since 1957. A season featuring only five victories started on a downbeat note with defeat by Middlesex at Lord's, and Kent found themselves up against two of the world's finest batsmen, Barry Richards and Zaheer Abbas, at the peak of their powers. Richards took three successive hundreds off the Kent attack that summer, and Zaheer gatecrashed Knott's benefit party by following up a double hundred in the first innings at Canterbury with a unbeaten century which brought Gloucestershire victory. The clear highlight of Kent's championship season was a 57-run win over Middlesex, the eventual champions, at Dartford. Kent followed on after being bowled out for 151, but half-centuries from Woolmer, Ealham and John Shepherd allowed them to set Middlesex a victory target of 195. Johnson and Derek Underwood shared nine wickets to complete a heroic fightback

There was a familiar ring to the official verdict on Kent's season: the power elite refused to accept that one-day successes compensated for shortcomings in the 'real' arena of the championship. Yet a repeat of the 1973 double of Benson and Hedges Cup and John Player League was achieved in heroic style, notably on the last Sunday of the season, when the BBC helicopter bearing the trophy hovered uncertainly between Cardiff, Edgbaston and Maidstone.

Kent were immediately up against it in the Benson and Hedges Cup when they were thrashed by Yorkshire in their opening group game, but still qualified for a quarter-final against Nottinghamshire. Kevin Jarvis, fast emerging as a useful spearhead for the attack, took four wickets and Underwood's stingy spell did the rest. Denness's 104 against Surrey in the semi-final was one of his best one-day innings, and a century stand by Johnson and Woolmer in the final against Worcestershire gave Kent an advantage which they maintained throughout, helped by an injury which restricted Basil D'Oliveira to four overs. Johnson claimed the man-of-the-match award by following his innings of 78 with four well-judged catches.

Jarvis remembers: "It was the first time I'd played in front of a huge crowd. It looked like we were in control of the game, but D'Oliveira, who'd pulled a hamstring, came in, stood on one leg and slogged. Gradually we could see the game slipping away, but fortunately we managed to get him out [b Jarvis 50] and the game changed again. It was just a fantastic experience."

A sub-standard batting display against Sussex had ended Kent's interest in the Gillette Cup three days earlier, but they were now able to give their full attention to the John Player League. Kent were being offered at a realistic 100-1 for the title after losing five of their first nine matches and though they remained in contention by winning six of their remaining seven games they also profited greatly from the frailties of their rivals.

A three-wicket win over Glamorgan kept Kent in touch going into the last round of matches, when five teams were still in with a chance of lifting the trophy. Somerset and Sussex, joint top with 40 points, were in prime position. Kent, Essex and Leicestershire were all four points behind but Kent, crucially, had won five away games and were shading Essex, the only other side to have recorded five wins on their travels, on run rate. It was too much to ask. Or was it?

Kent dominated from first ball to last at The Mote, Asif hitting a sparkling 106 as they made an unassailable 278 for five. Warwickshire were putting paid to Sussex's hopes at Edgbaston, so all attention switched to Sophia Gardens, where the closest of finishes was boiling up. The Kent players watched anxiously on television as Somerset needed three runs off the final ball to snatch the tie which would have denied Kent, only for Colin Dredge to be run out attempting the third. The helicopter set course for Maidstone.

James Graham-Brown's departure at the end of the 1976 season attracted rather fewer headlines than that of Denness. Despite his central role in the 1974 Gillette Cup win Graham-Brown's cricketing lot was to remain on the extreme fringes of the Kent side. However, he did feature prominently in the team, also including future Kent coach John Wright, who won seven out of 10 matches to carry off the 2nd XI championship. He was also part of a notable generation of players produced by the county's leading public schools, Tonbridge, Sevenoaks and King's Canterbury, in the late Sixties and Seventies.

Although Graham-Brown had his own ambitions at Sevenoaks he admits that his "role was much more about making the players coming behind me aware of the possibilities". The players in question were Chris Tavaré and Paul Downton, who both went on to play for Kent and England. "As a schoolboy Chris was peerless," Graham-Brown remembers. "Off the back foot he was one of the best players I've ever seen: a run-a-minute destroyer of bowling." Tavaré only began to do himself justice in 1976, his middle year at Oxford, and Kent were not to see the best of him until 1978, when he played a major role in the championship triumph.

Tavaré recalls of his early years with Kent: "Playing with the likes of Luckhurst, Denness, Underwood and Knott, and Colin Cowdrey in particular, whom I'd watched as I was growing up, was an awesome experience. I got a game when the Tests were on and there wasn't too much expectation. It was an ideal way to learn the game."

Charles Rowe attracted so much praise as a batsman cum off-spinner for King's Canterbury in the late Sixties that his subsequent, unspectacular achievements for Kent and Glamorgan had the dull ring of anti-climax. The same could hardly be said of the Tunbridge Wells-born David Gower, who assumed Rowe's mantle at King's, but sadly for Kent (and partly because of the perceived lack of guidance for Rowe) he was nudged towards Leicester rather than Canterbury.

Chris Cowdrey remembers rugby matches for Tonbridge against Sevenoaks (with Downton his opposite number at full-back) as vividly as he does cricketing confrontations; and if Sevenoaks prevailed with the oval ball, Tonbridge were next to unbeatable over 22 yards. The side Cowdrey captained in 1975 was spearheaded by Nick Kemp, widely considered to be the quickest schoolboy bowler at the time, and 15-year-old Richard Ellison.

Alan Dixon, who coached at Tonbridge in the mid-Seventies, has been recognised as the architect of the Ellison outswinger which played a big part in winning the Ashes for England in 1985, but he fondly recalls another eureka moment for the teenaged Ellison. "I was working with him in the nets at Tonbridge and I said, 'You bowl a good away swinger, Richard, but you don't make it go the other way.' He said, 'I can't do that.' So I showed him how to hold it, how to deliver it and he ran up and released the ball; it swung in as though he'd been bowling them all his life. The look on his face was an absolute picture."

Ellison, though plagued by injuries for most of his career, enjoyed some outstanding days in the sun, but Kemp frustrated both himself and Kent's management team with his inability to make the grade. Luckhurst, who captained and coached the 2nd XI in the late Seventies, reflected that Kemp "was an all-rounder with as much going for him cricket-wise as Chris Cowdrey, but unlike Chris he just couldn't put it all together when he got out into the middle". Colin Page, the first team manager, reported to the Kent committee that Kemp was "an enigma". He had "enormous ability which unfortunately he was not using to the best advantage".

Kemp points out that he was badly hit when his father died after top-edging a beamer on to his temple in a club match in 1979 – "my heart went out of it and I found I was just going through the motions" – but even before then he had struggled to recapture his instinctive schoolboy talent for quick bowling. "There was very little coaching in those days. You had to find a way of solving problems yourself because no one else was going to sit down and work it through with you. In the end I tried to do it differently. I went from being an all-out quick bowler at school, probably the fastest in the country at that age, to turning myself into a medium-pace dobber, which I shouldn't have done." Kemp played only four championship games for Kent in four years and left the first-class game after a single season at Middlesex in 1982.

He admits that the influx of public school players introduced a hint of social tension in the Kent dressing room. The triumphs of the late Sixties and early Seventies had been achieved with Colin Cowdrey as the privately educated head boy in a team built on working-class virtues. "There was a slight sense of resentment," Kemp says. "Some of the senior players on the staff at that time had come through the hard way; they'd been club and ground, they'd cleaned the boots, pushed the bloody roller and all that sort of nastiness, and suddenly there were these young professionals coming in in the Seventies without any kind of apprenticeship."

THREE

1977-78: Two Championships and a Crisis

THE LAST thing Kent needed at the start of the 1977 season was more controversy, but it was dumped on them in the shape of an announcement on 9 May that Australian tycoon Kerry Packer had given birth to World Series Cricket. Asif Iqbal, Alan Knott, Derek Underwood and Bernard Julien had all signed up and Bob Woolmer was to follow. Although Julien was promptly told that his contract would not be renewed at the end of the season, a more general solution proved elusive. The county's initial stance, voiced through chairman Walter Brice in a meeting with Asif, Knott and Underwood during the championship game against Middlesex at Lord's, was that as long as WSC did not impinge on their availability for Kent they were in the clear. The illusion of calm did not last for long.

As captain Asif was neither from Colin Cowdrey's school of analysis nor Mike Denness's academy of meticulous planning; he favoured the instinctive ploy. Kent knew when they appointed Asif that he was an unknown quantity, but his joyful approach to batting and infectious optimism were important hints. Woolmer, a team-mate with his own captaincy ambitions, could only applaud. "Everything he did went right. When he changed the bowling, he got a wicket nine times out of ten. His leadership was inspirational."

Asif and Alan Ealham were the only players to pass 1,000 runs (Ealham achieved the feat without a single century), but young bloods Charles Rowe, Chris Tavaré and 19-year-old Chris Cowdrey all recorded maiden championship hundreds. Paul Downton was so highly regarded as a wicketkeeper that, on the strength of seven championship appearances, he was selected as Alan Knott's understudy for the winter tours to Pakistan and New Zealand.

Kent's season revolved around sustained challenges for the championship and Benson and Hedges Cup, though they only sneaked into the quarter-finals by virtue of a last-ball victory over Sussex at Hove. By a quirk of the draw, the sides faced each other again in the quarter-finals, and Kent drafted in Cowdrey to combat the gentle, but naggingly accurate left-arm swing of Mike Buss. Cowdrey, who opened with Woolmer, made an uninhibited 114, then the highest score by a Kent player in the competition and the kind of innings which would have been utterly alien to his father.

That, to Chris Cowdrey, was the precise objective: to make a distinct statement as a batsman; to avoid direct comparison. He recalls: "At school I wasn't leg side at all, but when I started becoming a player who people were looking at, from the age of about 16 onwards, I wanted to have my own identity, rather than people saying, 'He plays the off drive or cover drive well, but not as well as his father.'" It had already become evident that the younger Cowdrey was much more of an open book than his father; he was popular, less self-critical and, in the words of Derek Underwood, "the kind of person his father would have liked to have been".

Against Sussex, Chris Cowdrey may have shared the plaudits with Ealham, whose punishing unbeaten 94 enabled Kent to reach a tricky target with 17 balls to spare, but it was Cowdrey jnr who took the man-of-the-match award and fielded Frank Bough's predictable line of questioning with amiable patience after being asked to appear on *Nationwide*.

The bowling of Kevin Jarvis and Woolmer, who took three wickets apiece, was the key factor in a five-run win over Northamptonshire, and Cowdrey's return to the real world was confirmed when he was left out, in favour of the stodgier left-hander Grahame Clinton, for the final against Gloucestershire. Clinton was seen as someone who might blunt the fierce pace of Mike Procter, but Brian Brain was the man who bowled him for nought as Gloucestershire won by 64 runs. Asif could scarcely believe that Kent had played so badly. "I feel we didn't do ourselves justice," was his understated verdict. "For once in Kent's successful limited-over history, their middle batting capitulated feebly," wrote Michael Melford in *The Daily Telegraph*. He also likened the lunatic fringe of Gloucestershire's support, who several times invaded the pitch in premature celebration, to "an out-of-season football crowd which has been sozzling all day".

There was no particular reason to believe that Kent would improve as a championship side in 1977, but John Shepherd bowled magnificently all season to take 87 wickets, a figure exceeded only by Procter and Ian Botham, at a shade under 20 apiece. Kent were competitive throughout and finally started to believe that they might actually claim the title when they won both games in Folkestone Week. Jarvis, one of the least distinguished No 11s in Kent's history, had the satisfaction of hitting the winning run in a one-wicket victory over Essex after they had collapsed from 168 for four to 183 for nine.

Jarvis admits that his super-rabbit status would now make it difficult, if not impossible, for him to hold down a place in a county side. He even received letters on the subject from Jim Swanton. "He was quite amused at the fact that I got more wickets than runs in first-class cricket. His line of inquiry was never

All-rounder John Shepherd in contemplative mood in 1977

Picture: Kent Messenger, PD1673763

about how good my bowling was, it was about how bad my batting was." Asif, when captain, accepted Jarvis's inability with a shrug and told him to put all his energies into bowling. Woolmer, on the other hand, refused to accept that his close friend was a lost cause. "Being the supreme coach that he was he couldn't come to terms with the fact that I couldn't bat. He tried long and hard to make me a better batsman and I did improve to the point where I was able to stay there, not to score many runs, but to allow players like John Shepherd and Graham Johnson to manipulate the strike."

When Jarvis's Kent career finished in 1987 his wickets total, 631, was almost twice his runs aggregate, 321. He finally improved his highest score from 12 to 19 in 1984, but recorded 52 ducks in 180 innings for the county. At least, in 1977, he proved adept at finishing not out, but as the climax to the season approached Kent were dealing neither in runs nor wickets: the weather intervened cruelly to wipe out seven successive days' play. They were able to muster only six points in three games and not a single ball was bowled in their match against Essex at Colchester. Kent's sense of injustice was compounded by the fact that Middlesex had been allowed to postpone a championship game against Somerset in favour of settling their delayed Gillette Cup semi-final against the same opposition. Asif later described the decision as "crazy"; he also found himself having to explain to the Kent committee why their over rate had fallen fractionally below the approved figure of 19.5 an hour.

Gloucestershire enjoyed a five-point lead over Kent and Middlesex going into the final round of games, and extended their advantage when both their rivals failed to take a single batting point. Kent made only 118 against Warwickshire at Edgbaston but, thanks to five for 63 from Shepherd, they were able to limit the first-innings deficit to 63. Shepherd emphasised his all-round value with a knock of 77, leaving Warwickshire needing 254 to win. Jarvis's three-wicket burst with the new ball reduced them to 29 for five, and Kent weathered a Geoff Humpage-inspired fightback to clinch a 27-run win just after tea. They knew by then that victory would bring them level on points with Middlesex, who had already beaten Lancashire at Blackpool. The first shared title since 1950 was confirmed when Hampshire made light work of a target of 271 at Bristol.

It was a notable achievement for a side who, on top of the customary Test calls, had to cope with Johnson's cartilage injury and Norman Graham's absence for almost the whole season. The one consolation for the hugely popular pace bowler was that he could give his full attention to a benefit season which brought in the exceptional pot of £58,000, more than twice the amount raised for Knott a year earlier. Visiting pubs was not the hardship it might have

Kent's players examine the fruits of their success after sharing the championship in 1977
Picture: Kent Messenger, PD1673762

been for less sociable beneficiaries, but did Graham really take in 1,000 hostelries, as reported at the time? "It was only 727," he insists. "Mind you, my wife reckons that I went back to every one of them to thank them." He adds: "People forget that we had to pay for everything in those days. To make decent money you had to spend a lot of money to get it in."

Graham's retirement at the end of the season coincided with the formal announcement that Julien would not be re-engaged after eight seasons at Canterbury. His bowling figures were respectable, but a highest score of 98, even allowing for his often lowly place in the Kent batting order, did not do justice to an exceptional all-round talent. He was already testing the committee's patience when news of the Packer revolution broke. Minutes from a meeting in May 1977 revealed that Julien had failed to let the club know that he had been injured in a car accident in Trinidad. Julien claimed that he had asked a friend to relay the news, but the committee expressed "disapproval of his behaviour"; he finally arrived in the country to discover that he had been fined a week's wages.

Shepherd, who was something of a mentor to the Trinidadian, feels that he was misunderstood and misrepresented. "Bernard lived with my first wife and I when he came over and I used to keep an eye out for him. We shared rooms when the team was playing away. Bernard got a lot of bad press and he really didn't deserve it; he had a bad heel and that was what finished his career. People thought he was swinging the lead. That guy sat in bed at night crying because he thought people didn't believe he was injured, but he genuinely was." Shepherd adds: "He was unfortunate that because he was so talented everyone started giving him the next Gary Sobers label which was not very helpful for a youngster like that."

For uncomplaining loyalty it was hard to top David Nicholls, who played his final championship game for Kent in 1977, but remained part of the one-day set-up until 1980. For 14 seasons he had cheerfully accepted his role as Alan Knott's understudy, unmoved by the prospect of being recognised as the first-choice wicketkeeper at another county.

The whole of the 1977 season was played out against the not-so-distant rumble of World Series Cricket. No county had more to lose from the fall-out than Kent, and they looked to higher authorities for a lead. Knott and Underwood both played against Australia in the summer Tests, but at the end of July the International Cricket Council plotted an unwise collision course with Packer and the law courts when they banned WSC players from Test cricket. Emboldened, the Test and County Cricket Board extended the ban to participation in the county game, then waited for the result of the inevitable High Court challenge brought by Packer.

Woolmer viewed the debate from a distinct perspective, first as enraged county pro, convinced that his team-mates were selling out the game as a whole to feather their elite nests, then as born-again Packerite. Woolmer was one of the players canvassed soon after the news had broken by Johnson, who found himself in a slightly invidious position as vice-captain to Asif, representative for the Professional Cricketers' Association and unofficial in-house shop steward. His reward for speaking his mind was to be overlooked when Kent came to choosing an eleventh-hour candidate to replace Asif as captain just before the start of the 1978 season.

Johnson reflects: "In retrospect, I was probably more upset at what happened at the Packer stage than at the Mike Denness handover stage. As a county pro with aspirations of getting higher I was probably a bloody idiot, because I just said what I felt was right. I remember speaking at a committee meeting, when I was standing in for Asif. I'd gone round the players to ask their opinion on Packer, and the general view was 'they can't have their cake and eat it too', because there was a huge threat to what was going to happen to domestic cricket. With the benefit of hindsight, and looking at the broader picture, perhaps you'd say the Packer era did a hell of a lot of good for cricket, but at the time there appeared to be a huge threat to the local pro."

Woolmer's conversion began in early July, on a long coach trip to Swansea for a Sunday League game which was rained off. The following month brought the first solid evidence that WSC riches could trickle down: on the eve of the fourth Test sponsors Cornhill Insurance promised England players not signed to Packer a spectacular rise from £200 a game to £1,000. Neither Woolmer nor the team-mates attempting to persuade him would know it at the time, but the basic pay for a capped Kent player shot up from £2,750 in 1977 to £4,000 the following year. The Packer package on offer equated to about £15,000 for three months' work.

On 24 August Woolmer was asked if he wanted to join the circus, but delayed to sound out Kent about his future captaincy and benefit prospects. If he expected a positive steer from Brice he was to be disappointed. Ironically, given the committee's indulgent tolerance of Colin Cowdrey's frequent absences, Woolmer was told that he was unlikely to be considered while he was still playing for England. "They wanted the continuity of leadership which they had not had under Mike Denness because of his Test commitments."

Asif, Underwood and Knott all found that friendships were tested to breaking point after they had committed to Packer, and Woolmer was to learn the same painful lesson when he finally decided, in early October, to join WSC. It was as if there was some unwritten loyalty clause which bound Kent players more subserviently to the wishes of the committee and hardline members than any other county. Woolmer's specific regret was that a close friendship with Cowdrey was put into cold storage for two years. He wrote: "The one person I never spoke to about Packer was Colin Cowdrey. I had discussed with him most of the decisions which I had made during my career, but not this very important one. I can't remember why I didn't, but perhaps, on reflection, it was because I knew subconsciously that he would try to persuade me not to go."

Because of his late defection Woolmer faced a supplementary charge, "that when I signed for Packer I knew that if I did so I might not play for the county again. That just wasn't true... to be accused of not wanting to play for Kent was very wounding." As it was he remained convinced, though it was never officially admitted, that his decision to join World Series Cricket put paid to his ambitions of captaining his home county.

There was certainly no unanimity among the rank-and-file Kent players about their international colleagues' defection. Norman Graham chose the unlikely setting of the Kent Village Cricket League's annual dinner, in November 1977, to make his opinions plain. "Kerry Packer has done the game a great favour... If the Kent committee had got off their backsides 10 years ago and done some fund-raising – and manager Colin Page is with me on this – the players would have been paid properly and there wouldn't be a need for Packer or benefit years. You've read all this rubbish in the press about 10 weeks' cricket for £20,000. But I'd go, wouldn't you? Good luck to them." An alternative view, and one expressed more widely when the Packer players were reprieved six months later, was that they had held the county to ransom.

On 25 November 1977, the seven-week High Court hearing ended in humiliating defeat for the authorities. The Kent committee were still intent on adopting a stern line with their World Series contingent and, after ploughing scarce resources into expensive legal counsel, hatched a plan designed to deal with both the general and the specific. They reiterated that the Packer players' one-year contracts would not be renewed after the 1978 season and effectively called time on Knott's career by saying that Paul Downton would play instead of him. A statement concluded: "The club and player are parting on extremely amicable terms and Alan Knott has agreed that his registration shall remain with Kent for the 1978 season."

Amicable was not a word which any of the affected players would have used at the time. They were left feeling more like errant schoolboys than world-class cricketers who, whatever the rights or wrongs of their bedding-down with Packer, were only employed by Kent from April to September. Derek Underwood articulated the feeling of general disillusionment among Kent's Packer players when he wrote in his 1980 book *Deadly Down Under*: "Nothing hurt me personally as much as the intensity of feeling over the whole affair in my own county of Kent."

John Pocock, the cricket committee chairman, confirmed in a meeting with Woolmer and Underwood that they would have to find new employers for 1979. Underwood recalled: "We just could not believe that all we had done for Kent in the years before could be discounted in a two-and-a-half hour meeting. To say their action was hurtful was the understatement of the year. What we could not fathom was why we should be dismissed from Kent simply because we wanted to play cricket under another banner in another part of the world during the winter. They talked about our disloyalty to Kent and we wondered just where their loyalties lay. I reckoned, without being conceited, that I had contributed to Kent's post-war success as much as any other bowler and yet here I was being fired from the club I had served in what was a dedicated way for 16 seasons."

Underwood was soon made aware that even if Kent were too principle-bound to soften their stance other counties would be happy to take a more pragmatic view. Eddie Barlow, the South African all-rounder who was then captaining Derbyshire, said he would be welcome at Derby if Kent stuck to their guns.

1978

The decision to replace Asif Iqbal – Kent's cricket committee recommended his reappointment in resigned expectation that the general committee would vote against him – was confirmed only three weeks before the start of the 1978 season. Asif had been full of sympathy for Mike Denness when he was deposed in 1976, arguing that he was "a successful captain of a very good team", but felt equally aggrieved at his own treatment. "We shared the championship and I was sacked for reasons which had nothing to do with cricket," he reflects.

In plumping for Alan Ealham as captain the county put their faith in someone of more grounded virtues. Colin Cowdrey may have described him as the only outfielder he had seen worthy of comparison with the South African Colin Bland, but Ealham was solid, dependable and straightforward, an Ashford-born lover of fish and chips. He has been portrayed as the reluctant captain, but Ealham insists that he was not caught completely unawares when the call came. "We knew the captaincy was going to change in 1977 because the county weren't happy with Asif being involved with Packer. As the winter wore on Colin Page asked me if I'd be interested in doing the job and I said yes. Basically I think it was between me and Shep." Brian Luckhurst, who had taken over as captain and coach of the 2nd XI, had also volunteered his services towards the end of the 1977 season, but there is no evidence that the cricket committee ever thought seriously of looking beyond the first team squad.

Ealham found himself having to deflect concerns that if he was in charge the side would be forced to sacrifice his outfielding ability. "That was one of the things that came up when they were deciding who was going to be captain. I said, 'Hang on, you can't use that to make the actual decision.' I did have to field closer in, but it was a bit of a blessing in disguise for me because by then the old arm was starting to go a bit."

John Shepherd believes that the choice may have been made on more than cricketing grounds: "I thought I would have got the captaincy and I wasn't the only one who thought that. I remember playing against other counties and they'd all say, 'Why aren't you captain?' I was given some paltry excuse that I didn't have the right temperament. It would be wrong or foolish of me to say that there were any underlying issues, but I don't have to spell them out. To be honest, I don't know whether Kent were ready for a black captain. Obviously you could say, what about Asif, but in the pecking order Asians and Indians don't quite fall into the same category. Even in South Africa during apartheid they were on a different rung of the ladder from the blacks."

Ealham and Johnson have different interpretations of how the vice-captain under Asif came to be overlooked when the number one job was vacant. "Graham had poor years in 1976 and 1977," says Ealham. "I think the committee must have thought they needed someone who was going to take the side forward and fortunately for me I'd had a couple of good seasons. If he'd had a couple of good years he'd have been the captain without a doubt, but I guess they thought they couldn't afford to appoint someone who might not be worth his place in the side."

Johnson sees it differently: "I'd invested quite a lot of time and effort into being vice-captain, so it was a bit tough when they chose Alan instead. I got the impression talking to people afterwards that they regarded me as more of a risk than Ealy, who was seen as a safe pair of hands. I was probably seen as a bit of a rebellious type, with my LSE background. When asked for my view, I said what I thought rather than thinking about the audience. But I did feel let down. I remember speaking to people who were involved in the decision, elder statesmen shall we say, who having seen me later on thought they might not have made the right decision."

The tensions and jealousies of the previous 12 months were set aside and Ealham deserved enormous credit for ensuring that the side pulled together in common cause. The World Series players may have started the season with the sense that they were merely enjoying a stay of execution, but the effect was galvanising rather than dispiriting. As Bob Woolmer put it: "Perhaps having the sword of Damocles hanging over our heads for much of the summer made us more determined. Team spirit was exceptionally high, and as far as we could see very few, if any, of the other players were against us."

The rallying cry in Ealham's three years as captain was a simple "right lads, fill your boots". The phrase has become a popular part of cricket parlance, though Ealham is not claiming authorship. "It was an expression I picked up in the motor trade," he admits. The origins are unclear (it is more likely to refer to a vessel for storing wine than the back of a car), though Ealham says that he employed it as a general form of encouragement, rather than as a specific demand for runs in easy batting conditions.

It was not until the second week in February 1978 that Kent's general committee finally confirmed, "in the light of the High Court decision", that they would be offering terms for the following season to Asif, Knott, Underwood and Woolmer. The committee were still painfully aware, from the high volume of letters they received, that many members opposed the merest hint of reprieve, and admitted that their decision would be met with "far from universal approval". The committee's statement also said they would "pursue a selection policy which aims to give their young players the fairest possible chance of development in the interests both of Kent and of English cricket".

Les Ames's impassioned defence of players he had helped nurture was a critical factor in the county's change of heart. The depth of feeling, on both sides of the argument, was shown when Ames, one of the most respected figures in the county's history, was jeered by a section of the members at the annual meeting on 3 April. He said: "The sacking of these players is a repugnant and distasteful decision. I have always considered these four to be model examples of how professional cricketers should behave. This is not going to solve the Packer problem. I am very anti-Packer, but another way must be found to solve the problem."

Despite Ames's intervention, the 250 members at the meeting voted overwhelmingly against a proposal to overturn the committee's decision. The moderate wing of the membership, however, were undeterred and launched a petition at the AGM with the objective of forcing a special meeting. Kent's highly encouraging start to the season, and the eye-catching performances of the Packer players, furthered the petitioners' cause, and the prospect of further blood-letting was averted by a dramatic climbdown. Underwood observed: "Kent, who had a tradition of success and wanted to guard it jealously, could not bear the thought of my joining another county and playing against them."

Ealham remembers: "One of the first things I said in committee after I'd become captain was, 'You've got to rescind the decision not to offer the players new contracts.' It got round to a week before the Benson and Hedges final. I said, 'They've got this weight hanging over them. Can't we take the pressure off them and just get on with the game?'" This time the official line was that the Packer four would be offered extended terms "in the best interests of Kent cricket". Woolmer said he was "obviously pleased"; Asif declared himself "totally delighted". Underwood added: "Now I can hopefully look forward to playing for Kent for many years, which is what I have always wanted to do."

The timing of the announcement prompted accusations that the World Series players had threatened to boycott the final unless they were offered new contracts. Woolmer's denial – "it was a complete nonsense" – was echoed by his similarly reprieved team-mates. The nonsense, as far as broadcaster Brian Johnston was concerned (and vociferous critics who expressed their outrage in the press), was that Kent had put parochialism before the good of the nation. He cancelled his membership in protest. There was also collateral damage closer to home: former captain and chairman David Clark, who as president of MCC also chaired the International Cricket Council, felt obliged to resign from Kent's general committee.

The season itself was spectacularly successful, even by the high standards Kent had set themselves over the previous 10 years. The "saddest" aspect, according to Woolmer, was Knott's absence, though the player himself seemed remarkably relaxed about the arrangement. "I went off and worked in my sports shop in Herne Bay and hardly missed cricket," was his matter-of-fact verdict. Still under the impression that his Kent career was effectively over, Knott contented himself with the knowledge that he would be on WSC duty again the following winter. Later in the season, prompted by Paul Downton's decision to finish his law degree at Exeter, he agreed to play for Kent in the first half of the 1979 and 1980 seasons.

Typically, given the ever-shifting sands of Kent cricket at the time, there was a fresh take on the wicketkeeping debate a year later. Knott turned down an offer to play in the second half of the 1979 season, on the reasonable grounds that he had already made business and holiday arrangements, but once again the prospect of one of the county's favourite sons plying his trade elsewhere helped to shape policy at St Lawrence. Nottinghamshire were among the clutch of counties who made informal approaches to Knott.

When he and Downton were both offered new four-year contracts by Kent, Knott accepted a deal which gave him an initial salary of £10,700 and guaranteed him annual increments of 12.5 per cent. Prompted by his previous inquiries about the feasibility of switching counties in mid-season, a committee meeting at the time reflected concern "that we were getting near a transfer system on the lines of soccer, which was undesirable". Downton pragmatically declined the offer, though the prospect of usurping Middlesex's gloveman in possession, Ian Gould, made Downton hesitate before switching to a side who, in the early Eighties, became the dominant force in county cricket. Ealham was convinced that Downton was being unnecessarily impatient. "He was only a youngster learning his game. You can't walk into first-class cricket and just think you're going to turn it on. You've got to serve an apprenticeship."

A damp summer and a fully available Derek Underwood were an irresistible combination for Kent in 1978, and he passed 100 wickets again the following summer. In an ideal world Underwood would have wanted to carry on serving both county and international masters, but the domestic game was a perfect environment for the continuity which his bowling had always thrived on. Thirty a day could have described his addiction to overs as much as to cigarettes.

The Kent side, and not just the Packer players, found that the simplicity of sport was a welcome refuge from the complex debate which was being played out in committee rooms, media circles and even the corridors of power. Tough selection choices were inevitable, but there was little evidence of factionalism as the season began with a Benson and Hedges Cup win over Yorkshire. They achieved early momentum in the championship as well, taking maximum points from a victory over Hampshire in which Ealham scored his first championship century for two years.

An innings defeat by Essex proved to be just a blip as Kent reeled off eight wins in 10 matches to build a sizeable advantage at the top of the table. On the strength of his performances for the 2nd XI, Graham Dilley had been identified as a hugely promising and distinctly quick pace bowler, and for once the fanfare seemed to be justified. He had just turned 19 when he made his championship debut against Middlesex at Lord's and included Mike Gatting, Roland Butcher and John Emburey among his victims in a five for 32 return which set up a seven-wicket win.

Kent could absorb the minor irritations of an indifferent season with the ball from Shepherd and Downton's lack of runs – the side rarely required heroics from him at No 9. Woolmer and Asif averaged 40 and 49 with the bat while Charles Rowe, though he failed to make a hundred, was a consistent opening partner for Woolmer. Chris Tavaré was both a dependable run-scorer, topping 1,500 runs for the first time, and outstanding as a regular second slip to the pace bowlers and a lone slip to the spin of Underwood and Johnson. By taking 48 catches (49 in all matches) he passed the county record of 45 set by Jim Seymour when Kent won the championship in 1913.

Tavaré pinpoints an innings of 87 against Essex on an awkward Folkestone pitch as not just his most satisfying batting performance that season, but also one of two innings which gave him the greatest pleasure in his entire time at Kent. The other was a more assertive 152 against Worcestershire in 1987. He looks back on the 1978 season as the most enjoyable of his career, in a county context anyway. "It was my first season after coming down from Oxford and the first year when I felt established in the Kent team."

He has a typically mundane explanation for his catching exploits that year: "Wickets were probably a bit livelier than normal and we had some excellent bowlers in all conditions. There were still uncovered pitches for Derek Underwood to bowl on, and it was just one of those years when the ball kept coming to me. It's much easier that way than when it feels like you're waiting for weeks for a chance to come your way."

Two outstanding catches stick in his mind from that summer, both off Kevin Jarvis. The first came early in the season when he dived away to his left to intercept an edge from the Hampshire left-hander David Turner in a championship game at Canterbury; the second was witnessed by a television audience

One to remember: Chris Tavaré catches Alan Hill brilliantly during the 1978 Benson and Hedges Cup final

Picture: Kent Messenger, PD1673764

as he flung himself to his right to catch Derbyshire opener Alan Hill in the Benson and Hedges Cup final. Jarvis, who benefited from 10 Tavaré assists in the championship, enhanced his claims for international recognition by taking 80 wickets, easily his best season to date.

Tavaré also figured in 18 dismissals for Underwood, who was at his most destructive in an innings defeat of Surrey at the Oval. Figures of nine for 32, the second best of his career, completed an extraordinary match return of 13 for 49. Ten days later he picked up another 11 wickets in a victory over Derbyshire. Kent's capacity for chasing down seemingly impossible targets was shown as they beat Leicestershire with seven balls to spare after being set 286 in 165 minutes.

The championship was as good as theirs when Asif made 171, his highest score in England, at almost a run a minute to lay the foundations for a 10-wicket win over Gloucestershire. Kent were now 41 points clear of Essex, and when the two sides drew at Folkestone the outcome became clearer still. Kent could even afford the anti-climax of defeat in their last two matches.

A disappointing John Player League season – Kent won only six matches – could also be seen in the light of the side's focus on the championship. Indif-

ferent one-day form also spilled into a quarter-final defeat by Somerset in the Gillette Cup, but they were a more determined proposition in the Benson and Hedges Cup. They edged a little nervously into the knockout stages by beating Surrey narrowly in a game which needed three days to be settled. In the quarter-finals a barrage of shots from Ealham and Asif enabled Kent to avenge defeat by Nottinghamshire in the group stages. They were then a little fortunate to

Alan Ealham shows off the Benson and Hedges Cup after Kent's Lord's triumph in 1978

Picture: Kent Messenger, PD1673766

enjoy the better of the conditions in a semi-final against Somerset which also seeped into the third day. With morale buoyed by the decision to reprieve the World Series contingent, Kent swept Derbyshire aside in a limp final. Jarvis and Shepherd exerted an iron grip in the early stages of Derbyshire's innings which Kent never relaxed. Woolmer's best one-day score, 79, meant that they won with 13 overs to spare.

Underwood described Kent's twin triumph in 1978 as "perverse", admitting: "I found I was living on a knife-edge, especially in terms of the hostility and pressures off the field." He added: "Luckily I was able to divorce myself from the never-ending arguments by shutting them out of my mind when we were actually out there playing for Kent. It helped that I received a great deal of sympathy and understanding from my Kent team-mates, otherwise I'm sure I could never have taken over 200 wickets in the next two seasons."

Even when Kent won the championship in 1978, he sensed the antipathy of committee men who wished it had been achieved without the Packer players. "I found that attitude small-minded and upsetting," he wrote. "I look upon those wickets in 1978 and 1979 as my crowning achievement for Kent, yet they were appreciated with muffled gratitude." Ealham, who admits that the harmony in the dressing room in 1978 was not matched off it, was soon reminded that job security had become an alien concept at Kent. "I was a bit taken aback to be told after that season, 'You do realise that this is an annual appointment. Just because you've had a good year it doesn't guarantee anything about the future.' It did take the gloss off it a bit for me. You're thinking that you and the side have done a half-decent job and it comes as a bit of a knock-back to be told something like that."

PART II

WILDERNESS YEARS

By Clive Ellis

FOUR

1979-84: Leading Questions

KENT WERE expected to swagger to further triumphs in 1979 – England calls were again unlikely to interfere – but Alan Ealham soon detected that something was different. "The atmosphere wasn't quite the same behind the scenes as it had been the year before," he admits. "We were another year down the road and I think, after we'd won the two competitions under me in '78, a couple of players began to think, 'I could do the captain's job as well.'"

The one distinct advance from 1978 was a much more convincing showing in the John Player League. Kent rose from 11th to second, but could and should have gone one better. The side's never-say-die qualities were amply illustrated, five games into the season, when they went top of the table with a startling one-run victory at Canterbury. An indifferent batting display by Kent left Northamptonshire needing only 146 to win and the task of scoring 17 runs off the last five overs, still with eight wickets intact, should have been routine. Kent, however, bowled with such discipline in the final stages that seven runs were required off the last over and two from the final ball. George Sharp drove it to mid-on, where Ealham gathered and threw down the stumps.

Kent batted erratically, but won crucially against Somerset to convert a two-point deficit into a two-point advantage with two games remaining. The position was unaltered when they met Middlesex at Canterbury in their last game. Ealham remembers: "I got blamed for losing that game, because I went out there, hit a couple of boundaries and then I swept John Emburey, which I'd no need to do at that stage, looking for the short boundary. I was hoping it would go for six but I got caught on the boundary. People said, 'What the hell did you do that for?'"

Ealham's dismissal left Kent on 64 for four and they finished 55 runs adrift of Middlesex's total. Meanwhile Somerset, who had won the first title in their history, the Gillette Cup, the previous day, added the Sunday League title when they beat Nottinghamshire at Trent Bridge. They had seen off Kent in the Gillette quarter-final at Taunton, where the combination of a pitch of inconsistent bounce and Joel Garner were too much for a side low on batting confidence. Garner took five for 11, and Kent's total of 60 remains their lowest in one-day cricket, though they looked equally fragile in being bowled out for 73 by Middlesex in the Benson and Hedges Cup.

There were too many misfiring parts for Kent to contemplate a repeat of their championship-winning form of the previous two seasons. Derek Underwood finished strongly to pass 100 wickets for the second successive year, but John Shepherd suffered the curse of the benefit and Kevin Jarvis was a pale imitation of the bowler he had been in 1978. There was some compensation in the form of Graham Dilley, whose 49 wickets earned him a place on the 1979-80 tour of Australia. He was 20 years and 210 days when he played in the Perth Test, becoming England's youngest debutant for 30 years, but there was a warning attached to Dilley's precocity: the bread-and-butter demands of county cricket quickly lost their attraction. Charles Rowe's batting form fell away after a bright start and Chris Tavaré and Bob Woolmer were the only players to exceed 1,000 runs. The job-sharing arrangement involving Alan Knott and Paul Downton was an uneasy compromise.

Successive innings victories over Hampshire and Glamorgan brought Underwood 24 wickets; the game against Glamorgan at Cardiff also featured the championship innings which Asif Iqbal looks back on with the greatest pride. He made 152 out of 299 on a pitch difficult enough for Glamorgan to be bowled out for 46 in their second innings and reflects: "I remember Derek and Knotty saying they couldn't believe how I'd managed to get so many runs on that track." It meant that Kent went into their final match with hopes of finishing as runners-up to Essex, but they reverted depressingly to type with the bat, losing to Warwickshire by an innings and 174 runs, and had to settle for fifth place. It was their biggest championship defeat since 1948.

1980

There were more encouraging signs in the development of batsmen like Mark Benson, Neil Taylor and Simon Hinks in the 2nd XI, under Brian Luckhurst's approving eye. Both Taylor and Benson were blooded by the first team in 1980 as the county made a policy decision to give young players a chance to establish themselves, but the fall guy was the player still expected to maintain the winning formula as captain: Alan Ealham.

The bald, depressing facts of 1980 were that Kent finished 16th in the County Championship, a position they had last occupied in 1956. Not since 1897 had they won as few as two matches. Ironically, given the side's lack of success, England came calling for Underwood, Knott, Woolmer and Tavaré, though all four were discarded as the season wore on.

Ealham's own form fell away after he had made 145 in a narrow defeat by Essex in early May. Kent built on that performance to beat Hampshire convincingly, Charles Rowe and Bob Woolmer both making hundreds, but they had to wait until August before recording their only other championship win of the campaign. Derek Underwood, deprived by the poor weather of the bowling rhythm on which he thrived, took wickets with his more customary regularity towards the end of the season.

For once Kent did not even have the get-out of superior form in the one-day competitions. Yorkshire ended their interest in the Gillette Cup at the second-round stage, they won only one of their group games in the Benson and Hedges Cup, and fell away after winning three of their opening four fixtures in the John Player League.

A rare moment of levity came in Kent's championship match at the Oval towards the end of August. With Surrey needing three to win, Ealham was persuaded to let Alan Knott bowl. His first delivery was blocked by Alan Butcher, Surrey's left-handed opener; the second looked like an open

invitation to end the match with a six. Woolmer recalled: "Butcher lunged down the pitch and attempted to hit Knott out of the Oval and into the Thames. It turned viciously past the outside edge and no sooner had it passed the bat than the keeper was there whipping off the off bail. Alan Butcher returned to the pavilion while the bowler, Alan Knott, and the wicketkeeper, Bob Woolmer, stared at each other in disbelief and then fell about laughing."

The very serious reality for Ealham was that he was stripped of the captaincy and saw his distinguished Kent career coming to an untidy end. "We always felt we were playing catch-up in 1980 because of the

Bob Woolmer: discarded by England in 1980

weather," he recalls. "I was given a vote of confidence, but then suddenly it was goodbye. I suppose they looked at me personally and thought I wasn't doing enough. All these things built up. Other senior players were canvassed about the situation. Colin Page had warned me that things were going on. I said, 'At the end of the day I've done my best – I thought I'd done a decent job – but if that's not good enough for you, so be it.' I worked hard that winter, thinking, 'Right, I'll show you lot.' It was the same mental approach I'd shown when I was young. But they never even gave me an opportunity: I was left out in the first game and made 12th man. It was a bit of a kick in the teeth to be honest; it was just the way they did it. I wasn't very happy, but there wasn't much I could do because I'd been given a benefit for the following year." He was offered, and turned down the 2nd XI captaincy in 1981, when Brian Luckhurst replaced Colin Page as first team manager, but did agree to do the job in his final season before going back into the motor trade.

Ealham realised, when he was "welcomed back with open arms" to coach and captain the second team in 1988, that his dignified stoicism in the face of undeniably callous treatment had been the best policy. "I'd left on pretty good terms. It helped that I remembered what had happened to other players. I'd seen Alan Brown go, John Dye go, David Sayer go. Alan had said he'd play for half the money because it was his benefit year. They said no and it ended up costing him because he was getting no salary from the cricket. I said to myself, 'Alan, that's going to happen to you one day. You don't want to feel too hurt, accept that it's part of life and move on.' I reckon the wife was more upset than me."

As Ealham's career wound down he was able to take a more detached view of the changes, both to dressing-room culture and personnel, in the early Eighties. Gone was the almost deferential respect which the young player making his way in the game felt for the senior professionals. "The attitude was different when people like Graham Dilley came into the side," Ealham confirms. "They wanted more noise on the field. Players like myself and Alan Knott and Derek Underwood weren't used to that." Sticklers, and Jim Swanton in particular, complained that players were wandering around in tracksuits rather than whites; a committee meeting in June 1981 was told that "bad habits were creeping into the behaviour on the field".

Much as Colin Cowdrey had shaken his head and bitten his lip as he surveyed the casually dressed Kent players at the Grand Hotel in Leicester in 1970, Ealham concluded that progress, whatever the decibel level, could not be reversed. He admits that when he took charge of the 2nd XI he was "making as much noise as any of them". He was more concerned by the negativity and cynicism which, he felt, began to infiltrate the Kent dressing room as the automatic success of the 1970s, and hand-in-glove solidarity, evaporated. Luckhurst retained the respect of the emerging players in the second team, but found himself the subject of ridicule and derision when he replaced Colin Page as first team manager. Luckhurst also struggled, in his new role, to re-establish a working relationship with players who before had just been his equals as team-mates.

"The attitude was just starting to change," remembers Ealham, "and Brian did get stick from the younger players. I also remember Derek Underwood being called an old tosser, which really upset him. Players don't need all that: you should be trying to encourage each other. We always used to be told by Colin Cowdrey, 'Your players are the best in the world even if you hate their guts.' He thought the image of the side was important. You don't want too much animosity because that just breeds problems within the team. Let's face it, cricket is a bit of a selfish game, but when I was coaching I used to say, 'I don't mind you being selfish as long as it doesn't interfere with the team and you're not trying to say you're number one.' "

1981

Bob Woolmer believed that Asif Iqbal was "harshly and wrongly treated" in 1980, though there was no obvious logic to Asif's reappointment as captain for the 1981 season, especially given his championship aggregate of 208 runs from 16 innings the previous summer. The side now seemed to consist largely of experienced potential captains who for various reasons were destined to be overlooked (Shepherd, Johnson and Woolmer) and players still considered too inexperienced for the job (Tavaré and Cowdrey).

Asif recognised the hand of cricket committee chairman John Pocock in giving him a second bite at the captaincy. "He was a bit like Colin Cowdrey: he had immense faith and belief in me." Asif is also refreshingly self-critical in admitting now that he should have retired from all cricket after ending his Test career at the start of 1980.

> "I had lost my desire for the game. I realised that there was nothing to play for and I was being selfish in accepting the captaincy and continuing to play because of the benefit that Kent had bestowed on me in 1981. Had it not been for that I would have retired from cricket straightaway when I announced my retirement from Test cricket. At the same time I would have been foolish to have done that because I had worked

reasonably hard to earn the benefit. Once it was over my heart was not in cricket and as a player it's unfair to carry on when you're not giving your best. It became an effort to play cricket whereas in the past it was a joy, for me and for the spectators. There were players who were sitting and waiting and dying to play and I was stopping someone from getting into the team. Being captain the responsibility is huge so I didn't feel I was being honest."

For all that Kevin Jarvis, who played under five full-time captains during his 13 seasons with the county, has no hesitation in putting Asif top of the list. "He was just one of those guys who expected to win. He bred that enthusiasm and belief, to the extent that we did just expect to win. That was a fantastic era to be involved. Whether it was luck or the players involved we got into a habit of winning."

Jarvis was also painfully aware of the pendulum shifting. "Suddenly the habit goes the other way and you're more used to losing than winning. It becomes hard then to turn it round again; you're always chasing the earlier glories and the pressure mounts. The expectation through the Seventies was such that when we moved into the Eighties and didn't do so well the pressure was always on and we always seemed to be struggling." Asif also believes that Kent were, in a sense, the victims of a gradual levelling-off in the county game. "I always thought that other counties would catch up," he says. "It wasn't so much a case of us getting worse as the rest getting better."

Despite his apparent lack of motivation, Asif put in his most consistent season with the bat since 1975. Although the closest that Kent came to silverware was a semi-final place in the Benson and Hedges Cup they performed to a more respectable level than in 1980. Chris Tavaré was outstandingly consistent, and feels now that the years between 1981 and 1983 represented his peak as a batsman. He also has a characteristically modest take on his failure to reproduce his county fluency on the international stage. "When you get to that level you have to have flair to take on bowlers and I don't think I was quite good enough to do that. I like to think that I did a reasonable job for England, and we had more than enough stroke-makers at the other end."

Mark Benson underlined his promise by passing 1,000 runs in his first full season and his future opening partner, Neil Taylor, who had made a hundred on his first-class debut against the Sri Lankan touring side in 1979, fell agonisingly short of a maiden championship hundred when he was out for 99 against Sussex. Kent won that match and a heroic spell of six for 29 from Derek

Underwood almost conjured another victory at Lord's when Middlesex, needing only 94, edged to a one-wicket win. Underwood also contributed a rare fifty and nine wickets to a victory over Hampshire and reached the 2,000-wicket landmark in the return match.

The game was also notable for a precocious debut by 23-year-old Derek Aslett, drafted in at the last minute, whose unbeaten 146 was the highest score by a Kent player in his first appearance. According to Chris Penn, a team-mate of Aslett's in the mid-Eighties, he became increasingly weighed down by technical thoughts and was only 29 when he quit the first-class game in 1987. This was one of three championship matches in which Woolmer captained Kent in 1981. He confessed that he had lacked motivation after being dropped by England, but the captaincy gave him fresh focus, even if his first game in charge, against Leicestershire, coincided with Botham's Test at Headingley. Two wins and a draw (Worcestershire finished nine down in the third game) were a more than respectable return and though Alan Ealham believes that Woolmer had "too many theories" to be a coherent captain, Alan Knott disagreed. "He had a very good cricket brain and tremendous enthusiasm for the game," he wrote.

Kent finished their championship programme with a victory over Surrey, notable for the sustained hostility of Jarvis, which enabled them to finish ninth. Jarvis's match return of 12 for 147 gave him 81 wickets for the season, one more than he had managed in the championship-winning campaign of 1978. Ironically, it was in the course of a much less successful 1982 season that Jarvis came within an ace of making his Test debut; he was 12th man for games against both India and Pakistan, but was again painfully aware that his lack of ability with the bat counted against him.

Once more Somerset stood between Kent and the prospect of another one-day trophy. Kent qualified for the knockout stages of the Benson and Hedges Cup despite losing to Somerset in a group game, and they were outclassed by the same opposition in the semi-finals. Kent lost as many games as they won in the John Player League and exited in the second round of the NatWest Trophy despite Underwood achieving a personal record for maidens in a one-day game. Underwood's return of 12-8-12-0 could not prevent Nottinghamshire rallying from 79 for six to reach a modest victory target of 155.

The saddest aspect of Kent's season was encapsulated in the minutes from a cricket committee meeting towards the end of July, confirming that Nick Kemp, Charles Rowe and John Shepherd would be released at the end of the season. Kemp had never fulfilled the great promise he had shown as a schoolboy; the same could be said to a lesser extent of the bookish Rowe; Shepherd was, and is, one of the best loved of Kent cricketers. He never regarded himself as an overseas player and Kent supporters saw him in the same light.

The undeniable facts were that the statistics in what turned out to be Shepherd's final three seasons for the county were modest, but the all-rounder himself had little or no inkling that his future was under consideration until Woolmer, the players' representative on the cricket committee, broke the news to him during a championship game at Derby towards the end of July.

"It was the first time I'd been sacked, so it was a real blow," Shepherd remembers. He had always believed that he would be able to dictate his own career moves. "I would probably have played in the 1982 season and then fallen into a coaching role at Kent because that was all I ever wanted to do. That was the natural progression in those days."

Shepherd was given a fresh perspective on his future when he was reminded by local journalist Stephen Brenkley, now cricket correspondent for the *Independent*, that he was only 47 wickets short of his 1,000 in first-class cricket. "I had no idea – I was just wrapped up with playing cricket. I never thought of statistics."

He was left out of the side after playing in a championship game against Essex in mid-August, but decided to float a loose proposal to Brian Luckhurst, who had become first team manager at the start of the season.

"I sat down next to Luckhurst at a Sunday game and said, 'I need 47 wickets for my thousand. I don't want a contract, I will just keep myself fit. Next year you're going to have injuries, people out of form; there are going to be countless reasons why you might need someone. You can just pay me on a match-by-match basis and I'll turn up, play and get my 47 wickets. And then I'll do a John Wayne and just ride into the sunset.' And Luckhurst said to me, 'What you must realise is we're not running a charity.' He's dead and gone and I never took it up with him afterwards, but that was the closest I've ever come to smacking somebody because that was the ultimate insult. I'd given the best 16 years of my life to Kent; I wasn't even asking for a contract. That is one of the things which still sticks in my throat. The same Luckhurst was telling the newspapers in one breath, 'He's the best overseas player ever to come to this country,' and in the next breath he's telling you that they're not running a bloody charity. You can't be that bloody hypocritical."

It was only thanks to a personal plea from Les Ames, the former secretary-manager, that Shepherd agreed to play against Worcestershire in the final Sunday League match of the season at Canterbury. "As far as I was concerned I'd rather have stuck two fingers up to the club, but Les sat me down one day and told me that the members wanted me to play." He did not bowl and made just two before being dismissed by fellow Barbadian Hartley Alleyne, who seven years later became one of Kent's less successful overseas players. Champagne flowed in the dressing room afterwards, but Shepherd was moved to ask his team-mates why he was celebrating being sacked.

He said Kent tried "to do everything to prevent me playing for another county, because they could see what was going to happen". The Lancashire League side, Nelson, and Oxfordshire were both mooted, but Shepherd was recruited instead by Gloucestershire, who saw him as the closest available thing to an ideal replacement for Mike Procter.

"It was just the impetus I needed," he remembers, "and sure enough the first hundred I got after I went to Gloucestershire was against Kent. You might call it poetic justice. Anyhow, I think I proved that I wasn't past my sell-by date." The figures support the claim: Shepherd took 63, 67 and 72 wickets in his three seasons with Gloucestershire and in 1983 passed 1,000 runs for only the second time in his career.

He admits that the manner of his departure from Kent still hurts and regrets that he has never had the chance to give something back to the county which gave him so much. "I never put myself forward to be on a committee or anything like that, but there again nobody at Kent has ever asked me to get involved. I'm not going to tell you that I would have been the best coach in the world, but I'm sure that there was a little niche somewhere where I could probably have helped out."

Various overseas options were being considered as Kent went into a period of transition from which they have never quite emerged. Minutes from June 1980 show that the committee were "disappointed with the form of Asif Iqbal and John Shepherd". Sunil Gavaskar's agent had inquired about the possibility of the Indian opener joining on a two-year contract, but the official response was: "The committee confirmed that they wished, as far as possible, to engage English-born players and that we had no wish to engage Mr Gavaskar." Graham Johnson tried to broker the signing of Graeme Pollock, the outstanding South African batsman of his generation, early in 1981, but there was a general feeling that the county's most pressing need was for a fast bowler or all-rounder.

1982

In 1981 Kent were able to field three overseas players, John Shepherd, Asif Iqbal and new arrival Eldine Baptiste, in the same side, but regulations were tightened for 1982 so that Baptiste could only play when Asif was missing. Baptiste, when only 18, had been identified by manager Colin Page as a potential replacement for Shepherd when he visited Antigua in 1979. That promise rarely surfaced in 1982, even though Asif, who had already announced that he would retire at the end of the season, was happy enough to stand down so that Baptiste could play, and missed the last six championship games. A paltry 12 wickets at 56 apiece were hardly what Kent were looking for; his batting, a secondary suit, was moderately successful. Opinion was divided about the advisability of replacing him with Abdul Qadir, the Pakistan leg-spinner, for 1983, but Baptiste survived a marginal 4-3 vote by the cricket committee and was given another chance to prove his worth.

Rumours of an unofficial England tour to South Africa had begun to circulate during the 1981 season and when the plans came to highly secretive fruition, Derek Underwood, Alan Knott and Bob Woolmer were all signed up to pocket £10,000 for three weeks' work in spring 1982, under the guise of a South African Breweries XI. To the arguments which had been batted to and fro about World Series Cricket could be added a complex series of moral conundrums: was it better to involve or isolate through sport?

Again the players faced an England ban, again the counties had to decide on a stance, though this time they were armed with the inevitable knowledge that if they sacked the rebels they would face potentially ruinous litigation. Kent chairman John Pocock met Underwood, Knott and Woolmer on 5 April 1982, and committee minutes recorded: "He had told them of the committee's extreme displeasure and had offered them one of three choices: to continue to play for Kent; to have a free transfer to another county; to negotiate a severance agreement. The three players had been surprised at the committee's strong reaction and, after consideration, had opted to continue to play for Kent."

Woolmer, someone for whom South Africa was by now a second home, had no moral qualms about taking part. He was more concerned with the practical implications of his decision (a benefit was uppermost in his thoughts). Discussions with Brian Luckhurst had already convinced him that he was not being seen as a successor to Asif. The county's argument was that Woolmer's age – he turned 34 in May 1982 – counted against him. Chris Tavaré, 27, and Chris Cowdrey, 24, were both seen as better long-term prospects, though Woolmer

A corps of keepers: Kent glovemen (from left) Howard 'Hopper' Levett, Les Ames, Alan Knott, Godfrey Evans and Derek Ufton

Picture: Kent Messenger. PD1673768

was still convinced that his involvement with World Series Cricket was the real reason that he was being overlooked.

Neither Tavaré nor Cowdrey were comfortable with the decision to give them joint vice-captain status in 1982, "with the clear suggestion", as Cowdrey put it, "that he or I would ultimately take over". Almost 30 years on, Cowdrey is still convinced that it was a misguided, divisive call. "It was a strange decision and a bad one. It put pressure on both of us to try to impress rather than concentrating on doing a good job when we got the chance. You're either vice-captain or you're not. I don't think either of us had the chance to show what we'd actually be like when we were captaining the club. It's easy to go out and captain on the field – I never found that any problem. It's very different when you're actually captain of Kent. There are so many more aspects of the job that come into play."

It was soon apparent that the crucial balance that Shepherd brought to the side as a third seamer had gone. Kent were hard to beat in the championship – they lost only four games – but did not have the firepower to bowl sides out twice. Three wins, two in the first six games, and an eventual 13th place were the outcome. They had to wait another 16 matches before Dilley, showing the form which had encouraged other counties to make approaches at the end of the 1980 season, set up a win over Leicestershire by taking 10 wickets in the match.

There was more to applaud on the batting side; Woolmer made a maiden double hundred at his home ground, The Nevill. Mark Benson's breakthrough season in 1981 was matched by Neil Taylor's rise in 1982 and Tavaré was again the most reliable performer with the bat. Much was expected of Laurie Potter, who had committed his future to England after captaining Australia at Under 19 level, and the Bexleyheath-born all-rounder, still only 19, did not disappoint, averaging more than 40 with the bat. Chris Penn, who made his first team debut in 1982 and was also a team-mate of Potter's in the England Young Cricketers side who played West Indies that summer, remembers: "He was the most talented cricketer I'd been around."

Taylor was so prolific in the Benson and Hedges Cup that he won the gold award in three of his first four games. Unfortunately for Kent and Taylor, his identical scores of 121 against Sussex and Somerset were both in a losing cause. The total of 305 for five made by Sussex at Hove was the highest one-day score against Kent since the same opposition had reached 314 in 1963, the first year of the Gillette Cup. Taylor played such a lone hand in the quarter-final against Somerset that, in a total of 207, Cowdrey (40) was the only other player to make more than eight. Somerset edged to a three-wicket victory with two balls to spare. Kent's encouraging start in the John Player League – they won their first four games – fizzled out as they finished fourth, and they were overwhelmed by Essex in the second round of the NatWest Trophy.

Asif's retirement, a year after Shepherd's sacking, seemed to symbolise the end of a glorious era for Kent cricket. The county's supporters had no opportunity to bid an extended farewell; Asif's last championship appearance on home soil was in early July and his final outings for the county were a championship match and Sunday League fixture against Middlesex at Lord's. Asif contributed little, but at least had the muted satisfaction of bowing out with a one-run victory.

Events, rather than any unofficial pecking order, dictated that Cowdrey was in charge for seven championship games in 1982. Tavaré, who played in all six Tests that summer, captained the side only twice, but the cricket committee voted 5-2 in favour of recommending his appointment. Luckhurst sided with Tavaré and the general committee came to the same conclusion in a desperately close 12-10 vote. The official explanation given was that Cowdrey had yet to command a guaranteed place in the side. "I can't deny that I was disappointed," he admits. "I didn't have an issue with Chris Tavaré – he's a very nice, quiet guy and a friend of mine – but I did have an issue with the way it was handled." Tavaré himself now insists: "I'd never really given much thought to the captaincy. I was surprised when someone mentioned it to me a couple of years earlier, but I'd thought that Bob Woolmer would get the job when Asif retired."

Cowdrey, who had been given the chance to captain Derbyshire four years earlier, now had to weigh up three more captaincy offers from other counties. "I nearly left," he says, "but when it came to it I couldn't really imagine myself going anywhere else. The fact remained that I was very keen to captain. I'd always captained the school and enjoyed doing it. I didn't assume that I'd get the job, but I felt that most of the other players believed I would. People thought that I was cut out to do the job and Chris Tavaré wasn't a natural captain because he was quiet. There again, Mike Brearley was quiet, but he was a great captain. It's just that I don't think anyone knew what kind of captain Chris might be. The committee took the chance and there was probably a feeling that I was too much one of the lads, and they thought that wouldn't work well. It was a difficult decision for them, but it was still a shock."

The Kent committee decided against appointing a vice-captain for the 1983 season, but announced that "when C. J. Tavaré is not playing and C. Cowdrey is in the side on merit, then he should be the captain". At the same time there was clearly an unspoken inference that once Cowdrey had established himself in the side he, rather than the less charismatic Tavaré, would be seen as the natural leader.

Cowdrey himself denies that there was an automatic succession, and insists: "I never thought I would do the job after that. I genuinely believed that Chris Tavaré would do the job for five, six, seven years, whatever it was, and I don't think I would have moved just to become captain somewhere else. The hardest part was that a lot of people never forgot it. There was a major split and people rowing about the captaincy in committee. That wrangling just went on and on and filtered through to the dressing room."

The one positive for Cowdrey was that he re-assessed himself as a cricketer, and particularly as a batsman, while playing grade cricket in Sydney in 1982-83. He admits that Tavaré was instrumental in the process. "He thought I was underachieving as a player, so he helped me quite a lot. I decided I needed to start playing as a proper batsman again. I'd been playing purely as an enter-tainer, trying to win games; I was never very interested on a flat pitch, when we were going to make 400 anyway, grinding out a 70, just to help my average. The problem is I should have played more like that because when you have a bad run those seventies keep you in the side, in the limelight. Chris was right that I needed to get my head down and play better."

1983

Although Chris Tavaré impressed with his quiet authority, attention to detail and calmness under pressure, it is hard to avoid the impression that he was merely keeping the captaincy seat warm for Chris Cowdrey. The only obstacle was Cowdrey's capacity to transform himself into a consistent top-order batsman, and he was quick to show the benefits of his winter makeover. Mike Gatting was the only English batsman to improve on his average of 56.83. Curiously, Cowdrey also captained Kent more often in the championship than Tavaré, who was required by England both for the World Cup and for the four Tests against New Zealand.

The hundreds flowed all summer for Kent players. Neil Taylor matched Cowdrey's total of five, finishing the championship season on a particularly productive note. In a statistical oddity Mark Benson and Derek Aslett scored two centuries in a match in successive games in mid-season. John Shepherd delivered a pointed riposte to the county who had released him in 1981, making his first century since joining Gloucestershire and taking four for 42 to boot. Kent's last-wicket pair, Graham Johnson and Kevin Jarvis, denied Shepherd the additional satisfaction of a victory.

Eldine Baptiste's low-key introduction to county cricket in 1982 had suggested that Kent would feel the lack of overseas inspiration even more keenly the following season, but Baptiste played a full part in a much more encouraging season for the county. He took 50 wickets and batted with freedom and flair to make 755 runs at an average of almost 36. A stand of 191 with fellow century-maker Aslett, laying the foundations for a victory over Surrey, was one of Kent's batting high points for the season. The wider benefit for Baptiste was a place in the West Indies' Test team the following winter; the knock-on effect for Kent was that when he was also picked for the tour of England in 1984 they recruited Terry Alderman as an inspired replacement.

Underwood was now 38, but his appetite for bowling was undiminished and his motivation still strong despite the fact that the rebel tour to South Africa had effectively ended his England career. He got through 919 overs and was the joint leading wicket-taker with 106 wickets, matching Essex's John Lever. Richard Ellison began to show the form which would earn him a Test debut the following year.

Seventh place in the championship represented a significant improvement, and Kent were satisfyingly competitive in all three one-day competitions. They were still in with a chance of winning the John Player League until losing to Somerset in their penultimate match and, despite indifferent batting, reached the semi-finals of the Benson and Hedges Cup. They appeared to be doomed to defeat in the quarter-finals, scoring only 198 then watching, helpless, as Gordon Greenidge and Paul Terry added 131 for Hampshire's first wicket. Inspired bowling from Ellison, Underwood and Bob Woolmer allowed Kent to squeeze home by five runs, but the game was up when they made only 128 against Essex at Canterbury.

The momentum was maintained all the way to Lord's in the NatWest Trophy, though again their progress was far from straightforward. Cowdrey's unbeaten 122, a one-day best, was the ballast to Kent's total of 274 against Essex in the second round, but Graham Gooch replied in kind and Essex were cruising on 210 for one before Ellison inspired a heroic fightback and four-run win. Kent eased past Warwickshire in the quarter-finals and Cowdrey's best limited-overs bowling figures, four for 36, enabled them to beat Hampshire.

The first half of the final, against Somerset, went roughly according to plan. Graham Dilley delivered the traditional eve-of-tour-party-announcement nudge to the England selectors, maintaining pace and accuracy to take four for 29. Kent, not for the first time, found runs desperately hard to come by against Joel Garner, but the inquests, after Kent's 24-run defeat, all centred on the bowlers they had used (or, more pertinently, not used) in Somerset's innings. As Tony Lewis put it in *The Sunday Telegraph*: "There was an oddity about the match – all this written with hindsight. Tavaré, captain of Kent, chose not to bowl Underwood, one of the most economical slow bowlers in the country, whereas Botham turned quickly to the combined spin attack of Marks and Richards." Just to prove that strange forces were at work on that day Alan Knott dropped a catch, standing back to Cowdrey.

Taylor, who had scored a hundred against Leicestershire in the championship game immediately prior to the final, was puzzled by his omission from the starting XI at Lord's, and no less bemused when he made another century, pointedly against Somerset, the week after. He also thought that his chances of selection had improved when Woolmer sustained one of cricket's more unusual injuries: he hurt his back while washing his cricket trousers in the sink at St Lawrence after making a hundred against Surrey.

One of the more forthright individuals in the Kent dressing room in the Eighties and early Nineties, Taylor explains: "I hadn't been playing in the one-day games, but after my hundred at Grace Road I thought I'd got a pretty good chance of playing at Lord's. I probably only found out at half past ten on the day of the game that they wanted to play an extra bowler, so Graham Johnson was going to open the batting. But that didn't really rub with me because Derek

Graham Dilley strains for pace during the NatWest Trophy final in 1983

Underwood, who was our best one-day bowler, didn't bowl a ball. I wouldn't say that was one my fondest memories from my time with Kent."

There was no indication at this point that Tavaré's tenure was under threat. Woolmer, who applauded his calmness in the heat of battle, went so far as to write in his 1984 autobiography: "It looks very much as though Tavaré will hold the reins for many more seasons to come."

1984

Both captain and county should have been able to look forward to the 1984 season with reasonable optimism, but injuries conspired against them. The most serious case of absenteeism was that of Graham Dilley, who had to return early from England's tour of Pakistan and required a bone graft from his hip to repair a neck injury. Unsurprisingly, Dilley missed the whole season and Bob Woolmer was forced to retire because of a back injury. A cartilage operation kept Mark Benson out of action until mid-June and, with Chris Tavaré falling short of his normal high standards, there was a fragility to the batting which legislated against a top-three finish in the County Championship.

In the circumstances they did remarkably well to win eight games and finish fifth. For once the seam bowling was reliably penetrative, helped by the recruitment of Terry Alderman. The Australian took 76 wickets and both Richard Ellison and Kevin Jarvis enjoyed productive seasons. Derek Underwood remained the county's most reliable match-winner with the ball, but it was a batting performance which gave Underwood one of the most cherished and unexpected achievements of his lengthy career.

As a batsman he had never been short of courage, even when subjected to a short-pitched bombardment from Lillee, Thomson and assorted West Indian quick bowlers, but his technique was far from watertight. Underwood's jabby range of shots was as far from Colin Cowdrey's silky repertoire as it was possible to be. The presence of Norman Graham, and later Jarvis, guaranteed that he would go in no lower than No 10 for Kent, but it was only as night-watchman that he could dream of playing lengthy innings. At the start of the 1984 season, the 22nd of his career, there were just two half centuries on his CV. His career-best score of 80 was made going in at No 3 against a high-quality Lancashire attack in 1969.

It was somehow both appropriate and ironic that Underwood's finest hour, or approximately four hours, should come at Hastings, a ground where he had bowled with such relish and distinction throughout his career. His best first-class figures of nine for 28 were recorded there in 1964 and, 20 years later, he returned to claim his finest one-day return, six for 12, in a John Player League game.

The Sunday match was the filling in the familiar weekend sandwich; Kent began their championship fixture on the Saturday, 30 June, and only edged to an all-out total of 92 on the back of opener Neil Taylor's dogged 50. It was the lowest ever Kent score in which a batsman had made a fifty. Seamers continued to hold sway as Sussex were bowled out for 143, then nightwatchman Underwood, who throughout his career had maintained an almost unblemished record for keeping his wicket intact until the following morning, clung on after Taylor went early in Kent's second innings.

The real drama unfolded when the match resumed on the Monday. Sussex's bowlers disposed of Kent's front-line batting efficiently enough – they were soon 86 for six – but Underwood remained, as Garth Le Roux, in particular, showed a bone-headed lack of imagination. "I'd played with Garth in World Series," Underwood recalls, "and he was just trying to knock my block off." The batsman responded, according to Doug Ibbotson in *The Daily Telegraph*, with "hunch-shouldered hooks and square drives"; Tavaré contributed just a single to a third-wicket stand of 44. Underwood reached his fifty off 65 balls and a career best came into view as Ellison and Alan Knott, at eight and nine, stuck around.

Unfortunately for Underwood, however, the last two Kent batsman were Alderman, a No 11 in most company, and Jarvis, one of the least able batsmen in Kent's history. When Knott was eighth out at 155, Underwood was still well adrift of his hundred, but Alderman captured the almost surreal mood to play his own innings of a lifetime. He raised his career best from 26 to an unbeaten 52 as Underwood marched on with what *The Times'* Marcus Williams described as "a delicious mixture of brave defence and orthodox and idiosyncratic stroke play".

He was convinced that he had been caught only to discover, when he had already begun his walk back to the pavilion, that a no-ball had been signalled. On 96 he was obligingly dropped at slip by John Barclay, the Sussex captain, and celebrated the reprieve with a hooked four, the 14th of his innings, off Ian Greig. He was finally out for 111, the product of 219 balls and 254 minutes, but even Jarvis caught the mood in a last-wicket stand of 35 with Alderman which nudged Kent's total to 243.

The game could have finished there and remained as an indelible part of Kent folklore, but it also provided a memorable finish. Sussex slumped to 89 for five on the final morning before Colin Wells wrested the initiative once more with a forthright 81. At lunch Sussex were 186 for six, needing only seven to win, but Wells went immediately after the break, then Ellison struck twice with successive balls. Two nervous singles enabled Sussex's final pair to bring the scores level before David Smith, the reserve wicket-keeper, edged Alderman to Tavaré in the slips to produce the first tie in the championship for 10 years.

Kent themselves had not been involved in a tie since 1950, but the laws of statistical improbability

Terry Alderman enjoyed two excellent seasons for Kent in the mid-Eighties

were stretched to breaking point when they figured in another two weeks later at Northampton. On this occasion the bulk of the match was mundane; Kent led by 126 on first innings after dismissing Northamptonshire cheaply, and had the luxury of being able to declare for the second time, setting a target of 331 on the final day. Inspired by a maiden century from Duncan Wild, Northamptonshire were apparently cruising to victory on 232 for three before panic set in. *The Times'* version of events was this: "When Wild eventually went for 120, attempting another boundary, 17 runs were needed with 14 balls remaining. The last pair were together and Northants still needed a run off the final ball of the last over bowled by Alderman. Griffiths was run out by Knott as he tried to scramble a bye off the final ball."

But for Lancashire's final pair holding out in a match notable for the lone hundred of Chris Penn's career, Kent would have won four successive championship matches in the early part of the season. A first defeat resulted from another John Shepherd backlash, and match figures of nine for 69 for Gloucestershire, but Kent finished their championship campaign in convincing style with three wins and five draws in their last eight games.

Benson contributed three hundreds to the sequence and Underwood reverted to his major suit, bowling sides out, in an extraordinary show of stamina against Hampshire. He operated unchanged in both innings to record figures of 27-13-34-4 and 42-15-87-8 and also played his part in a brilliant victory over, on paper anyway, a much superior Essex side at Colchester. Essex were reigning champions and on course to defend their title successfully; Kent were so depleted that they were forced to go into the game with three half-fit players, Cowdrey, Alderman and Jarvis.

Cowdrey, captaining the side in Tavaré's absence, may have been a very different technical specimen from his father, but there was a shared determination to rise above adverse conditions or circumstances. Essex were bowled out for 90 on the greenest of pitches, designed to help their own seamers and neutralise Underwood. Cowdrey's challenge, when batting, was not just to keep out bowlers like Neil Foster and Derek Pringle but to avert further damage to a cracked knuckle and cut finger. Cowdrey wrote in his book *Good Enough?*: "Every ball from Pringle hit the splice of my bat, forcing my hand off the handle on impact. Any shot off the front foot I could play without pain." He made an unbeaten 125 out of a total of 201 as Kent wrapped up a 10-wicket victory in a day and a half.

The dispiriting side-effect for Cowdrey was that the game, and his own performance, only served to highlight the air of cynical suspicion which had consumed the club at this time. He remembers: "I'd got a hundred on a terrible pitch, we'd beaten the county champions, but still there was a wave of ill-feeling coming my way. People said that I only ever played well when I was captain. It was a really hurtful thing and completely untrue. I never had any problem playing for Tav."

Kent were also no strangers to close finishes in the one-day competitions in 1984, though the results all seemed to go against them. Their chances of reaching the knockout stages in the Benson and Hedges Cup ended when, in quick succession, they lost by two wickets to Somerset with two balls remaining, and to Sussex by one wicket with one ball left. Early in an indifferent Sunday League season they made an imposing 255 against Derbyshire and still contrived to lose by one wicket.

Those disappointments were just flesh wounds compared to the grievous harm inflicted when they lost to Middlesex off the last ball of the NatWest Trophy final. The form which took Kent to Lord's for the second successive year suggested that the traumas of the defeat by Somerset had been buried. They bowled out Hampshire for 99 to wrap up an overwhelming win in the second round and landed a psychological counter-punch by beating a Garnerless Somerset in the quarter-finals. A Tavaré hundred was pivotal to that 10-run victory, and Benson's unbeaten 113 guided them home with two overs to spare against Warwickshire in the semi-final.

Kent had to draft in Stuart Waterton for the final when Knott failed a late fitness test, but Waterton was to have little impact on a game remembered as one of the most gripping one-day showpieces. The fundamentals were that Kent were given crucial momentum in the final 20 overs by Cowdrey's 58 off 56 balls, an innings which was widely taken to have clinched his place on the winter tour to India.

A total of 232 was competitive, but no more. Middlesex were uneasily placed on 88 for three when Underwood, the fifth bowler used by Tavaré, bowled the dangerous Roland Butcher and reduced the flow of runs to a trickle. The game may have turned on Tavaré's much-criticised decision to take Underwood off when he had bowled nine overs for 12. Clive Radley, the canniest of one-day players, and former Kent man Paul Downton lifted the tempo, but when both were out in quick succession the match was back in the balance.

The gathering gloom simply added to the drama in what Tony Lewis described in *The Sunday Telegraph* as a "dark and mysterious last three overs". He summed up: "When eventually Middlesex needed 13 runs off 18 balls they looked strong favourites; when they wanted six from five Kent were, if not firmly in the driving seat, at least riding side-saddle."

John Emburey and Phil Edmonds, more accustomed to sharing wickets than runs, faced the final over from Ellison, and nibbled away at the requirement with a leg bye, single, two, single, single. The scores were now level, but Kent knew, or at least suspected, that if they denied Middlesex a run they would win by virtue of their superior scoring rate in the early overs. Emburey, however, removed the need for such calculations by hitting a four wide of square leg.

Taylor, who had laid the foundations for Cowdrey's assault by making 49, sympathises with the dilemma which faced Tavaré: "There were a lot of comments suggesting that he was sacked because he'd taken off Underwood when he'd gone for next to nothing and then bringing him back when Radley and Downton were pinging it all round the park, and Deadly certainly didn't have the same impact as he did in his first nine overs. Obviously Tav wanted to have one of his better bowlers to bring back at the end in case we needed to tie it up. It didn't work out that day; it's the nature of the job."

Tavaré's removal as captain was, predictably if simplistically, traced to his tactics in the two NatWest finals, but in reality a change of captaincy had been agreed a few weeks earlier. Tavaré accepts that interpretation, though he also confirms that he knew that he was being removed as captain just a week before the change of leadership was formally announced.

He remains reluctant to discuss his feelings at being ousted, but admits: "I didn't play very well in 1984, though I don't think the captaincy had anything to do with that. Three years with England had left me mentally exhausted and one or two flaws crept into my batting technique as a result." Tavaré also believes that the side had performed more than respectably during his two years in charge. "It was much more disappointing to lose in semi-finals than in finals. When Middlesex beat us they were at their absolute peak, so it was no disgrace to lose to them. And despite the result, it was a fantastic game."

John Woodcock, writing in *The Times*, had an interesting take on the change at the top, even if his note of optimism proved to be wishful thinking. The sentiment could as easily have been drawn from Jim Swanton's pen. "It is a pity that the switch in the Kent captaincy from Chris Tavaré to Christopher Cowdrey should have been interpreted as a 'sacking' for Tavaré. It is in Tavaré's own interest quite as much as Kent's, that he be relieved of a job which, for the past two seasons, has had an adverse affect on his form. His loyalty, modesty and dedication are such as to beget blessing rather than blame." Woodcock added: "Cowdrey could captain England one day: Tavaré probably never will. Between them, as good friends, they could take Kent into a golden age."

The unavoidable fact was that Tavaré's pride was deeply wounded. In November he made it clear that he wanted to leave Kent (despite the offer of a new deal which would incorporate a benefit). The county, predictably, said that he would have to honour the remainder of his contract. The Professional Cricketers' Association felt powerless to back him, though in the current climate they might well have argued that there had been an irretrievable breakdown in the relationship between club and player. The new season was only a month away when Tavaré announced, with obvious reluctance, that he had agreed to sign a four-year contract.

He explained: "My reason for wanting to leave was not due to the loss of the captaincy but the way in which the matter was handled. I felt that my loyalty and trust had not been reciprocated by the club. The executive committee of the club, however, turned down my request for release which meant I had to stay with the club or retire from the game. I considered that to pursue the matter either by litigation or prolonged argument would have been damaging to Kent cricket."

FIVE

1985-92: The Cowdrey Inheritance

WHATEVER THE merits of the decision, or how it was arrived at, the plain truth facing Chris Cowdrey when he replaced Chris Tavaré was that the differences of opinion expressed two years earlier had escalated into a full-scale feud. The job which Cowdrey had cherished and been encouraged to regard as a simple family inheritance now appeared to be more of a curse than a compliment. He admits: "If they made the wrong decision to appoint Tav as captain in the first place they certainly made the wrong decision to change it when they did. They should have been backing a bloke who had just led us to a final. He was doing a very steady job, a better than steady job, and everyone would have happily carried on playing for him.

"It's hard to sit here and say I think they made the wrong decision to appoint me as captain but I think they did."

The same opinion was held by Brian Luckhurst, who was nominally still first team manager but rapidly losing authority. Two years earlier his was a respected voice when Tavaré was appointed. Now he was not even consulted, but he made his thoughts plain in his memoirs *Boot Boy to President*: "It was against my wishes as the team manager at the time and, in my view, it was the worst decision that the county has made since the war."

The added complication for Cowdrey was that he was trying to give his full attention to England's tour of India, a trip critical to his ambitions of claiming a regular place in the international side. "It was very strange going from playing in a county team to all of a sudden finding that I'm captaining Kent, while on an England tour playing all five Tests. Everything completely changed in no time at all. I had no time for preparation; you fly back and you've got about three weeks before the season. You're captaining a team with a guy in it who's just been sacked and there's ill-feeling among public, players and committee. That's a period of my life which I enjoyed less than any. It was ridiculous in many ways because that was what I was good at, that's what I should have done. It shook the club."

He also realised, when confronted by the thankless task of trying to bring some harmony to the Kent dressing room, that positions had become entrenched. "A group of Chris Tavaré supporters really hit me hard on this. They thought that I planned the whole thing and they accused my father of being behind it, both of which were rubbish. They accused Jim Swanton of instigating secret lobbying. These are not just friends and colleagues, these are players as well, so I actually thought when I was on tour, 'Shall I bother doing it?' I nearly arrived back and said I'd just carry on playing for Tav. I got a lot of stick from people, for something which had nothing to do with me. If I was going to lobby I would have done it three years before."

Alan Knott, along with Graham Johnson and Graham Dilley, was firmly in the Tavaré camp. In his autobiography, published just after the captaincy had changed hands, Knott wrote that Kent had done "superbly well" under Tavaré, whom he described as "marvellous under pressure". He added: "He believes in discipline and applies it cleverly, making his feelings known, but with the knack of stopping the development of any situation which could be getting out of control. During his captaincy, for example, he made it perfectly clear that he wanted his players fit in the morning before the day's play and that he was not going to tolerate late nights or heavy drinking." The disciplinarian tag is, incidentally, not one with which Tavaré readily relates.

Cowdrey was soon given a vivid indication of the depth of feeling. "Possibly the most senior player we had in the dressing room said, would I mind if he didn't come to the team meeting on the first day of the season. I'd got the full staff in there and five minutes before he told me he didn't want to come in. I said, 'You have to.' This is someone I respected more as a player than probably anyone I'd ever played with. He said, 'I can't sit there and listen to you talking.' I said, 'Why not?' He said, 'Because everything you say which will be different from last year will be to disagree with the job Chris Tavaré did.' I said, 'Don't come in then.' He did in the end."

Everywhere you looked in 1985 there seemed to be disgruntlement of various degrees and origins. Richard Ellison's spectacular part in England's Ashes summer, and brief dalliance with fame beyond the cricketing norm, was a welcome distraction from Kent's mood of gloomy introspection. Ten wickets at

Richard Ellison became an instant celebrity after his starring role in England's Ashes triumph in 1985

Edgbaston and seven at the Oval, the reward for high-quality swing bowling, helped England to back-to-back innings victories.

There was some reflected glory for Cowdrey, his friend and fellow Old Tonbridgian, who earlier in the season had threatened to leave Ellison out of the Kent side unless he lost weight. "I could murder a pint, Cow" became a recurring wistful line as the pounds were shed. Cowdrey wrote: "He and his moustache became front page in most dailies, some in bowling stride, some with Fiona [his fiancée], some drinking beer, some drinking champagne." Ellison, who was to be cruelly treated by injuries for the rest of his career (he was then only 25), finished near the top of the bowling averages and got married just after the end of the season. Cowdrey, in his best man's speech, advanced the theory that Ellison's PE from Exeter University had stood for Pie Eating.

The genuine delight at Ellison's success – he was also picked for the winter tour of the West Indies – contrasted with the fortunes of the county at war with itself. Cowdrey had felt under critical scrutiny all summer, though he is quick to stress that the most obviously aggrieved party, Tavaré, behaved impeccably. "Chris was amazing. You wouldn't have known any difference; he just got on and did the job. There was wrangling, obviously, but he was never at the forefront of anything like that. A few wives got involved but he was exemplary. He supported me as I knew he would." Tavaré's stoicism was all the more remarkable given that he had also lost his England place after averaging only 29 in 1984, his worst season since 1977.

He laid down a significant marker by scoring a hundred against Hampshire in Kent's opening championship match and also made consistent runs as they set the pace in the John Player League by claiming four wins and two no-result points in their first six games. Tavaré's championship form was unspectacular but he still finished the season with more than 2,000 runs in all forms of cricket.

Cowdrey himself managed to deflect a little criticism by starting the season in decent batting form, scoring a career-best 159 against Surrey and making two more nineties in the opening five games, though none led to Kent victories. Meanwhile, Neil Taylor, after an indifferent season in 1984, was disappointed to be left out for the Hampshire game – "there was no expla-nation" – and played only twice in the championship before mid-July.

Kent's whole season was one of mini peaks and major troughs. Their Sunday League challenge disintegrated so badly that they failed to win any of their last eight matches. A brilliant 143 from Tavaré, his highest one-day score, helped Kent to beat his future employers, Somerset, in the group stages of the Benson and Hedges Cup, but the whole side batted so poorly in the semi-final at Leicester that no one made more than 15. A much more convincing display, led by 95 from Hinks, enabled them to chase down 294 to beat Surrey in the NatWest Trophy, but they were well beaten by Essex in the quarter-finals.

The side's showing in the championship was equally erratic. All four of their wins were condensed into a period of less than four weeks in mid-season. Mark Benson hit hundreds in victories over Lancashire and Yorkshire; Hinks made a maiden century in a win over Surrey which also featured a hat-trick for Graham Dilley. The surge of optimism as Kent moved up the table evaporated with equal speed and they were forced to settle for ninth place. Their NatWest victory on 17 July over Durham, then a Minor County, proved to be their last of the season.

Cowdrey's verdict, written in the immediate aftermath, was: "Having dried up with excuses I take to heart Kent's disappointing conclusion to 1985. If I enjoy the praise when we win four out of five and when the headlines feature my captaincy, I must also take and accept the criticisms. During my first season I learned a great deal about all aspects of choosing and leading a team, both on and off the field. I am optimistic about the future. There is plenty of reason to be."

The season was just part of the learning curve for Cowdrey, but 1985 had deeper and more lasting significance for two members of Kent's all-conquering Seventies side. Luckhurst was sacked as first team manager; Graham Johnson was released as a player. Their falling-out was one of the sadder aspects of a traumatic year for the club.

Although Johnson had made little impact with bat and ball he was shocked to the core when he was told, towards the end of June, that he was being released at the end of the season. "We were playing Essex at Chelmsford," he remembers. "I was asked to go up to the Essex committee room and John Pocock, our chairman of cricket, told me that I wasn't being retained. They needed to bring the youngsters on and Laurie Potter was a key element of that – they wanted him to take over from me as the bowling all-rounder. I already knew at that stage that Laurie was going to leave, so that made it worse. So I said, 'Fine, what does this mean for the rest of the season?' They said if they picked the best team I'd be in it. And I said, 'Sorry I just don't understand what you're saying.' What they wanted me to do was to stay fit. I said, 'I've been at this club for 21 years. I would find it very difficult, the way you're talking to me now, to go on to the field and give 100 per cent. I don't think I can do that and I don't think it would be fair to the rest of the team.

"It came to a head at Canterbury, when we were playing against the Australians. I got a message to say that I was playing. I said, 'I beg your pardon,

I thought we had an agreement.' I went down there on the morning of the match and said I wasn't prepared to play. Call it pride, but we'd agreed at the Chelmsford meeting that that was the way it would be. Brian Luckhurst got quite emotional. He said, 'Johno, please don't do this.' I said, 'There was an agreement and now you're telling me I must play. I'm not playing.'

"That was it. I left the ground. The last thing I said to Brian was, 'Me doing this means that you're going to achieve one of your ambitions.' He'd always wanted to play in the Fifties, Sixties, Seventies and Eighties. I got on a ferry to go to France with some friends that day. What happened on the Sunday was that someone in the press box had heard some rumblings and asked Brian to go up to the box. 'Is it true Johnson's refused to play?' he was asked. He didn't know what to say. Brian called John Pocock, and he came over and they asked the same question. Pocock didn't know what to do so he said, 'Effectively he's sacked on the spot.' When I came back I was told I'd been sacked and wouldn't get paid for the rest of the season."

Alan Dixon, who was on the cricket committee at the time, insists that the motive for telling Johnson in mid-season was a compassionate one. "We told him early purely on the basis that it would give him time to establish himself with one or two contacts so that when the season finished he could move seamlessly into commerce. That fell absolutely flat; he couldn't believe that it was happening to him and just lost it and said he couldn't play any more. He refused to play and they had to sack him. That's the true story from the committee side."

Luckhurst, though he was retained in an administrative capacity, subsequently admitted that he had enjoyed his five years as first team manager less than any other phase of his 50 years' service to the club. Johnson, in common with most people who knew him, held Luckhurst in high regard, but believes he found it hard to adapt to the different demands of his managerial role. "Brian was a lovely guy. He and I were pretty close, but there were times when we did disagree and it was normally about man management. I thought you should set out a vision of the way things should be done and stick with it. He didn't like the idea of giving bad news; if there was a nice way of saying something that's what he wanted to do."

Taylor, one of the players brought through the ranks by Luckhurst, says: "I think Brian just enjoyed seeing younger players that he worked with come through. There's more pressure on the first team because it's more results-orientated, whereas with the second team you want to win games, but your job is to produce the next batch of county players." Cowdrey describes Luckhurst as "the nicest bloke in the world", but adds: "The pressure was too much for him at times. He was so passionate about Kent cricket it was almost scary. If the side had had a bad morning he'd have his head in his hands: it was as though he was still playing. He put players under pressure for the right reason – he so much wanted them to do well – but cricket's a long game; you do need to sit back a bit."

Alan Knott's retirement, at the end of the 1985 season, was as sudden and understated as Johnson's departure was drawn-out and acrimonious. Team-mates had always expected that Knott would make his exit without fuss or ceremony and he did not disappoint in that respect. A recurrence of the ankle injury which had kept him out of the NatWest Trophy final in 1984 was the clinching factor in his decision to give up, announced on the penultimate day of the season.

The clearest evidence that Knott's wicketkeeping standards had barely slipped was the suggestion earlier in the summer that he be recalled by England. The bare statistics of Knott's final season with the bat did not make pretty reading – he failed to top fifty in his last 29 innings – but he was frequently relegated (without complaint) to nine and 10 in an effort to push younger players up the order.

His captain, Chris Cowdrey, preferred to remember him for an extraordinary unbeaten 87 which demonstrated perfectly Knott's versatility as a batsman. "He played an unforgettable innings at Northampton. The wicket was seaming. We had collapsed to 120 for eight. For his first fifty he met the ball with a stroke as straight as the MCC manual; then suddenly he played every kind of game with the bowlers." Cowdrey was reminded of a typically idiosyncratic pre-season routine in which Knott would use his time in the nets to recreate various match situations: everything from an occupy-the-crease championship innings to a Sunday cameo of impudence and improvisation.

Knott deserved a more heroic finale than to be run out for one and nought in his last two innings: in a championship game at Worcester and in a Sunday League match against Derbyshire at Folkestone, but the final two weeks of the season at least gave Kent a chance to run the rule over Steve Marsh and Stuart Waterton, the keepers in waiting. Marsh was ultimately preferred and Waterton moved to Northamptonshire. The last sighting of c Knott b Underwood, a scorecard staple which had opened its account with the wicket of Leicestershire's Paul Munden in July 1964, was the dismissal of Warwickshire's Paul Smith at the St Lawrence Ground on 15 August 1985. In total, Knott was responsible for 107 catches and 54 stumpings off Underwood's bowling when playing for Kent.

Chris Penn, who was still trying to pin down a regular first team place when Knott retired, remembers: "I travelled with him for years. He had to stop at the Westmoreland [hotel] in London because that's where he got the best bacon in town. I hung his pants up to dry, because I was permanent 12th man for a few years; I listened to him trying to convert me to Christianity. But underneath he was one of the hardest and toughest cricketers who had ever played the game." Journalist Dudley Moore, who was also Knott's agent, gave the county first option on Knott's coaching services in 1988, but terse committee minutes reveal: "The meeting was not enthusiastic."

Knott's departure was, inevitably, felt most keenly by Underwood, who described him as the best wicketkeeper in the world. Ten years earlier he had explained their uncanny on-field rapport. "He has kept to me so regularly over the years that he knows what type of delivery I am going to bowl before even I have made up my mind." Raised eyes and a surreptitious point to the ground were Knott's coded suggestions for a ball tossed up or the fast yorker.

Underwood also became wistfully aware that his own final chapter was approaching. "It was like Colin Cowdrey must have felt towards the end of his career, a little bit out of it," he recalls. "The boys were very kind to me, but it makes you feel a little lonelier when you're 40 and the next oldest person in the side is probably about 30. They wouldn't want me to see that they'd got a bird on their arm for instance." As senior pro he had to call a halt to card games "when young players were losing more than they could afford to"; he also saw first hand how the dressing-room hierarchy had changed. Gone was the reverential respect that players like he and Luckhurst had for Colin Cowdrey. "The young players would say, 'Morning Deadly,' and I was quite comfortable with that, though perhaps 30 years ago it wouldn't have been acceptable."

1986

The 1986 season followed a similar pattern to the previous summer, though there were also shades of 1984 in another final defeat, once more at Middlesex's hands. The Lord's loss represented the conclusion of a dispiriting four days in which Kent were also dumped out of the NatWest Trophy by Nottinghamshire. The summer as a whole was most notable for an outstanding championship campaign for Terry Alderman. He missed the opening two games after the birth of his first child and, but for a shoulder injury which kept him out of the last two matches, would almost certainly have become the first Kent pace bowler since Norman Graham in 1967 to pass 100 wickets; his final tally was 98.

Alderman's success had much to do with a job-share arrangement in which he threw all his energies into three-day cricket, while the more versatile Eldine

Baptiste took the overseas player's berth in one-day games. Kent also had cause, in retrospect, to be grateful that Alderman's younger Australian team-mate, Craig McDermott, turned down their original offer.

The season began on a reasonably encouraging note: Alderman contributed nine wickets to an early win over Essex, the eventual champions, in which Graham Dilley claimed his second hat-trick in successive seasons. Baptiste shone with bat and ball in a tie against Surrey which followed victories for Kent in the first three Sunday League games. As in 1985 they could not sustain the form – batting inconsistency afflicted them in all competitions – but still managed a respectable sixth-place finish.

Despite Alderman's consistency, and an effective combination of swing and out-and-out pace when Dilley was available, Kent were unable to achieve much winning momentum in the championship. One current England bowler, Richard Ellison, proved so ineffective that his 23 first-class wickets in 1986 cost almost 48 apiece; a future international, Alan Igglesden, made a telling impact before succumbing to a side injury. Innings of 90 and 97 not out, easily the highest of the match, showed Mark Benson's technical expertise in a win at Southampton, and earned him a Test debut against India 10 days later. While Benson was joining the ranks of one-Test wonders Kent were contriving to lose at Derby, despite leading by 132 on first innings after Alderman had taken eight for 46. Even when he recorded match figures of 14 for 144 against Leicestershire, the best in the championship that season, Kent flirted with defeat before edging to a nervy five-run victory.

Derek Underwood was as hard to get away as he had ever been, but without rain-affected pitches to bowl on he was forced to work that little bit harder for reward. Remarkably, he had to wait until Kent's penultimate championship game of the season before recording his one five-wicket return. Even in a career full of eye-catching figures, an analysis of 35.5-29-11-7 against Warwickshire – helped by five close-in catches for Chris Cowdrey – was noteworthy.

Kent reached the knockout stages in the Benson and Hedges Cup despite a narrow defeat by Surrey and a heavy one by Middlesex. They then picked up momentum by beating Derbyshire in the quarter-finals, thanks to an unbeaten 63 from Cowdrey. Chris Tavaré and Neil Taylor both made 68 as they edged past Worcestershire in the semi-finals.

Excellent bowling from Ellison and Dilley, who was considered a doubtful starter because of an ankle injury, enabled them to restrict Middlesex to 199 for seven in the final, a notable landmark for Underwood in that he became the first player to participate in 10 Lord's finals (he had a won three, lost six record going into the game). The fragility of Kent's batting once again returned to haunt them on the biggest domestic stage, but 22-year-old Graham Cowdrey, one player without the baggage of previous defeats to weigh him down, almost conjured a famous victory from the ruins of 72 for five. Cowdrey, whose no-nonsense batting style had more in common with his older brother's hard-hitting approach than the subtlety of his father, made 58 off 70 balls to loosen Middlesex's grip, but Kent were left with too much to do in the latter stages and, despite a six from Steve Marsh in the last over, finished an agonising three runs short of their target.

The match concluded in near darkness and heavy rain. Tony Lewis, writing in *The Sunday Telegraph*, said: "Kent had themselves to blame for having to bat in atrocious light." They were fined after managing only 51 overs in the time allotted for the Middlesex innings. If Kent were criticised for their lack of urgency in the field, Graham Cowdrey and Baptiste earned praise for staying on when, with 84 needed off 10 overs, Kent were offered the chance to suspend the innings. Cowdrey has no recollection of this, but suggests that the conditions were so bad that they were more of a handicap to the fielding side than to the batsmen.

The "nightmare" of pulling Simon Hughes to Clive Radley with victory within grasp is still imprinted on his mind. He adds: "I remember feeling almost no nerves when I went out to bat – it shows you what youth is I suppose – though before that I'd probably only played in front of the odd crowd of eight or nine thousand at Canterbury. It wasn't the greatest innings at the ground, but it was an extraordinary finish. I had very mixed emotions at the end because obviously as a young man it was great to score a fifty, but if we'd just crept over the line I think it would have been my finest hour." His brother suggested afterwards that Kent had paid the penalty for being a little too cautious when they were trying to rehabilitate the innings.

Their NatWest fate had been sealed earlier in the week when they made only 161 for nine in the second-round tie against Nottinghamshire at Trent Bridge. A century opening stand between Tim Robinson and Chris Broad guaranteed that there was no way back for Kent.

Every close season brings negotiations and far-reaching decisions, but 1986-87 was of more than usual significance to Kent. Doubts about Alderman's fitness legislated against his return – though he did play a final season of county cricket with Gloucestershire in 1988 – and they were also sweating on Dilley's response to the offer of a new, and by Kent's standards lucrative, long-term contract. It is easy to deduce that the carrot was being dangled in vain.

Dilley had first been courted by other counties in 1980, soon after making his Test debut as a 20-year-old. He was never fully settled at Kent and the likelihood that he would move turned into a full-blown certainty when Tavaré was deposed as captain at the end of the 1984 season and Graham Johnson was sacked the following year. Dilley had asked then to be allowed to leave, but was told that he would have to honour the final year of his contract.

Chris Cowdrey broke off from a holiday in Australia to speak to Dilley, who was touring with England. It was reported back to the Kent committee that he was 90 per cent sure that Dilley would stay, but in reality Cowdrey was never that optimistic. He also insists that the parting was the right outcome for both player and county. "I just wanted to know if he really wanted to play county cricket, on a cold day at Folkestone for instance, and the answer was no. I asked Graham Dilley one question. I said, 'Do you really want to play for Kent?' And he said, 'No.' That was good enough; I didn't really need to ask him anything more.

"Graham Dilley was a Test player, not a county player. Losing Graham was seen as a disaster in Kent's cricket history. To me that's rubbish: look at his record for Kent. Graham Dilley was a friend of a lot of players, but he was also caught up in the ill-feeling of the Tavaré captaincy situation."

Johnson, whose sister married Dilley, feels that there was a domino effect to the series of decisions which were made in the mid-Eighties. "The three of us, Tav, myself and Dill, used to travel around in a car together; we were quite close. I got sacked, Tav got shafted and Dill didn't like what was going on. So when Worcestershire made a good offer to him he could see a future there and took it. You could argue that someone like that should have stayed and had a benefit at Kent, but the atmosphere was such that he didn't want to."

1987

The removal of Terry Alderman and Graham Dilley from Kent's attack had already left them dangerously short of firepower for 1987 and the county had to face another setback when Richard Ellison returned from a winter stint with Tasmania suffering from a back injury which was to keep him out for the whole summer. The good news, as far as Chris Cowdrey was concerned, was that he had brokered the recruitment of Bob Woolmer as coach, if only on an initial one-year contract. The appointment also brought to an end a period of almost 30 years in which Kent, based on Les Ames's belief that top players could find their own technical answers, had operated without a coach.

"I saw Bob as a brilliant coach," Cowdrey explains. "He probably had more coaching knowledge than anyone I've ever met. He called himself a student of the game, but he was also a fanatical Kent supporter and his passion for the game was second to none. I had a feeling that we were missing out on a very special coach."

There would have been no shortage of players to endorse Cowdrey's view. Some had already been coached by Woolmer at the Avendale club in Cape Town, where he championed multi-racial cricket. Steve Marsh, preferred as Alan Knott's wicketkeeping successor, worked with Woolmer before the 1986 season and countered suggestions that Stuart Waterton was a superior batsman by averaging more than 30 in first-class cricket. Another Woolmer fan was Vince Wells, yet to force his way into Kent's first team, but ultimately an important all-round component in the Leicestershire success story in the 1990s.

"My cricket really kick-started when Bob Woolmer came over," he recalls. "At that stage I was a keeper-batsman. I used to muck around in the nets bowling, but Bob could see something there. He invited me out to Cape Town and I spent three winters with him at Avendale."

Coaching expertise was not quite enough for Woolmer, who found that his familiarity with the surroundings – he had finished as a player only three years earlier – was a hindrance rather than help. Cowdrey reflects: "I thought having a Kent player who'd been away a while would work. It proved when he came back that it was too close. There was baggage with him because he was such an enthusiast. He never stopped talking in the dressing room. He irritated team-mates when he played because he was so excited about his batting. I thought he would change, I thought as a leader in the dressing room, as a coach-manager, he would be awesome. It didn't really work. Too many people remembered him, they were too close to him. Not that they didn't like him as a person, but they didn't like his antics in the dressing room."

Chris Penn, who claimed a regular place in 1987 after five seasons on the fringes, says: "He came over as a bit of a plonker to the younger players, but as a source of knowledge he was superb." Graham Cowdrey believes that with extra coaching miles on the clock Woolmer could have transformed him into a much more consistent batsman.

Woolmer was also reminded that he had foes in the committee room, the same ones who had never forgiven him for his involvement with the Packer revolution or part in the rebel tour to South Africa. The formidable Jim Swanton was also a great believer in keeping up appearances. A committee meeting in August 1987 was told: "The captain said that R. A. Woolmer thought he ought to have more authority over the players. He and Woolmer try to get the team to wear smart clothing on the first and second days of a match but relax this on the third day. E. W. Swanton said he thought Woolmer was the worst offender against dress regulations when he wore shorts. The captain replied that Woolmer felt he was entitled to wear shorts in the nets during long sessions on hot days."

The implacable Swanton also complained that the batting during Canterbury Week had been "deplorable", wondered if Woolmer had been any help to Chris Tavaré and thought Chris Cowdrey should bat higher than six. Cowdrey's official response was that the players did not enjoy playing at Canterbury, which was described as "the worst wicket in the country, with no pace". Two years later, Kent committee minutes recorded the unease of groundsman Brian Fitch at being "requested to do things he did not want to do to produce result wickets".

Kent needed heroism from unexpected sources to compete in 1987 but it was inevitable, given their paucity of pace-bowling resources, that they would have to look to the one-day competitions for their only chance of success. They were convincing winners of their second championship game, against Glamorgan, thanks to hundreds from Neil Taylor and Chris Cowdrey and a first five-wicket return from Alan Igglesden, but had to wait another 13 matches before recording their second and final championship victory of the season. The one-wicket win over Middlesex was particularly memorable for Kevin Jarvis, who took a hat-trick then played a passive role to enable Marsh to see Kent home.

Taylor, Tavaré and Chris Cowdrey all had their moments with the bat, but the beacon of consistency was Mark Benson, whose aggregate of 1,725 runs was comfortably his highest to date. He hit five first-class centuries, all outside Kent, and was also out for 97 and 98. The leading wicket-taker was Eldine Baptiste, who claimed career-best figures of eight for 74 in what turned out to be his penultimate championship game. Baptiste, similarly to Bernard Julien, always promised more than he delivered (even his heroic haul against Warwickshire ended in defeat). One of the cheerier aspects of the season was the emergence of medium-pacer Danny Kelleher, whose 34 wickets cost less than 26 apiece. Sadly, the promise was not maintained. He was released in 1991 and though he subsequently signed for Surrey he never played for them and died of a drugs overdose, aged only 29, in 1995.

Kent's season of misfortune seemed to be summed up by a semi-final defeat by Northamptonshire in the Benson and Hedges Cup. They had almost slipped up against Gloucestershire in the quarter-finals when, needing 251 to win, they slid from 228 for four to 246 for nine before Derek Underwood held his nerve to see Kent over the line off the final ball of the 55th over. A first

Chris Tavaré on the attack during Kent's Benson and Hedges Cup semi-final against Northamptonshire in 1987

Picture: Roger Vaughan, Kent Messenger, PD16737

trophy since 1978 would have been the appropriate send-off for Underwood in his final season, and they did most things right against Northamptonshire. An imposing total of 275 was built around 78 from Chris Tavaré and 87 from Chris Cowdrey, then Baptiste produced an exemplary opening spell in which he conceded only eight runs from six overs.

Critically, however, Baptiste was unable to complete his stint after injuring his groin and side in the field, and even Underwood came in for unaccustomed punishment as an inspired Allan Lamb strong-armed his way to an unbeaten 126. There was an odd finale when Northamptonshire, believing that they had won by levelling the scores with three balls remaining, began to troop off; on their return Lamb edged a clinching boundary. The minor consolation for Kent was that they were able to recruit Roy Pienaar, the South African who was to play a major part in the side's renaissance the following summer, as a temporary replacement for Baptiste.

Kent were competitive throughout in the Refuge Assurance League, again finishing sixth, but they unexpectedly suffered a one-wicket defeat to Derbyshire in the second round of the NatWest Trophy. The first-round victory over Scotland was utterly routine, but did yield the best one-day figures of Underwood's career, eight for 31. They were also, at the time, the best analysis in the competition's 25-year history, but surpassed by Derbyshire's Michael Holding the following season.

Holding was also instrumental in redefining Graham Cowdrey's repertoire of shots in 1987. Cowdrey recalls: "I went in at three up at Derby and made 68 in the first innings. I remember going back to the hotel that night thinking, 'Crikey, this it. I've made it.' Then, of course, in the second innings Michael Holding smashed my jaw first ball and five teeth came out on to the pitch; I was never quite the same to be honest. Although I wasn't frightened that people were looking to pin me again I never really pulled or hooked after that and if you're not a puller or hooker you're never going to be a quality player. I improvised most of the time. I tried to cut them if it was wide but if it was straight I ducked or weaved and I didn't do it particularly well."

Even by Kent's standards the 1987 season was one of upheaval, though nothing else could match Underwood's retirement for sheer impact. He reflects: "I could still churn out the overs in the championship, though I found that I was struggling physically the day after, but it was the fielding which had become a nightmare. Batsmen just used to drop the ball and run and I thought to myself, five or 10 years ago I might have saved that single. Or they used to push it past you. 'Look for two, it's Deadly.' That was like a knife in the back. So that was the major reason for calling it a day. You couldn't afford to go for runs as well as give them away in the field."

Underwood, whose 1,951 first-class wickets for Kent (out of a grand total of 2,465) place him third on the county's all-time list, could hardly be in more illustrious statistical company. Tich Freeman and Colin Blythe are ahead and Doug Wright and Frank Woolley immediately behind.

Swanton's appreciation for *The Daily Telegraph* combined genuine admiration with a cryptic reminder that Underwood had never quite conformed to the purist's ideal. "The fact is that Derek has followed no one's prototype. His pushing-through style, slowed down a bit at some stages on some pitches, has been peculiarly his own. I doubt whether in modern times there has been such an accurate bowler of any sort, nor such a devastating one whenever the pitch was susceptible to turn and lift."

Underwood had long since agreed to disagree with Swanton on the question of his bowling method, but he did not forgive so readily when the writer hid behind Victorian protocol the following year. Underwood asked his mother to accompany him to the launch of Dudley Moore's Kent history, but when Swanton discovered that she did not have an official invitation he asked her to leave. Her disgusted son was right behind her.

Even after calling time on his county career, Underwood was in demand and played for Bankfoot in the Bradford League in 1988. "I was offered a contract to play once a week, £500 a match, over 26 weeks. They played 50-over games and they wanted me to bowl 25 overs at one end. I said, 'I'm 42, no way.' I ended up playing 13, three at the beginning, five in the middle and five at the end, and we gained promotion in the last match, so it was exactly the way I wanted it."

Underwood, like Alan Knott, was able to bow out on his own terms. The same could not be said of Kevin Jarvis, Derek Aslett, Baptiste and all-rounder Steve Goldsmith, who were all released. Goldsmith was a bigger fish in a smaller pond at Derbyshire, while Jarvis moved to Gloucestershire after an injury-troubled benefit season. "It was very disappointing," he remembers, "because our supporters were very loyal and I got fantastic backing from the supporters' club and from people around Kent and it was sad that I left. You don't really get the chance to thank all the people who put in those hours on your behalf, so it would have been nice to have gone back the following season and thanked those people in a more leisurely way."

Chris Cowdrey is not alone in believing that the talented Aslett, whose first-class career ended when he was 29, should have been given another chance to succeed. "Aslett was probably my one big disappointment in terms of feeling that I'd let someone down as a captain. I knew the county were trying to trim players – things were a little bit dodgy financially – and the bottom line was that they told me we had to lose a senior batsman. At one point it actually looked as though we might have to get rid of two out of Benson, Taylor, Hinks and Aslett, and that at a stage when all four were playing. I said that was ridiculous. I had a view that Simon Hinks was going to kick on and be a bit of a Gower – he was a freak timer of the ball. He didn't, he just did OK and didn't get any better. Derek Aslett was going through a bit of a difficult trot when it came to that period. It was a no-brainer that it was between Hinks and Aslett, but I never felt comfortable with that one. I thought Hinks could be a bit of a Gilchrist, but he couldn't."

Hinks, who was admonished by Kent's committee for his "behaviour on and off the field" was given a new one-year deal. Matthew Fleming, a future Kent captain, was left in no doubt that he would have to improve or look elsewhere. Committee minutes revealed that he was considered to be "not yet a potential first-class cricketer"; he was registered at this stage but only offered a contract a year later.

1988

There was no reason to believe that life after Derek Underwood would be anything other than traumatic for Kent, though in Richard Davis they had a tall slow left-armer with a model action and decent prospects. As it turned out, Davis was little more than a stock-bowling presence in a seam attack which somehow managed to be much more than the modest sum of the parts in 1988. Kent supporters had become wearily accustomed to underachievement and near misses in the previous 10 seasons; again a title narrowly eluded them, but this was heroic failure on a grand scale. A five-month adventure ended with a hugely unexpected runners-up position, just a point behind the winners, Worcestershire.

This was the season in which the County Championship dipped its toes into the uncharted waters of four-day games. The longer matches were played at the start and end of the season; the standard three-day formula applied for the rest of the campaign. The first set of four-day matches appeared to demonstrate two things: that first-innings totals of 400 plus guaranteed nothing and that the weaker teams (on paper including Kent) were more likely to be found out over four days than three.

A double-century opening stand between Mark Benson and Neil Taylor set up a declaration at 400 for seven against Essex, but a remorseless 275 from Graham Gooch meant that Kent trailed by 216. A seventh-wicket stand of 222 between Graham Cowdrey, whose innings of 145 was his maiden first-class hundred, and Steve Marsh almost removed the possibility of defeat, but Essex chased down 170 at eight an over to win an extraordinary game.

This chastening experience seemed to traumatise the Kent side, who were bowled out for 99 as they lost to Hampshire then slumped to an innings defeat against Leicestershire, despite Taylor carrying his bat. Cue the kind of soul-searching exercise which had galvanised Kent at Maidstone in 1970, transforming a tentative top order into championship-winning cavaliers.

This time the catalyst for change, and dramatic improvement, was Jim Woodhouse, "a very punchy individual" in Chris Cowdrey's words, who was then the county's chairman of cricket. Woodhouse had become a Kent member as a 12-year-old in 1946, the start of a love affair which has never dimmed. He played for the 2nd XI in the Fifties and admits: "I got my fingers in the butter tub and never let go. I've loved it and I've argued against it and I've argued for it." In 1987 he had prepared a paper, 'Thoughts on the Future of Kent Cricket', which advocated the formation of the Cricket Element, an elite group who would take pressure off the captain and participate in the selection process.

Cowdrey remembers: "I spent a lot of time talking to Jim about why we were underachieving, and about all the baggage which was left after the Tavaré situation. We decided that it was time to do something a bit more positive about it. We did try to raise the players' ambitions, but it didn't happen straight away. After we'd lost the first couple of championship games, Jim said, 'Right, the time's come to do something. We can't carry on like this.' "

He drove up to Leicester, where Kent were playing their third championship game, and challenged the players to offer their own solution. "I said, 'I've paid people and I've run a company in the City, but how do *you* want it happen? They were all prepared to talk because I was the only person there. There was no one from the management side. They could let their hair down and say what they liked." Cowdrey takes up the story:

> "He said to them, 'On paper you're not a bad side. You're not playing very well, so what's the problem?' We sat there for three hours and he said, 'As far as I'm concerned I'm prepared to do anything I can, whatever you need. I'm going to make it easy so you never have any excuses again. I'm fed up with listening to excuses.' They came up with some pretty mild, pathetic schoolboy-type comments. 'Our meal allowance is £10.50 a day. It's ridiculous, we should be getting £11.' 'Right. Next point.' 'We need a proper coach.' 'Who do you want?' John Inverarity's name kept cropping up. 'Right, we'll ring him in an hour, let you know tomorrow. And if we can't get him, who else do you want?'
>
> "We sat there and said, 'We've at last got someone from the committee coming into the dressing room and supporting us. Right, now we've got to get out there and play, forget about everything else.' Sure enough he got everything they asked for and made it happen. We played brilliantly. We had a belief that you wouldn't believe. We just thought we were going to win every game."

Inverarity's track record as a former Test player demanded respect, but there was also a schoolmasterly sensitivity – he had spent a year teaching maths and coaching cricket at Tonbridge – to his dealings with individuals; he was described as a counsellor rather than a coach. Chris Penn, the spearhead of Kent's attack according to Cowdrey and "phantom quickie" in his own more modest estimation, says: "Inverarity got us thinking in the right direction, but Bob Woolmer had set up a lot of stuff the year before. It couldn't have been that great a team if they were picking me regularly, but we just got on a bit of a roll. It wasn't a normal Kent team, full of internationals, it was a side that tried hard and played for each other. I have to say that season Chris Cowdrey captained better than anyone I played with in my time at Kent, not necessarily tactically but as a person. He started to make contact off the field; he'd phone you at home to make sure everything was all right."

Penn, who finished with 81 first-class wickets, excelled in what he described as "a bit of a pop-gun attack". Richard Ellison, restored to fitness, was another player who benefited from Inverarity's combination of coaching knowledge and man management skills. Chris Cowdrey says: "He was brilliant for confi-

dence. I remember we went down to Hampshire and Richard had slightly lost his way. He was bowling wides, the ball was swinging all over the place, but he couldn't bowl straight. And John Inverarity just took him out and changed his action on the morning of the game. Suddenly he felt good and bowled beautifully. He was very good at picking up players, and that's what a captain needs. They don't need these tracksuit managers making you run round the ground a hundred times. You need someone who knows the game and can work with individuals."

In a summer notable for result pitches Kent consistently outbowled the opposition. Roy Pienaar, though primarily a gifted batsman, also took important wickets. Cowdrey enjoyed his most productive summer with the ball and Alan Igglesden finished the season strongly, taking 10 wickets in a victory over Hampshire. After the Leicester showdown Kent put together a run of six straight victories and held their nerve impressively in tight

Chris Penn, Kent's 'phantom quickie' in an exhilarating championship campaign in 1988

finishes against Yorkshire, Nottinghamshire and Northamptonshire. There was a remarkable game at Dartford, where Nottinghamshire trailed by 247 on first innings after being bowled out for 65; it was only thanks to an unbeaten 38 from Cowdrey that Kent edged to 111 for eight and victory.

Cowdrey was not just an inspiring and charismatic leader, a "D'Artagnan figure" according to Marsh, but one of the first captains to preach the virtues of diving around in the field. He even managed to convince Pienaar, a reluctant fielder in any position, that grass-stained whites were a price worth paying. Gone were the days when Stuart Leary, an immaculately turned out Kent player in the Fifties and Sixties, would complain to Colin Cowdrey about the grubby state of team-mates' kit.

Chris Cowdrey was, in a sense, a victim of Kent's success and his own part in it. England, already 2-0 down in their Test series against the West Indies, hoped that the Kent effect could rub off. Cowdrey, the third of four captains used by England that summer, was drafted in for a mission impossible at Headingley in late July. He maintains: "We'd have won the championship without that, no question. We were on such a roll we'd have won by 30 points, but that disrupted things. It wasn't so much the fact that we would have won the games that I missed, it was the fact that the momentum changed, and then I got injured and we slightly ran out of puff."

Cowdrey admits that his selection then rejection by England (he missed the final Test because of injury) was "hurtful", adding: "The fact is that I was chosen to do the England job for the winter. They wanted me to captain the side to India and I was given those couple of games against the West Indies just to settle me into the job. Of course it went wrong and I was left out for Graham Gooch and then it took its toll." Cowdrey vented his frustration with a broadside at the selectors – his godfather, Peter May, was chairman – which attracted the headline, 'England can stick tour job', in the *Sun*. The paper graciously picked up the tab after Cowdrey had been fined £500.

Kent, having scented victory in their penultimate championship game when they led Middlesex by 122 on first innings, were ultimately grateful to hang on for a draw at 129 for nine. The net result was that they trailed Worcestershire by a single point going into the sides' final games, and that slenderest of margins remained as both claimed maximum points in innings victories. The highlight of Kent's win over Surrey at St Lawrence was a devastating spell of six for four from Igglesden, as Surrey collapsed from 70 for no wicket in their first innings to 109 all out. Igglesden had earlier made a career-best 41 as he shared a last-wicket stand of 82 with Ellison. Penn's reward for his wicket-taking feats that season was £2,000 in unit trusts.

Doug Ibbotson wrote in *The Daily Telegraph*: "Among the members who gathered beneath the players' verandah, however, were some who believed that the champagne grapes had been soured by events at Edgbaston in June. This was the occasion on which Warwickshire, though dismissed within 100 overs, had two men absent and Kent, under the bonus regulations, were thereby denied an opportunity to take the extra bowling point which ultimately cost them a share of the championship title." Cowdrey still looks back with pride on Kent's performance in 1988. "Let's face it, nobody even thought we were a good side – on paper we were probably the 12th or 13th best team – so it was a great year."

The one-day competitions took an inevitable back seat for Kent in 1988. They won three of their last four games in the Refuge Assurance League, but were outclassed by Middlesex in the quarter-finals of the NatWest Trophy and lost to both Surrey (despite a one-day best of 137 from Taylor) and Middlesex in the group stages of the Benson and Hedges Cup.

Cowdrey realises, looking back, that 1988 was destined to be a glorious one-off, rather than proof that the glory days were back, though they would have been more competitive if they had persuaded Phillip DeFreitas to join them rather than Lancashire. "We'd gone as far as we could with a fighting side. I don't think anyone reported back the following summer thinking, 'We can do this again.' We just hoped we could." He also became aware that his brief dalliance with the England captaincy had taken its toll. "I didn't realise it at first, but it was quite a distressing time. I thought I'd be fine when the next season started, but I'd lost a bit of drive and I don't think I did a very good job from there to be honest. It was also my benefit year, which didn't help. It was absolute chaos."

1989

The side's prospects were hardly enhanced when Chris Tavaré decided to leave at the start of 1989. Despite the distractions of his benefit he believes that his batting had been in better order in 1988 than in any of the three previous seasons. He contributed 1,430 first-class runs, four centuries and 29 catches to the cause, maintaining the same level of professionalism that he had shown throughout his Kent career. There were committee-room mumblings over his departure immediately after his benefit – it was even suggested that the disappointment be put on record – but Tavaré insists that his original intention was to retire when a job outside cricket cropped up. It fell through and though Kent made sure that he was classified as a contested registration, preventing Northamptonshire from signing him, there was no shortage of rival suitors. Essex were regarded as the front-runners, but he eventually elected to join Somerset, initially on a one-year contract. In the event he spent five years at Taunton, the last four as captain, before retiring to pursue a teaching career.

"I hadn't ever expected to leave Kent," he says, "and on reflection I would have liked to have finished my career there. It was a fantastic county to play cricket for, with the tradition, the wonderful support and the lovely grounds. Certainly, when I look for the results now it's Kent first, Somerset second and I don't bother much with the rest."

The player who benefited most obviously from Tavaré's departure was Trevor Ward, a flamboyant stroke-maker who would delight and frustrate Kent supporters in equal measure. He converted only one of his 10 fifties into three figures, but still passed 1,000 runs comfortably. Roy Pienaar and Mark Benson averaged 59 and 54 respectively in the championship, though both players missed more matches than was healthy for Kent.

By sharp contrast with 1988, when it seemed that in any game Chris Cowdrey could turn to half-a-dozen seamers in confident expectation of a wicket, Kent's bowling was far less reliable than the batting. Chris Penn's 41 wickets cost almost 44 apiece and Pienaar was only able to bowl a handful of overs after knee surgery. The signing of the West Indian Hartley Alleyne as an auxiliary overseas player did nothing to compensate. Richard Ellison again struggled to stay fit, and another injury-prone bowler, Alan Igglesden, was alone in passing 50 championship wickets. His reward was a Test debut against Australia.

It was hardly surprising in the circumstances that Kent struggled to win matches. They recorded only one victory in their first 17 championship games, and seemed doomed to finish bottom until Pienaar found a rich vein of form, hitting centuries in three successive matches. The result was back-to-back successes over Yorkshire and Glamorgan, the only two sides to finish below them.

There was little to cheer about in the one-day competitions either. The batsmen made hay against Dorset's modest attack in the NatWest Trophy, a thunderous stand of 102 in 38 balls between the Cowdrey brothers carrying Kent to a record one-day score of 359. Normal service was resumed when they lost to Warwickshire in the second round. Despite two defeats in the group games, Kent reached the knockout stages in the Benson and Hedges Cup; Ellison was the all-round architect of a quarter-final victory over Northamptonshire, but their hopes of reaching the final effectively vanished when they were taken for 296 in 55 overs by Nottinghamshire.

Kent's Refuge Assurance League season ended on a reasonably optimistic note with three wins in the last four games, capped by a sparkling 76-ball hundred from Graham Cowdrey against Leicestershire, which lifted them to a mediocre 11th place. The younger Cowdrey's poor form in the championship, after an unbeaten hundred against the same opposition towards the end of May, was one of the more disappointing aspects of a lacklustre year for the county. It also highlighted the selection minefield which Chris Cowdrey had to negotiate throughout his six years as captain: whether or not to pick his brother.

Graham, who shared his father's natural reserve and insecurity (though not his social ambition), admits that he was too easily weighed down by family baggage. "I don't think Chris was overly bothered by it, albeit he was the first one to have to face the comparisons. Really by the time I turned up it shouldn't have bothered me, but I was a lot more sensitive to it all than Chris. And then when Chris was captain I was sensitive about those issues, particularly when I got selected instead of somebody else. We were all adults, but there was a lot of, 'Bloody Cowdrey,' and I took that to heart, though I shouldn't have done."

Only in 1990, Chris's final year in charge, did Graham make an unanswerable case for a regular place in Kent's championship side; yet although he was an automatic choice for three seasons, he still insists that he never felt fully established. "In 14 years I never did and that was a great disappointment to me. I probably put it down to the fact that my route into the team had been as a one-day player and so in many ways I allowed myself to think that I was a one-day player. As such I almost moulded myself as someone who improvised and probably didn't have the right technique to be a top-four batsman."

Jim Woodhouse, instrumental in Kent's dramatic playing improvement in 1988, had been given the chance to shape the county's future off the field when he was appointed as Kent's first chief executive at the end of the year. After 10 months he was told his contract would not be renewed. "It was thought I was too much on the players' side," he says. "About three weeks later they rang me to set up a meeting. 'This is rather a difficult thing to ask you, but there's been a deputation from the players. Would you come back as chairman of cricket?' I suppose if I'd been tougher I'd have said, 'Stick that on the wall,' but I was so thrilled to be asked back I said, 'Yes of course,' and I did another five years."

Woodhouse's reappointment as chairman could easily have coincided with Chris Cowdrey's removal as captain. At much the same time that his father was taking over as chairman of the International Cricket Council, Chris and 15 other English players were ruffling the feathers of the establishment by committing to an unofficial tour of South Africa. In 1978, Asif Iqbal had been stripped of the Kent captaincy because of his involvement with World Series Cricket. In comparable circumstances Chris Cowdrey remained in charge for the 1990 season.

1990

Statisticians may have enjoyed themselves in 1990, but bowlers and Kent supporters did not; it was a summer of unhealthy dominance of bat over ball. Kent's batsmen, and in particular Neil Taylor, shared in the bounty, though Taylor refuses to attach exaggerated importance to his feats. The fact remains that in the course of two seasons he scored 3,785 first-class runs at an average of 59. In the same golden phase of his career, Taylor twice managed a double hundred and century in the same game, and made 14 hundreds in all. Only a chronic failure to convert fifties into centuries prevented him reaching the same heights in 1992, though he still averaged almost 54.

Taylor believes that various factors contributed to "the best part of my career". For one thing he was older … and wiser. "I'd just turned 30 and at that age you know more about yourself and how to handle yourself and everything that goes with being a batsman or a cricketer. I'd signed a new three-year contract and I knew I'd got a benefit [in 1992], which tends to make you more relaxed. You might also say that it was the couple of years when they took the seam off the ball."

He insists that international cricket was never on his personal radar. "If I'd been playing the way I did after 30 when I was 23 then I might have been more disappointed, but people like Atherton and Stewart were that bit younger. It never really worried me; I certainly didn't find that every time an England team was being picked I'd be glued to the television screen."

Kent had failed in an attempt to recruit David Gower over the winter – he joined Hampshire instead – but runs were rarely in short supply in 1990. Graham Cowdrey and Mark Benson, despite breaking a thumb, both scored consistently; the bowling, by contrast, was a huge disappointment. Alan Igglesden and the strongly built West Indian, Tony Merrick, played together only twice in the championship because of injury, and Merrick's overseas locum, South African Fanie de Villiers, recalls the "incredible frustration" of the Dukes ball which refused to swing. "I had all this time on my hands to think about how badly I was bowling." Such was Kent's lack of wicket-taking potential that Igglesden's 30 championship victims placed him second in the county charts to slow left-armer Richard Davis. At least there were a couple of pointers to future prosperity in the emergence of Matthew Fleming, though more with bat than ball, and spinner Min Patel.

Most of the excitement in Kent's championship campaign was concentrated on the first few weeks of the season. They should have beaten Hampshire, but lost by six runs after losing their last five wickets for 18. This was balanced by a six-run win over Glamorgan, when Benson, captaining the side in place of the injured Chris Cowdrey, employed his own bowling to revive waning interest in a run chase.

Depressingly, however, Kent won only one of their last 18 championship games and had to rely on Middlesex beating Sussex in their final game to avoid finishing bottom. There was little more than statistical satisfaction in the stand of 366 between Simon Hinks (234) and Taylor (152 not out) against Middlesex which beat a county second-wicket record set by Bill Ashdown and Frank Woolley in 1934 and was also Kent's highest partnership for any wicket at the time. Kent flattered to deceive in the Refuge Assurance League, winning seven of their first eight games before going winless in the second half of the season. They also made negligible impact in either of the knockout competitions.

Team-mates had sensed that all was not well with Chris Cowdrey – his frustration at Kent's lack of success was compounded by injuries and his own indifferent form – but his decision to stand down as captain was still an abrupt one. He remembers: "I suddenly woke up one morning and thought, 'I shouldn't be doing this any more.' We'd had this massive high in 1988 and ever since then it had drifted away."

He broke the news to the players in early August, just before a championship game against Leicestershire which he missed because of injury; he told the county's committee that his resignation could take effect when they saw fit. Cowdrey also said that he would be happy to play out the final year of his contract. The match at Dartford was notable both for Kent's third and final championship win of the summer and for the feat of Davis and Patel in becoming the first pair of slow left-armers to take all 20 wickets for the county since Colin Blythe and Woolley in 1912.

Jim Woodhouse describes Cowdrey's decision as "a horrendous thing", but still managed to take a dispassionate view. "A lot of people might have sat him down and said, 'Come on, you don't want to stop.' I always ran the businesses I had on the basis that if someone said he didn't want it anymore I didn't try to persuade him to change his mind if it was made up. So I said, 'Fine, you've done it for five or six years, don't worry about it.' About a week later his wife [Christel] rang me up and said, 'Can't you persuade him to go back?' And I said, 'No.' And she said, 'Why not?' I said, 'Because he made a decision and you can't make people change their minds.' You can, but it doesn't do any good."

Taylor saw Cowdrey's resignation as a natural process of erosion. "The bottom line was that we weren't winning matches, but I think it's the same

The pain of it all: Chris Cowdrey berates himself after getting out against Lancashire in 1990, his final season as captain

Picture: Kent Messenger, PD1673772

with managers, coaches, captains: you have a sell-by date. If you've got the same group of players you've got to be doing something different to keep them interested. Or you get a new group of players. Five or six years is enough for most people who captain sides, with all the stuff which goes with the job, off the field as well as on it." Taylor himself had captained the side when both Cowdrey and Mark Benson were missing, but for once there was little complaint about a committee decision. "I had no real ambitions in that direction and if I wasn't going to be captain, there was no one I would rather have seen as captain than Mark. He was the best person for the job."

Graham Cowdrey, though saddened by his brother's departure, enjoyed the experience of being captained by someone else. He was also a great admirer of Mike Gatting's ultra-positive brand of captaincy and came very close to joining Middlesex when Keith Brown was on the verge of a move to Glamorgan. "I never really discovered why Keith changed his mind," says Cowdrey. "I would have liked a change of scene, just to get away from that Cowdrey thing at Kent and be my own person somewhere else. I think it would have been a good thing for my career; it could have been the making of me."

Mike Procter, the great South African all-rounder, had expressed an interest in coaching Kent at the start of the year, but Benson and Woodhouse looked to Australia for a right-hand man. Daryl Foster had put together an impressive CV as Western Australia's coach, but Woodhouse was quickly reminded that Jim Swanton (even at the age of 83) regarded himself as the ultimate authority on such matters. "He said at a meeting, 'What are you going to do about a manager?' And I said, 'I've got one.' 'You've *got* one? Who have you got?' I said, 'I've got Daryl Foster from Western Australia.' 'How did you do that?' And he was absolutely shattered that no one had come to him and said, 'Who do you think we should have, Jim, because your experience is so good?' I had come across Daryl Foster and I thought he was really rather a good egg."

Benson says: "Daryl's brief was to bring in a tougher mentality to the group as a whole. People had become accustomed to losing and not expecting to win, so I had to try to change that mentality."

1991

The much-improved results in 1991 reflected credit on both Mark Benson and Daryl Foster though Chris Cowdrey, for one, found himself at philosophical odds with the Australian from the word go. "I remember the first practice at Canterbury. He said, 'Right I want the slip fielders over here, and the rest of you over there for long catches.' I said, 'I've been fielding slip for 10 years.' He said, 'Not today you're not.'

"It wasn't Benny's fault at all, but Daryl Foster was awful for me. It was the only time in my Kent career when I lost all enthusiasm for the game. To me, Foster was everything that a coach shouldn't be, though probably for the side as a whole it was a good move. We needed to become more professional and we needed to be a fitter, stronger side. But for me he was hopeless because he didn't want me there from day one. I think he would have just liked to have got the brush out, and said, 'Old players, go. We'll start with a new captain and a new team.' Probably I shouldn't have played that year."

In retrospect, Cowdrey also feels that he made a mistake in playing for Glamorgan as a one-day specialist in 1992. He was flattered with the suggestion that, as a hard-hitting No 5 who could bowl a bit and field brilliantly, he was the final part in their jigsaw. " 'You come in and we'll win everything in one-day cricket,' they said, and I was very excited by that. Unfortunately they didn't win everything, until I left, then they won everything the following year. I started OK, but I hated going in to bat with just a couple of nets."

If Kent were not suddenly transformed into world-beaters in 1991, they were certainly tougher opponents, losing only three games in the championship as they rose from 16th to sixth. Benson himself laid down a significant marker when he improved his career best from 162 to 257 in the opening match at Southampton. Chris Penn signalled a return to form with eight wickets in an innings victory over Surrey, then Benson and Neil Taylor benefited from fallible catching to figure in a county-record opening stand of 300 against Derbyshire which set up another win. A diving catch to remove Middlesex's Angus Fraser enabled Steve Marsh to equal the wicketkeeping world record of eight catches in an innings, and he followed up with an unbeaten hundred. Marsh enjoyed an excellent summer and Trevor Ward, still only 23, showcased his exceptional talent with an unbeaten 235 against Middlesex.

Kent also had significantly more wicket-taking options than the previous summer. Richard Davis was less effective, but Alan Igglesden largely stayed fit to take 48 wickets in the championship, and the longer-term prospects were improved by Mark Ealham's bright showing with the ball in the final three games. Foster had also used his connections to bring in Martin McCague on an initial one-year contract. The 6ft 5in, muscular McCague had already played for Western Australia but, by virtue of being born in Northern Ireland, did not class as an overseas player. He was an uncut diamond of a fast bowler, capable

Full throttle: Alan Igglesden puts in maximum effort in 1991

of genuine pace when the working parts were in concert.

McCague recalls: "At the time I'd just been drafted by Melbourne Football Club to play Aussie rules and had a choice to make: cricket in England or stick with Aussie rules. That summer I'd played four Sheffield Shield games for WA and got a taste for first-class cricket. I'd also got the travel bug because I'd never settled down in any one place as a kid so when the opportunity came to develop my game in another country it was too good an offer to turn down."

Tony Merrick delivered much more than he had in 1990 – he was the county's leading wicket-taker – but his finest hour for Kent, in another tie with Sussex, coincided with the news that he had been released. Taylor extended a gluttonous sequence of run-making to five centuries in seven innings with 111 and 203 not out; Mark Ealham weighed in with the first of 19 five-wicket returns for Kent. A target of 437 looked to be beyond Sussex, even on a superb batting pitch, but centuries from Alan Wells and Paul Parker lifted them to 371 for four before Merrick, with three wickets in 10 balls, revived Kent's hopes. Sussex's last pair were at the crease, with the scores level, at the start of the final over, bowled by Min Patel. Off the first ball, the non-striker, Ian Salisbury, was almost run out after being sent back. Patel's next delivery turned out of the rough and was edged by Tony Pigott to Chris Cowdrey at second slip. Merrick, playing his last game for Kent, emerged with heroic figures of seven for 99.

Taylor's most cherished innings that summer, if not in his whole career, had come six weeks earlier, against the touring West Indies. "It was my birthday [July 21] and my mum and dad were both there, which was normally the kiss of death for any innings I played," he recalls. "I made an unbeaten 138 out of

247. It wasn't their strongest attack – they had Walsh, Patterson and a couple of their young quickies – but Viv Richards, Brian Lara and Desmond Haynes were all in the team. To score a hundred with players like that around was something I'll always remember." The game itself had a memorable finale, Graham Cowdrey and Matthew Fleming both hitting hundreds as Kent were bowled out only five short of their target of 342.

Excitement was in short supply for the county in the one-day competitions, though they also tied with Essex in the Refuge Assurance League. They were seen off by Surrey in the second round of the NatWest Trophy and lost a high-scoring Benson and Hedges Cup quarter-final to Worcestershire.

Merrick and Cowdrey were not the only players to leave Kent at the end of the 1991 season. The left-handed Simon Hinks, who had never done full justice to his batting talent, moved to Gloucestershire, and did very little for his new county. By contrast, Vince Wells, understandably frustrated by his peripheral role in the set-up, proved to be an excellent signing for Leicester-shire. "It was just a question of wrong time, wrong place for me," he says. "There were a lot of senior players around who were in the prime of their careers. I remember getting a hundred against Oxfordshire in the NatWest [in 1990], getting the man of the match and I didn't even make the squad for the next round. That's sport. Kent offered me a new contract, but it was time to move on because I desperately needed to play first-team cricket."

1992

There had been too many trophy-free seasons for Kent supporters to read much into 1991's improvement, but the following year was about as encour-aging as it was possible to be without the actual proof of silverware. Rarely have fortunes been shaped so completely by the form of one player. While Martin McCague was misfiring Kent were helping to make up the numbers, particularly in the championship. Once he had found confidence and rhythm they seemed capable of beating anyone.

At the end of June, McCague had managed six first-class wickets at 96 apiece. By the end of the season he had mustered 53 wickets at just under 27. There were shades of 1970 in Kent's rise from 13th place to an eventual second, though first place was never within realistic reach. Essex, the runaway champions, beat Kent by an innings in mid-May, but that was one of only three defeats in an admirably consistent campaign. The other two losses, incongru-ously, were both at the hands of a Glamorgan side who could only finish 14th overall.

Kent picked up the pace in the course of three wins in four games in July; their victory against Surrey at Guildford was achieved, unusually, after following on. Centuries from Trevor Ward and Carl Hooper, their new overseas signing, kept Kent afloat, but a target of 149 should have been within the compass of a strong batting side. The innings, however, imploded from 53 for one to 76 all out, Surrey's lowest score in 50 championship matches at Woodbridge Road. The following week brought victory over Somerset at Canterbury, though Kent were only spared a 25-point pitch penalty after arguing that a severe water shortage in the county had hampered preparations.

McCague moved into overdrive at the start of August, taking a Sunday League hat-trick against Glamorgan (he claimed 49 one-day wickets in 1992). He was awarded his county cap on the first day of the championship game against Hampshire at St Lawrence and celebrated with figures of eight for 26, the best of the season. He followed up with seven for 52 in an innings victory over Leicestershire, and 10 wickets in the match helped inflict a thumping defeat on Gloucestershire.

It was far from a one-man show. Richard Davis bowled superbly to take 67 wickets in the championship, and Hooper offered the bonus of back-up off-spin. All-round versatility was at the heart of Kent's success in the late Sixties and Seventies, and now both Matthew Fleming and Mark Ealham were capable of telling feats in all forms of the game. For once there was a heart-warming solidity to Kent's batting in the championship. Neil Taylor and Graham Cowdrey both averaged more than 50, and Trevor Ward, Hooper and Mark Benson were all comfortably above 40.

Kent's one-day form was more inconsistent and they made a tame exit from the NatWest Trophy at the quarter-final stage, unable to cope with Warwickshire's skilful seam bowling on a tricky Edgbaston pitch. They had edged nervously to a two-wicket victory over Hampshire in the previous round, a game and result which assumed added significance in the light of the teams' date, three days later, in the Benson and Hedges Cup final. Christopher Martin-Jenkins, writing in *The Daily Telegraph*, applauded the calmness under pressure of Ealham, who contributed 12 tidy overs, a crucial unbeaten 33 and "some fielding reminiscent of his brilliant father Alan" to win the gold award.

Fleming had been the leading light in Kent's progress to the Benson and Hedges final. He won gold awards against both Somerset and Yorkshire as Kent swept through their group games, and again got the vote in a tense semi-final against Surrey. The match was still in the balance when Fleming was eighth out, but Kent's ninth-wicket pair, McCague and Davis, were equal to the task of taking seven off the last over.

The reprise with Hampshire was depressingly familiar in tone and outcome for Kent supporters, who were suffering the purgatory of a fourth successive defeat in a Lord's final. In gloomy conditions, Benson had hoped that Kent would gain some advantage from being able to put Hampshire in but, with the exception of Alan Igglesden, the bowling was undistinguished.

Kent were only eight balls into their reply to Hampshire's total of 253 when bad light intervened. The weather had improved when play resumed on the Sunday but, despite 59 from Benson, Kent struggled against a fired-up Malcolm Marshall and rarely looked capable of reaching their target. A capacity crowd of 22,000 had been in attendance on the Saturday, but there were about 8,000 in the ground as Kent were bowled out for 212. Hooper was left with the impression that priorities had been mislaid in the build-up to the game. "It was a big day for the club, but there seemed to be more preparation time spent organising tickets for wives and girlfriends than anything else," he remembers.

It was scant consolation for Kent when they recorded a comfortable Sunday League win, their fifth in six games, over Hampshire four weeks later. They went on to finish joint fifth in the competition.

Kent's captain, Mark Benson, is bowled trying to force the pace in the 1992 Benson and Hedges Cup final

Picture: Barry Hollis, Kent Messenger, PD1673774

PART III
FALSE DAWNS

By Mark Pennell

*T*HE GARDEN *of England was transformed into a cricketing hot-bed when Kent's team of the 'glory years' reaped 11 titles in 12 golden summers. The players' names tripped off the tongues of their adoring supporters as easily as those of England's World Cup winning football team. Yet in time the legacy of success simply became a 'monkey on the back' to those who succeeded them.*

Sides captained by Asif Iqbal, Chris Tavaré, Chris Cowdrey and then Mark Benson all tried and failed to create a new winning dynasty. So, by the time I started reporting the county's matches in 1993, Kent had already suffered 14 trophy-less summers. The club's serial underachievement had become a bone of contention for their now success-starved supporters and quickly evolved into a recurring topic for my comment pieces in the columns of the Kent Messenger. At one point my rants became so concerted that one committee man took to calling me 'poison Pennell', while the chief executive, Paul Millman, kindly told me (and my then editor) that he likened my writing, and what he perceived to be my negative slant on club affairs, to a super-tanker. He moaned: 'Mark, we can't stop you, and we can't easily turn you around!'

I had clearly struck a nerve and chose to accept Paul's analogy as a compliment. I always felt my role for the Messenger was to report the facts as I saw them: to act as the 'eyes and ears' of those supporters who could not get to the matches. Most cricket pundits claim that the averages never lie. That being the case, I never failed to unearth an indicator or statistic to support my views and those of the disillu-sioned Kent members, many of whom felt that the club was being mismanaged.

By the late 1990s, a handful of the players believed that Kent had degenerated into a team of 'chokers'. I also recall at least five occasions when one unhappy supporter or another started to collect the 100 members' signatures required to call for a special general meeting, and with it a potential vote of no confidence in the management board or, prior to them, the general committee.

As for the balance books, their slide into the red has mirrored the club's lack of achievement on the field, culminating in successive, record-breaking six-figure losses. The painfully protracted ground redevelopment plan and Kent's first taste of life in the Second Division of the County Championship were contributory factors, yet I am left wondering: is it just a national trend that the club's membership has plummeted from 7,500 to under 4,000 during these past two decades?

It would be wrong to point the finger of blame for Kent's difficulties in any one direction, because it remains a members' club and those of us who have supported, managed, coached, played or merely followed Kent's results over the past 20-odd years, are all culpable to one degree or another. While interviewing the players I was struck by their overwhelming candour and acceptance of the fact that they had, indeed, collectively underachieved.

Matthew Fleming, Kent's captain following the sacking of Steve Marsh in 1998, has no doubt as to why Kent failed to win more: "From 1994 onwards our big problem was that we were good enough cricketers, but we weren't always good enough people," says Fleming. "We had too many for whom cricket was a lifestyle and the game was just part of the fun of being a cricketer. There were also a couple of people who were pretty focused on averages and securing another contract come the end of a season. If we could have found a captain who was a combination of Benson and Marsh, it could have been a great side. But Benny was too quiet and thoughtful, and though Marshy was aggressive and pugnacious, there was always an element to him. What neither he or Benny ever managed to do was bring the club together beyond the playing staff."

Marsh himself sees the club as a missed commercial opportunity: "The only major sporting club in the huge county of Kent is the county cricket club. If they can't make money, bearing in mind they have a monopoly and get £1.4 million a year from the ECB, then they shouldn't really be in business. If I was the only man selling mobile phones in the county I'd clean up, I'd be a multi-millionaire, so you have to ask the question, why haven't Kent done better than they have?"

Former Kent coach Daryl Foster thinks his team of the early 1990s just about delivered what their collective talents promised. His successor, John Wright, reckons his side might have won more if he had taken a more relaxed approach to coaching. Whatever the interpretation, these past 17 years have been an intriguing period of my life: long, happy days intermingled with demoralising slumps. Overall, I believe it has been one of the most fascinating eras in the club's rich history.

SIX

1993-95: First and Last

BEING WORCESTERSHIRE born and bred hardly qualifies me as a Kentish Man, let alone a Man of Kent, but what first drew me to the county was the passion for cricket and fervent support for the county club. When I started work as the Kent Messenger Group's cricket writer in May 1993, I had only seen the county side play on a handful of occasions at Worcester or Edgbaston and did not know any of their players or officials. Yet even as an outsider I could see, on paper at least, that Kent possessed an improving side, a devoted fan base and a deep interest in cricket; something akin to that in Yorkshire.

Having mounted a courageous challenge for the County Championship in 1992 – as well as reaching the Benson and Hedges Cup final – the players had created a keen sense of anticipation and expectation within the club and county. My first impressions of coach Daryl Foster and captain Mark Benson were positive. Their working relationship seemed to be based on bedrock foundations: they both enjoyed the confidence, respect and backing of the players. As a club Kent appeared to be on the up.

Benson, a gritty opener and cerebral skipper, was softly spoken, with a Sahara-dry sense of humour. His poise around the ground and with the players reflected a successful playing career. "I guess I was lucky in that way," he says. "Sometimes I possibly wasn't as tough as I should have been as a captain but had I ever felt I'd lost the respect of the dressing room, there's no way I would have been arrogant enough to carry on. While it was a great honour to captain Kent it was never something I aspired to because I never felt I was a natural leader."

A masterly opening batsman of the old school, Benson had developed a distinctive defensive technique that eventually became known as the 'Kent leave'. His simple, yet ingenious method, entailed pushing down the line of his off stump and thereby well inside the flight of any delivery that either swung away or left him off the pitch. The technique was also adopted by Benson's team-mates, Steve Marsh and Neil Taylor.

Benson, who now lives in Florida, remembers the leave as "my one legacy in the game", adding: "It started to creep in during a time in 1985, when I scored 50 plus in nine or 10 consecutive innings. When I was playing well, I knew exactly where my off stump was, so I found it much simpler to push down that line rather than the more orthodox method of shouldering arms, or sticking your hands up in the air. It just felt easier, much less of an effort, and it worked for me.

"Marcus Trescothick jokes to me about it, because he does it a lot, and Jack Russell says he copied me too. It seems particularly effective for left-handers." It also worked for the right-handed Marsh, who believes that Benson would have played in 20 Tests, rather than a single one, if his defensive method had been more conventional. "To this day I think the England selectors probably thought he was playing and missing," says Marsh.

Even the inventor admits that his technique was misconstrued. "I will never forget opening the batting on a cold morning up at Scarborough and a chap called Chris Shaw opened the bowling for Yorkshire. I left every single ball of a rubbish opening over with my 'Kent leave'. He never once made me think of playing at the ball, but he got an ovation as he went down to fine leg because everyone thought he'd made me play and miss six times." Shaw had the last laugh though: he had Benson caught behind for 17.

As a captain, Benson was dependable rather than adventurous; a leader who would take calculated risks in order to steal a last-day victory rather than one who might gamble his lot on a whim or fancy. Developing a working relationship with the new local cricket reporter never appeared too high on his list of priorities and I often watched in horror from the St Lawrence press box when, at the end of a day's play, he by-passed the dressing-room stairs and walked off to drive home, leaving me to source my day's quotes elsewhere.

But where it mattered, in the dressing room and out in the middle, Benson was much admired, particularly by his right-hand man and vice-captain Marsh. "Had you been able to mix the personalities of Chris Cowdrey and Mark Benson you'd have had an all-time great captain," he says. "If Mark had had a few more guys in the side with the mentality and character to run through brick walls for him, then he'd have won a lot more." Marsh also remembers him as a captain who showed great faith in emerging young players.

My first game as a cricket correspondent was a turgid draw on a painfully slow early-season Lord's seamer against Middlesex. At least I was able to witness Benson's 43rd first-class hundred, together with Nigel Llong's maiden championship century, which included a huge straight six onto the top tier of the Lord's pavilion. Afterwards I knocked on the door of the visitors' dressing room and requested an interview with Llong. It was 40 minutes before he finally emerged, full of apologies. He believed the 'interview request' had been a dressing-room wind-up because, until that point, the Messenger had rarely covered away games. I learned to knock more frequently thereafter.

The corresponding Sunday League game heralded the advent of the white ball and Kent's new powder-blue strip. They marked their maiden 'pyjama game' with a comfortable nine-wicket win, but the kit, complete with its burgundy and navy blue 'V' emblazoned across sweater fronts, appeared more suited to rugby league than cricket.

In looking to instil a keen work ethic on the younger members of Kent's squad, Foster organised numerous training and fitness drills, which came as a culture shock to first-season professional David Fulton. Writing in his 2009 book *The Captains' Tales*, Fulton said: "He had based a lot of his success at Western Australia on tough physical conditioning. Perhaps he didn't understand the long grind of a county season, pushing us too hard at times, but it was something my generation grew up with."

Foster looks back on the era with great pride, saying: "The overall improvement of the entire squad meant Kent players were competing for positions and, as a consequence, began again to be noticed by the national selectors. To be fair, with the exception of Mark Ealham, no one quite cemented a permanent place in the England side, but it was further proof of Kent's emergence as a competitive county."

Both Foster and Benson felt that the side needed a dependable new-ball partner for Martin McCague, and Benson encouraged Dean Headley to make the short journey along the A2 from Middlesex. Headley was seen as a ready-made replacement for that season's beneficiary, Richard Ellison, who then retired after only three first-class appearances in his last two seasons and became cricket master at Millfield School in Somerset.

Headley recalls: "I wasn't very pleased with the way Middlesex wanted to treat me financially. They decided they would offer me a fixed-term contract but, in doing so, took away all my bonuses and match fees. That meant in my third year with them I would have earned less than my second, so I refused their contract offer. It was then that I had a call from Carl Hooper, who asked if I'd fancy going to Kent, so I met Mark Benson at a hotel near Dartford and agreed right then that I'd sign for Kent."

The Test and County Cricket Board ordered a disciplinary hearing to investigate claims that Kent had poached Headley, who explains: "Kent were due to play Middlesex in the first game of that season and I had to go before a TCCB committee to answer if I'd had any contact with Kent before the expiry of my Middlesex contract. Middlesex claimed that the first they heard of me moving to Kent was through the media, but the truth was, I'd told Bob Gale [then chairman of cricket at Middlesex] over the phone that I would not be signing their contract and would be moving. At that time, I'd not spoken with Kent.

"The TCCB pushed me further, so I said: 'I'll be truthful, I haven't spoken to Kent, but my dad [the former Worcestershire and West Indies opener, Ron] might have.' I made it quite clear that I didn't control my dad and that he might have acted independently. Instead of making the proper decision, they banned me for one game; it was my first and only ban."

There was a wider significance in Headley's signing: remarkably, he was the first English player since Peter Richardson[1] in 1959 to join Kent from another county. More than 20 Kent players had moved away from St Lawrence during the intervening period. With Headley eventually on board, Kent possessed a lively opening attack and had promising left-arm spinners Richard Davis and Min Patel vying for one berth. Hooper was their glorious, if enigmatic overseas star and Ealham and Matthew Fleming their budding all-rounders. Marsh, the side's chief motivator, was their dependable wicketkeeper and the final member of an experienced, if occasionally frail batting line-up.

Kent prepared for the summer with a short pre-season tour to Zimbabwe, where England Under-19 captain and promising left-handed bat, Matthew Walker, made his first-class debut. Walker remembers being puzzled by his taciturn captain: "I couldn't really work Benny out. He'd never speak, so going to him for advice wasn't really an option. He did make me laugh, though, because he never seemed to have all his own kit. He'd borrow other people's stuff and walk out wearing odd pads, different gloves, even someone else's bat. Yet he'd go out and score an amazing hundred against someone like Allan Donald. He was an unbelievably good player."

The opening championship matches of '93 went badly for Benson and his team. Despite a pre-season hundred at Fenner's and his century at Lord's, Llong was dropped to accommodate the late-arriving Hooper, yet still Kent suffered back-to-back defeats to Warwickshire and Nottinghamshire. They rallied with innings wins over Durham and Gloucestershire, despite injuries to Alan Igglesden and McCague. A rain-affected draw against Hampshire at Basingstoke ended the winning sequence, then Igglesden and McCague again broke down late in the game at Headingley, leaving the side to hold out for a draw.

Despite numerous ailments, Igglesden topped the national averages by late June; his nagging swing bowling and McCague's hostility earned both England

[1]See Notes and Sources

Test calls. Sadly, their fragility ensured that they never played international cricket together and while Igglesden occupied the physiotherapist's bench, McCague went on to make his England debut against Australia at Trent Bridge.

McCague reflects: "Bowlers stick together and Iggy and I became great mates. It's bloody hard work and we all have our aches and grumbles, but no matter what, the unit of bowlers tend to get on because you're all in it together. When we did play together for Kent the win percentage rocketed because we had different styles and techniques."

Both men missed a high-scoring draw against Essex at The Mote, a game that led to a wicket-less Kent debut for another Australian-raised firebrand, Duncan Spencer, who had also played under Foster at Western Australia. The former warehouseman, 5ft 8in in his bowling boots, possessed a short and straight run-up, uncoiling at the crease to generate express pace, sometimes in excess of 90mph. The effort could prove so great that on occasion Spencer would lose his footing on the follow-through and end up on all fours. When fully fit he was a real handful, but a suspect spine, which had already been under-pinned with a brace of steel surgical screws, ultimately finished his career.

Marsh's understudy, Graham Kersey, had joined Surrey at the start of the summer and with Marsh injured Kent signed former Hampshire wicketkeeper Bobby Parks on an emergency registration for a solitary championship appearance against Essex at Maidstone. Hooper, who grew to love the benign pitch at the county-town ground, notched 142 from 134 balls before Benson's declaration left Essex an unlikely chase of 341 in 82 overs. They were nine down after tea but survived the last five overs.

A draw against Surrey in Canterbury Week ended any championship aspirations and Kent slumped to an innings defeat against Worcestershire at New Road in mid-August, when Ealham hit the only half-century of an appalling batting display. Benson, absent in the second innings after being hit on the right knee, missed the remaining six weeks of the season. The knee had first troubled him in 1979, when he had a cartilage operation, and he now admits: "After that I could never bend my knee that well and couldn't really play the sweep shot."

Under Marsh's acting captaincy Kent gave rookie opener Fulton a late run in the side and finished the championship season with a flourish. A draw against Northamptonshire, during which Llong and Headley received their county caps, was sandwiched between wins over Lancashire and championship-chasing Glamorgan. The trip to play Lancashire at Lytham St Annes

Jim Swanton entertains then Prime Minister John Major during Canterbury Week in 1993

Picture: Mike Waterman, Kent Messenger, PD1673775

proved memorable for Patel's then best haul of seven for 75 (and match return of 12 for 182), marking his full recovery from cruciate ligament surgery – the legacy of running into a pot-hole while coaching rugby at Dartford Grammar School during the close season. The game also stuck in the minds of spectators who were left with blue-striped derrières after sitting on recently painted benches. The public address announcer attracted sniggers all round when he invited those affected to make themselves known at the club office to receive a contribution towards dry-cleaning bills.

Hooper marked the season's final four-day game at Canterbury with a sumptuous, unbeaten 236. His first double hundred also proved to be his highest score for Kent. The Guyanese finished the summer with 1,304 first-class runs at an average of 59.27. He also took 33 championship wickets and scored 954 runs in all limited-overs cricket to become the AXA Equity and Law League's player of the season.

By the end of that season the languid Hooper had replaced Hampshire's Barry Richards as my all-time batting hero. I felt privileged to report his exploits, yet during his time with county I never once saw him take part in a full-scale net session. If the county were batting he would take 20 pre-match throw-downs, usually wearing only one pad. Or if Kent were in the field he would snaffle 15 or so practice slip catches off the bat face before swaggering out to the middle to take his place as the best slip-catcher I had ever seen.

Hooper's team-mates must surely have regarded him as aloof on occasion, but I got to know him well and we have remained friends. I recall his indignation one season when Kent dared issue him with a diesel Vauxhall Cavalier as his sponsored car. His preference was for high-powered BMWs, and he vowed never to get behind the wheel of the Cavalier. I became designated driver for trips up to Maidstone to meet with his West Indies team-mate Richie Richardson at Lashings wine bar and restaurant.

As we chatted about Kent performances, it soon became clear that Hooper was on a different wavelength to players who lacked his god-given talent and innate fitness levels. When he looks back on his trophy-less seasons with the club, Hooper says: "I don't want to be too negative about people, but I lost count of the number of times when, at a key point of a championship season, we went into games without McCague or Igglesden." He adds: "It's OK to have a good side, but for some of the guys it wasn't all about winning the championship; it was about being retained for the next year."

Despite Hooper's contribution, Kent finished eighth in the championship which, coupled with an early exit to Warwickshire in the NatWest Trophy and a first-round knockout by Glamorgan in the Benson and Hedges Cup, left supporters and committee men frustrated once more. Sound performances in the Sunday League did, however, maintain interest until the final day of the campaign. Kent's 12 wins from 16 starts helped set up a televised title showdown with Glamorgan at a packed St Lawrence. On police instructions stewards were ordered to close the main gates by 3pm, only to leave them slightly ajar once a gaggle of enthusiastic Welsh fans arrived by taxi from nearby Manston Airport, where their chartered plane had landed late after weather delays.

Unbeaten in their nine previous league outings, Kent went into the finale level on points with Glamorgan, but nerves got the better of them when batting in front of a 12,000 crowd; after a steady start, inspired by Hooper's restrained 60, Kent fell away, losing their last five wickets for 14. A chancy, unbeaten 46 from Viv Richards saw Glamorgan past Kent's paltry total of 200 with 14 balls to spare.

The fiery Spencer split the fingers of Richards's batting glove and was convinced that he had dismissed him when he had made 14, only for a no-ball to be called. Fulton, playing only his sixth first team game, remembers drifting down the order from an original three to nine when Kent batted, and being almost redundant in the field. "Even when I was about to catch Viv Richards off that no-ball, Spence was so pumped up that he barged me out of the way and caught it himself, even though it would have been a dolly to me. He was going ballistic and I had to say, 'Listen mate, it's a no-ball,' but that moment summed up my game."

Following his penultimate innings before retirement, Richards sprinted towards the dressing rooms, only to drop to his knees and slide along the last few yards of outfield, punching the air in a rare display of emotion. His knock and Kent's questionable big-match temperament had guaranteed their eighth runners-up finish since 1978, yet it was still their best showing in the league for 14 years. Graham Cowdrey describes it simply as "a wet performance. We were at home; we should have won it."

Welsh celebrations at the Bat and Ball public house opposite the St Lawrence main drive were lengthy, loud and enjoyable that night. Tony Cottey, on acoustic guitar, led the rabble-rousing as the bawdy Dragons took turns to serenade the locals. As they did so, Kent's players snuck home licking their wounds.

Missing out on the closing four-day games and selection for the Sunday League showdown proved to be the final straw for Davis. Despite finishing with 36 wickets from his 14 championship appearances, more than double the victims of his chief rival Patel, the 28-year-old declined a new one-year deal with Kent and joined Warwickshire. Frustrated by his lack of first team opportunities, fringe batsman Jonathan Longley left to join Durham.

Barely a fortnight after the season's end Kent lost their affable chairman of only 18 months' standing, Bill Sale. Aged 60, he collapsed and died of a heart attack during a benefit event for Ellison at Knole Park Golf Club in Sevenoaks. The year also marked the passing of Kent stalwart Claude Lewis, who died, aged 84, after serving the club for 60 years as player, coach, administrator and scorer, through to his retirement in 1988.

1994

Kent's injury woes went from bad to worse as the summer of 1994 progressed; at one point or another, every member of their pace battery suffered a lengthy spell on the sidelines. Mark Benson and Daryl Foster turned to local doctor Julian Thompson – not to sort out their injuries, but to bolster their attack – though even he missed the second half of the season because of shin problems.

Martin McCague tore shoulder muscles in May, missing 10 weeks' cricket, Dean Headley developed ankle problems and then a hernia and, once McCague returned, Alan Igglesden went down with a bad back; it prompted conspiracy theories among Kent supporters that Igglesden and McCague were, in fact, one and the same player. After flying home to Australia in June for tests on his brittle back, Duncan Spencer threatened comebacks but never featured seriously again for Kent.

Left-arm swing bowler Tim Wren, Mark Ealham, Headley, Carl Hooper, Min Patel and Matthew Fleming, who battled on despite shoulder problems, carried the championship attack for long periods but, without their heavy artillery, Kent lacked the firepower to bowl sides out twice. They lost a thrilling opening championship game by nine runs inside three days to Nottinghamshire. Ironically, it proved the only occasion when Benson could select all four, first-choice pacemen in McCague, Igglesden, Headley and Spencer. Recalling how his seamers suffered, Benson says: "I hadn't realised until I started umpiring what a difficult profession being a bowler is. If you've a slight weakness in your knees or ankle, bowling is going to find that out. There's so much wear and tear and until I heard the bowlers running, over after over as an umpire, I didn't fully appreciate that."

Headley still treasures the days when the Kent pace attack were fully fit and capable of lifting the mood of the vociferous and adoring Canterbury public. "I used to love playing at St Lawrence, running in to bowl with the crowd chanting my name. Even when I came in to bat the crowd were always right behind me. I remember one occasion during a limited-overs match against Worcestershire, we had no chance of winning, but I still got a great ovation. Tom Moody turned round towards me, did a double take in my direction, and said: 'It *is* you, Deano, I thought for a second there Don Bradman was walking in.'"

A four-wicket reverse to Essex at Chelmsford proved memorable only for Hooper's 79-ball last-day century, the first before lunch by a Kent player since Bob Woolmer in 1979. He hit nine sixes, one of which smashed through a window in the members' pavilion. They were still searching for their first championship win when they lost to Warwickshire in late June. The result was a particularly bitter blow for a Kent side hell-bent on avenging their Benson and Hedges Cup quarter-final exit in May, following a controversial bowl-off in the Edgbaston indoor school.

On the designated morning of the match Kent arrived to find ground staff using industrial-sized hot-air blowers in an effort to dry one half of the pitch. When viewed from wicket to wicket, one side was sodden, the other reasonably dry and nigh-on playable. A failed bid to move the game to Derby only served to heighten Kent's indignation over the condition of the Edgbaston playing surface and the old wicket ends. Rightly, Foster and his players questioned why the second-city Test venue had not deployed the 'Brumbrella'.

In a bizarre press statement, Warwickshire's chief executive, Dennis Amiss, explained that use of the 'Brumbrella' had been suspended to prevent an outbreak of fusarium patch, a fungal infection prevalent in newly seeded areas of turf. In the absence of an agreement over switching the game to an alternative venue, Kent had little option but to take part in a bowl-out.

After practising at the indoor school some of the regular bowlers ruled themselves out on the grounds that the ball was swinging too much in the high humidity. The air of farce gathered momentum when Amiss arbitrarily decided to ban the press from reporting the bowl-out. He eventually relented and we watched Kent go out of the competition when Nigel Llong missed with both his attempts. The clubs exchanged angry letters, Kent lodged a formal complaint to the TCCB and, to this day, the affair still rankles with the players concerned. To rub salt into already weeping wounds, Warwickshire, inspired by Brian Lara, beat them twice more in Birmingham that season; by six wickets in the Sunday League, then by eight runs in the semi-final of the NatWest Trophy.

Inspired by Neil Taylor's first championship century in almost two years and five-wicket returns by Patel and a fit-again Headley, Kent landed their first championship win from eight starts against Yorkshire at Maidstone in early July. Taylor a burly, obdurate right-hander and hugely effective opening bat, never appeared the most animated of characters once back at the team hotel; he also earned the unwanted nickname 'Crime' (... never pays). In beating their fellow strugglers at The Mote, Kent pushed Yorkshire to the bottom of the table and avoided equalling their worst, winless start to a championship summer, set in 1972 and again in 1985.

Taylor's 139, scored over six hours, led to a narrow first-innings advantage, but it was the speed of Hooper's 183 in the second innings that gave Kent, and Patel in particular, with five for 68, time to whittle out Yorkshire on a shirt-front, last-day pitch. Forced to retire with a mild case of sunstroke and dehydration when on 38, Hooper returned to blast a record 10 sixes during his sublime 151-ball stay. Five of his sixes sailed over the hospitality marquees and onto the adjacent rugby field.

Benson describes Hooper as "the most naturally gifted player I played with at Kent". He also believes that he would have benefited from playing county cricket at a younger age – he was 25 when he joined Kent. "He may have developed quicker mentally if nothing else and would probably have gone on to have a more successful career for the West Indies."

Although a large St Lawrence crowd witnessed Kent's first win over the South Africans since 1924 they were then subjected to an appalling home

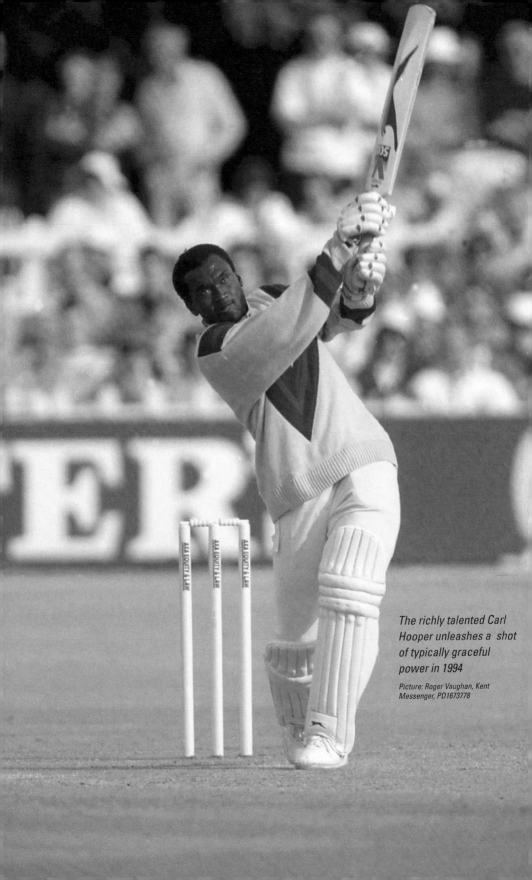

The richly talented Carl Hooper unleashes a shot of typically graceful power in 1994

Picture: Roger Vaughan, Kent Messenger, PD1673778

defeat by Worcestershire, sparking McCague's return to the fold and an improved second half of the championship season. Kent won at Abergavenny, where Trevor Ward scored centuries in each innings, and Cheltenham, where the right-hander reached his 1,000 runs and Benson chalked up his first hundred of the summer.

A beautiful player when in his stride, Ward could be incredibly stubborn yet he also suffered hugely from nagging self-doubt. According to Ealham, Ward was the most talented Kent-produced player of the generation. "Even at age group level he would 'munch' it everywhere. He'd smack a championship century for the first team, yet still come back to the dressing room and throw his bat in the bin because he'd not managed to break the ball!"

My own assessment of Ward was tinged with frustration. Now and again he would bat in 'stand-and-deliver' style, seemingly without regard for the quality of the attack, the condition of the pitch or the state of the game. On occasion, he would give away his wicket as a result. We fell out briefly after I wrote he had batted "like a millionaire", but happily a working relationship was quickly restored.

Returning home, Kent lost their Canterbury Week clash with Hampshire on an unpredictable, re-laid pitch at the top of the St Lawrence slope which umpires George Sharp and Bob White reported unfit for first-class cricket. Kent escaped censure and moved down the square onto a more predictable strip and reaped the rewards with a nine-wicket success over Durham. Fresh from winning his county cap, Patel took 10 wickets in the match – he also maintained his remarkable record against Lancashire with career-best figures of eight for 96 – and his season's tally of 90 wickets was the highest in the country. The luckless Benson missed the game with a groin strain, leaving acting captain Steve Marsh to lead from the front with nine victims and a season's best 85 not out in a match that also marked Matthew Walker's championship debut.

Marsh, who ended the campaign with a career-best 74 victims, had led the side to seven straight wins when deputising, but it was Benson's shrewd leadership that inspired McCague's outstanding analysis of nine for 86 at Derby in August, when Kent eased to a 69-run win. McCague's first-innings haul represented the finest figures by a Kent bowler since Derek Underwood's nine for 35 against Surrey in 1978. McCague went on to record match figures of 15 for 147, the best for Kent since John Shepherd's identical return against Sussex at The Mote in 1975.

Not surprisingly, McCague looks back on the game as his finest hour for Kent, "not just because I took 15 wickets, but I almost scored a fifty in our second innings. I bowled with consistent pace throughout the whole game. It was one of those matches when everything clicked. It swung a bit when it was overcast, but then the sun would come out and the ball did nothing. It was 'hard yakka' at times, but Benny was clever and just bowled me in short spells."

After a defeat at Northampton, Kent wrapped up their home fixtures with an innings win over Somerset at Canterbury, where Taylor hit his 13th century on the ground to surpass Frank Woolley's record of 12 St Lawrence hundreds. The championship season concluded with a rain-wrecked clash at the Oval, notable only for Walker's maiden championship hundred, leaving Kent ninth in the final table, one place lower than the previous year.

With an eye on the future, Foster made a point of taking Walker to one side after his eye-catching innings to stress the importance of maintaining a winter fitness programme. I watched in fascination as Foster, who had previously angered Fleming, among others, by banning ice cream from the St Lawrence dining room, chatted with Walker over a coffee in the members' restaurant. He handed him his close-season training schedule and returned to the dressing rooms, leaving Walker to finish his drink and mull over his winter plans. A moment later, Walker stood up, rolled the papers into a ball and consigned them to the bin.

"I can't remember doing that," Walker says, "but I wouldn't be surprised if it were true because I found Daryl very intense. The other thing I didn't like about Daryl was that he had his favourites. If you weren't in the first team shake-up or you weren't playing well, Daryl didn't have much time for you."

Foster did have major supporters in the camp, though, none more so than Benson and his vice-captain. Marsh, who formed a near "father-and-son" relationship with Foster, says: "He rubbed a few guys up the wrong way, but that was a positive for me because it gave us more steel. Looking back, it was the most enjoyable part of my career. He had

Over the top: Neil Taylor takes the aerial route in 1994

Picture: Derek Stingemore, Kent Messenger, PD1673779

*Mark Benson on the hop
against the short ball in 1994*

Picture: Roger Vaughan, Kent Messenger,
PD1673777

the Aussie mentality which I love. I felt he could see some of that in me because he said to me one day, 'I'd love to take you back in my suitcase to play back home.' That gave me a real buzz."

Marsh knocks down the suggestion, widely aired at the time, that Foster banned the Kent squad from associating with opposing players. "I still get asked about it by players to this day, but it's all rubbish. What Daryl said was something like, 'The thing is, guys, it might make us appear more focused and that bit tougher if, maybe one of the mornings, we don't speak to the opposing batsmen when they come to the crease?' Pretty soon, visiting players were coming up and asking if they were allowed to talk to me? In the end, we thought, 'Let's use this to our advantage.' We felt that if the other team were worrying about us not talking to them, then they had a problem, not us.

"Daryl was just looking to make us a more professional outfit, to take every possible advantage, be it through diet, training or psychology. He was trying to squeeze an extra one per cent from everyone's game and I didn't have a problem with that. I thought he was good, ahead of his time in many ways."

Foster's input into training drills and fielding practice had undoubtedly helped improve Kent as a one-day side and once again they challenged for the AXA Equity and Law League title in 1994, only to fall away at the final hurdle. The coach earmarked middle-order batsman Llong, an athletic fielder and tidy off-spinner, as a key member of Kent's limited-overs side and he responded with some match-winning displays.

Llong believes that Foster's arrival simply proved that Kent had been "fairly amateurish prior to that". He describes him as "no Alex Ferguson – he didn't need to rant and rave – but if he went quiet you knew you were in trouble and you'd soon find out what you'd done wrong." Fortunately for Chris Penn, Foster also proved that he could take a practical joke … and respond in kind. Bending down to put on his shoes after a net session, Foster discovered they had been glued firmly to the carpet. After unearthing the culprit, Foster exacted revenge the following week by stuffing cream cakes into Penn's bowling socks.

After losing in four of their first seven Sunday League starts and suffering their customary defeat to Warwickshire, Kent embarked on a county record run of nine successive wins, culminating in a nervy 66-run home success over Somerset that took them to within two points of leaders Warwickshire with one game remaining. Then, when seemingly on course for a comfortable victory over Surrey at the Oval in their final game, Kent conspired to lose their last nine wickets for 59 for a 24-run defeat that left them third. Meanwhile, Warwickshire secured the last trophy of an unprecedented domestic treble.

Hooper was named the league's most valuable player for the second successive year, but again he failed to collect the award in person. Disenchanted at having missed out on team silverware for a third straight summer, he had already left the country. Hooper's disappointment was mirrored by Ward who, after scoring 1,368 first-class runs for the season, appeared to surprise himself by ignoring the overtures of Middlesex, Derbyshire and Warwickshire to sign a three-year contract extension. Committee minutes of the day confirm that Ward was granted permission to speak to Middlesex, yet he eventually agreed his new deal with Kent and went on to reveal that not everything was rosy in the Garden of England.

During a frank interview for the *Kent Messenger* that November, Ward said: "It was a difficult decision and I'm not sure it was the right one. It was a case of sitting down, mulling things over and perhaps allowing my heart to rule my head. Certainly, I don't think it's done anything in terms of enhancing my chances of playing for England."

Ward refused to be drawn on suggestions that he and Foster no longer saw eye-to-eye, but the Australian was more forthcoming. In admitting his surprise at Ward's decision to stay, Foster added that he had "not been the easiest man to handle".

1995

If honest-to-goodness hard work was required to turn around Kent's ailing fortunes, then Mark Benson showed during the winter months that he, for one, would not shy away from it. By day, Benson worked as a court representative for Ramsgate solicitors Godfrey Davis and Waitt; by night he honed his batting technique in the Ames-Levett indoor school at St Lawrence. In a bid to improve on the previous summer's disappointing return of 737 runs at an average of 27, Benson called in a trusted long-time friend, Sussex batting guru Les Lenham, for a series of video coaching sessions.

Benson also had to find a locum overseas replacement for Carl Hooper, who was certain to be picked for the West Indies' tour of England in 1995. After being knocked back by a couple of Australian fringe players, Benson plumped for a virtual unknown to county followers, Sri Lankan batsman Aravinda de Silva. He had discovered, while on a trip to Sri Lanka in the mid-Eighties, that De Silva was regarded as both an outstanding batsman in the making and a useful off-spinner.

Benson admits, looking back, that he doubted his own judgment in the early weeks of the season. "I do remember thinking in the first few weeks, 'Oh my

God, I've made a huge blunder here.' " He was bombarded with letters from Kent members, some of them verging on hate mail. Benson told the *Kentish Gazette* at the time: "I got 150 letters or more, all simply asking me, 'Why?' "

De Silva's new team-mates also wondered what to make of him when he and a Sri Lankan chum arrived, four days late, for his first practice session. As Graham Cowdrey explains, Kent's players were even unsure as to which of the pair was De Silva. "He turned up at lunchtime with this other guy, pulling these great cases of cricket kit, but none of us could remember what he looked like. We all said hello. He said, 'Do you mind if my friend bowls in the nets?' I was the first man in the nets after lunch and this bloke came in bowling this extraordinary stuff and I was trying to slog him over midwicket. It was the great Muralitharan of course. Quite a few of the guys thought he was De Silva to start with because we literally didn't know what Aravinda looked like."

During his dismal early appearances in Canterbury, De Silva took to wearing three sweaters and would thrust his hands deep into his pockets in a bid to stave off the cold. On his Benson and Hedges Cup debut he contributed only 16 in the 93-run win over Surrey then, in his losing championship bow against Northamptonshire, he mustered two and 13. The clouds eventually parted and on 5 May, with the sun on his back, De Silva underwent a stunning metamorphosis to score his maiden championship hundred at Hove. Using a feather-light bat and with quixotic foot movement, he would flutter down the pitch to drive with grace, yet if the Sussex bowlers dropped short, the little man in the white helmet (he is 5ft 4in) rocked back to cut or pull with savage power. Batting like this, he was mesmerising. Characteristically, though, De Silva ran himself out without scoring in the second innings and, despite Dean Headley's then career-best return of seven for 58, Sussex cantered to victory with two centuries from Alan Wells.

For the next four months De Silva's batting was a sheer delight. His now adoring public dubbed him 'Ari' and, by the time of his departure in September, his sole season at St Lawrence had become the stuff of Kentish folklore. He posted 10 centuries in all forms of cricket, hit 1,781 first-class runs at an average of 59.37 and 722 in one-day cricket. My former *Kent Messenger* colleague, John Evans, wrote: "This was a cricketer to recall to your grandchildren." Steve Marsh rates De Silva as the best cricketer he played alongside. "In terms of overall contribution, Aravinda de Silva always gets my vote. He listened, laughed and wanted to be part of the dressing room and the team. Just a great player."

De Silva's Kent career could so easily have ended in tragedy towards the end of June; he was returning, as Min Patel's passenger, from the NatWest

Trophy win over Staffordshire when Patel's car was involved in a high-speed crash on the M6. After swerving to avoid a motorway cone that blew across the carriageway, Patel's car slewed into the side of an articulated lorry and was written off. Mercifully, both players escaped without a scratch.

Not even De Silva's batting exploits could successfully paper over the cracks of a brittle, somewhat schizophrenic Kent top order who continued to underachieve, particularly in the first innings of championship games. On the rare occasion when they did bat well first time around Kent beat Leicestershire by an innings inside three days after posting 575, their then highest total at Canterbury. Benson and Neil Taylor hit centuries, Martin McCague took six wickets in the match and Steve Herzberg five for 33 on his championship bow. Off-spinner Herzberg, the third Australian-raised player with a British passport to be unearthed by Daryl Foster, was the first Kent bowler since Eddie Crush in 1946 to claim five wickets in an innings on championship debut, but hardly featured after injuring a finger and was released at the end of the season.

On their travels, Kent landed a three-day success at Southampton and wrapped up an innings victory on their first visit to Chester-le-Street. Durham were toppled for 85, Headley's five for 32 fully vindicating Benson's decision to open up a rain-ruined game by forfeiting Kent's second innings and offering a tantalising target of 200 on the final day. With three wins, confidence appeared high but Kent's championship bubble burst thereafter. They failed to win any of their 11 matches after 5 June to finish bottom of an 18-county table for the first time and claim their first wooden spoon since 1895.

Benson insists that he was right to prioritise the Sunday League towards the end of the season. "Of course, it wasn't great to finish bottom and I got a fair pasting for it, but I probably wouldn't swap that. I remember being a bit surprised by the reaction from the AGM and it left a bit of a sour taste, but the supporters pay their fees and are entitled to their say. But we had a chance to win something and I chose to put all our eggs into one basket to the detriment of the championship. Can they really blame us for that? All these years later, I've still no regrets about doing it."

Patel finished as the county's leading wicket-taker, with 61 victims at 37.18, but there was little seam support for McCague and Headley, who took 50 and 44 wickets, both at 29 apiece. Matthew Fleming claimed only six wickets in 10 first-class appearances and Julian Thompson six in three, though he did have the distinction of dismissing Brian Lara in both innings of the tour match as the West Indian master recorded his first ever pair. Thompson said modestly afterwards: "Just because they're big names shouldn't alter the way I bowl at them, but Lara was something of an exception. I was slightly apprehensive about playing against him."

De Silva, the only Kent batsman to top 1,000 first-class runs, brought out the best in Graham Cowdrey. The pair, who became firm friends over the course of the season, shared several memorable partnerships, including a Kent record 315 for the sixth wicket against Nottinghamshire at Trent Bridge. But their pinnacle came during a run-feast draw with Derbyshire at The Mote in July. Combining for the fourth wicket, de Silva, with 255 from 313 balls, and Cowdrey (137) added 368 in 80 overs. It remains Kent's record championship stand for any wicket.

McCague recalls that De Silva's thirst for runs was still not sated. "I remember going in as nightwatchman in our second innings when Phil DeFreitas and Alan Warner were bowling. I played and missed a few times, but survived. Then, with four overs to go, Aravinda nicked the strike from the last ball of the over. He did the same to the last ball of the next over, so I went down in between overs and explained that wasn't how it was meant to work with a nightwatchman. He looked up at me, smiled, and said: 'Yes Martin, I agree, but you look like getting out every ball.' He ended up facing until stumps, went out the next day and scored yet another hundred."

For the fourth successive year Kent suffered an early-season NatWest Trophy defeat at the hands of Warwickshire. Unable to explain the phenomenon to this day, Matthew Walker says: "There was always this thing about Warwickshire being a hoodoo side for us. I hadn't played against them much and didn't feel there was a real problem, but it was clear that the rest of the lads did. There was such a negative attitude in that dressing room whenever we were drawn against them. You have to ask now, why did we do that to ourselves? With the quality of that side, why on earth would we groan about things that were out of our hands?"

Concentrating on matters they could control, Benson and Trevor Ward excelled in Kent's run through to the Benson and Hedges Cup final by posting a record five successive century opening partnerships. Ward reflects: "I probably played my best one-day cricket that year, but couldn't transfer it into the four-day game. That was so frustrating to me." He and Benson inspired wins over Surrey, Somerset, Ireland, Sussex and quarter-final opponents Middlesex, before adding 53 as Kent booked their seventh B&H final visit to Lord's with a 31-run home triumph over two days against Somerset.

The game ended on a downbeat note when Benson fractured his left thumb catching a skied slog from Mushtaq Ahmed. His wife Sarah, having discharged herself on the opening day of the tie from the adjacent Kent and Canterbury

Daryl Foster (right) joins in the celebrations as Kent reflect on their semi-final win in the Benson and Hedges Cup in 1995

Picture: Roger Vaughan, Kent Messenger, PD1673783

Hospital, where she was waiting for gall-bladder surgery, was back on her ward by the time Benson suffered his injury. He later admitted to crying when the club doctor told him the triple fracture would force him to miss the remainder of the season, the final included. "One of my big disappointments was that I got some stick from Kent supporters for not playing in the final," says Benson. "It didn't seem to matter to them that I'd got a triple fracture to my thumb and couldn't even get a batting glove on. It was the worst break I ever had in my career."

Marsh captained the side at Lord's, where Kent finished second best in their fifth successive final despite a heroic riposte by De Silva. Michael Atherton, with a steady 93, laid the foundations for Lancashire's 55-over total of 274 for seven, though had De Silva reacted more swiftly at long leg to a top-edged Atherton pull in Tim Wren's opening over, the outcome might have been different.

Kent made a shaky start in reply as Ward edged behind then David Fulton, wearing a wide-brimmed sun hat on his cup debut, fell leg before for 25. He insists that the choice of head gear was "down to insecurity rather than vanity. It wasn't a 'look-at-me moment', although a lot of people probably thought that was the case. The reality was I was really nervous. It was my competition debut and I'd never played in front of 25,000 people before. I've seen recordings of the game since and it looks like I'm chewing gum, but I didn't have any gum with me; it was just nerves."

Fulton had taken his cue from Adam Seymour, the Worcestershire batsman, who confessed that he had felt anonymous when playing in the previous year's final. A few days before the game Fulton discussed his concerns over a beer with Herzberg. "I remember saying I felt I needed a gimmick, a prop to lean on like a Pat Cash headband. So I came up with the idea of the sun hat. As soon as I put my hat on it was a way of telling myself that I was going out there to enjoy it. The other thing in my mind was, having played against Wasim Akram before, I knew his short stuff was a little easier to deal with than the full length, so if it wound him up to bowl bouncers, so much the better."

After Fulton's demise, Taylor yorked himself to make it 81 for three and bring together Cowdrey and De Silva. Prior to the big day in St John's Wood, De Silva's competition best had been a modest 39, leading him to say: "Perhaps God is saving all my runs for Lord's." He responded to the big-match pressure with a breathtaking 88-ball hundred, including 10 fours and three sixes that sailed over a short boundary into the Mound Stand as he and Cowdrey added 61 in 14 overs.

Cowdrey remembers sensing that the pendulum was starting to swing in Kent's favour. "When I came in Aravinda didn't have very many. They knew they'd won the game and they were cock-a-hoop. Then Aravinda started playing some extraordinary shots. I don't know how many we'd put on, but all of a sudden there was that magical moment as a batsman where they all got a bit niggly with each other. We certainly weren't anywhere near being favourites, but we'd got back in it."

Their fun ended abruptly when David Shepherd sent Cowdrey packing leg before when sweeping at full stretch against Gary Yates. Marsh, disappointed to this day by the decision – "it wouldn't have hit another set" – insists that a single umpiring decision changed the course of the match.

Cowdrey himself describes it as "an atrocious decision" and defends his choice of shot: "I remember that year I'd been sweeping really well. Mike Gatting had helped me a bit and I just made damn sure I was always outside the line. I'd played before against Yates and I didn't rate him at all. We met in the middle and Aravinda said, 'No big shots, let me play him.' And I went, 'OK, no problem.' I walked back to the crease and thought, 'Gary Yates, you're going out of the ground.' It was in his first over and it was a fairly short boundary on the Tavern side. I was certainly looking to get him out of the ground and couldn't believe it when I was given out."

Benson's take on the incident is different from that of his colleagues. "We only realised it was maybe an incorrect decision because TV were there to cover the final and we watched the highlights later. I don't particularly remember many people moaning that day. We just accepted it, at least I did. You can't blame an umpiring error for us losing to Lancashire. I felt we were struggling to win it at that stage anyway. You never know what might have

Mad hatter: David Fulton is dismissed in the 1995 Benson and Hedges Cup final

Picture: Derek Stingemore, Kent Messenger, PD1673784

Not by a long stretch: Graham Cowdrey is astonished to be given out leg before in the Benson and Hedges Cup final

Picture: Ady Kerry, Kent Messenger, PD1678847

Aravinda de Silva launches another six in the Benson and Hedges final

Picture: Ady Kerry, Kent Messenger, PD1675505

happened had Graham Cowdrey batted a few more overs, but we didn't bowl as well as we could have done first up in the morning anyway."

After Cowdrey's dismissal, De Silva prolonged his assault beyond tea and a brief break for rain but Matthew Fleming and Mark Ealham fell cheaply and, with 10 overs remaining, the asking rate had risen to 8.6 an over. In his final salvo De Silva pulled an Ian Austin bouncer into the Mound Stand but, in trying to repeat the stroke, picked out Graham Lloyd on the ropes at deep midwicket to go for 112. A dumbstruck Marsh shovelled Austin's next delivery into the hands of John Crawley and Kent tumbled to a 35-run defeat with 17 balls remaining.

De Silva had to be cajoled by his team-mates into accepting the man-of-the-match award from Ian Botham afterwards. If Botham, the chairman of the gold award committee, had got his way the medallion would have gone to Atherton instead. Barely 15 minutes earlier Botham had told his fellow adjudicators, *Manchester Evening News* correspondent Colin Evans, and me: "Well guys, the way I see it, Atherton has to get it. He created the pressure with his 93 at the top of the order and Kent cracked trying to get the runs." Colin and I had to enlist the support of the former England captain and BBC commentator, Tony Lewis, before finally convincing Botham. De Silva thus became the first and only gold award winner to emerge from the losing side in all 31 B&H finals.

Fulton suggests that some of the Kent players believed the outcome was effectively decided off the field. "Some of the lads said it was because Lancashire turned up on a coach and in matching suits, while we had rocked up in our cars and wearing training kit. This sort of thing became a legitimate gripe in the eyes of one or two senior players, who argued that Lancashire were much better prepared."

To their credit, Kent and De Silva dusted themselves down to make a late tilt at the Sunday League title. They had secured an edgy four-run win against Derbyshire at The Mote, courtesy of Ealham's record-breaking 44-ball hundred, before setting out on a six-match winning run stretching from 18 July through to the final game of the season. With two matches remaining they were joint top and, in a magnanimous show of unity, De Silva opted to extend his stay with the club by a week against the wishes of his home cricket board, enabling him to play a pivotal innings in a seven-wicket away win over Lancashire.

Having already missed Sri Lanka's opening Test against India, De Silva reluctantly said his goodbyes and told the *Kent Messenger* that he was disappointed not to be able to see the job through. "I was criticised in the newspapers back home but I didn't want to go back on my word to Kent. Now, I'm afraid, I have to put my commitments to Sri Lanka first." He then handed me a rustic, hand-crafted brass incense burner as a parting gift. An inscription underneath read: 'With the best compliments of Aravinda de Silva'. I have treasured it since.

Kent explored the possibility of registering Hooper for the final league game, but TCCB regulations prohibited it, so Fulton was asked to fill De Silva's boots at St Lawrence on 17 September, when Kent crossed swords with their old adversaries Warwickshire. Just 24 hours earlier Warwickshire had clinched their second successive championship title at the ground and had celebrated well into the night. Fulton remembers being struck by the contrast between the two sides' attitude. "They didn't even warm up for the Sunday game using a bat and ball, they just kicked a football about. Yet we had Ceefax up on the dressing-room TV and Benny asking people to stay out the back of the dressing room to give him weather reports. I couldn't believe it; there was no way we were going to win that game."

Invited to bat first in a match reduced to 35 overs, Kent infuriated an 8,000-strong crowd with a below-par batting display; when it mattered most they had again choked under pressure. Only Nigel Llong offered sustained resistance with 50 from 48 balls as Kent toiled to 166. Warwickshire emerged to savage an anxious home attack, Neil Smith biffing a 40-ball fifty before news arrived that the game involving favourites Worcestershire had been abandoned. In a surreal atmosphere of Kentish celebrations, Warwickshire

Despite defeat in their final game, Kent won the Sunday League title in 1995
Picture: Derek Stingemore, Kent Messenger, PD1673786

cantered over the win line with 10 balls to spare. Kent, Warwickshire and Worcestershire all finished level on 50 points, but Kent's superior run rate meant their 17-year wait for a trophy was finally over.

There was an overriding emotion of relief in the dressing room, where McCague playfully doused me with lager as I attempted to conduct interviews. With hindsight, Ealham believes the team's lacklustre performance was predictable. He says: "The way we lost the last game was a very 'Kent' thing to do at the time; to blow the important game had become a bad habit. That was disappointing, but because it was a league played over the course of the season, we still all felt we deserved to win the title. It was a huge relief and a great evening in the pavilion. It was a throwback to the old days when the players, supporters, committee and the office staff all celebrated together."

Llong recalls that although De Silva was in the middle of a Test match in Kandy, he still found time to contact his, by now, former team-mates. "He rang us on the dressing-room phone to congratulate everyone. That was typical of him, not all of our overseas players would have thought to do that." During a flying visit to Kent the following month, De Silva collected his richly deserved winners' medal.

Benson was not the only player to be made aware of the members' reaction to a season of such extreme highs and lows. Llong says: "If you saw us from Monday to Saturday we were awful, but come Sunday morning we always felt it was our day and did some phenomenal things to win games. We'd done something special, yet the members still viewed it as our worst season ever. But I have a winners' medal on my mantelpiece at home and that's all I care about now."

Both Benson and Foster maintain that the decision to leave key bowlers out of championship games was a correct one. Foster reflects: "I took the view that we needed to win and learn how to celebrate instead of being runners-up and disappointed. There is no doubt we should have avoided finishing bottom in the championship. However, I still believe that in the overall context of the entire season we made the right decision."

In honour of De Silva, five Kent players – Cowdrey, Marsh, McCague, Fleming and Igglesden – pooled resources to put a racing filly into training with Cowdrey's step-mother, Lady Herries. Cowdrey, nicknamed 'Van' after his musical hero, Van Morrison, had already attracted headlines for naming that summer's one-time Derby favourite, Celtic Swing, after a Morrison song. This time he chose Aravinda, and he and the other syndicate members pitched up to watch her maiden race. Disappointingly, she ran just as badly as her namesake and was soon put out to pasture.

SEVEN

1996-98: Good Cop, Bad Cop

EVEN THOUGH Kent's trophy famine was over, members still called for heads to roll after the county's worst finish in championship history. One supporter led an unsuccessful campaign to force an extraordinary general meeting, in a bid to oust the committee. Another, speaking at the annual meeting on 4 March, labelled Daryl Foster a mercenary, suggesting that his coaching credentials failed to compensate for a lack of passion for all things Kentish.

Although he was not at the meeting, Foster was clearly shaken by the accusations and said: "I can assure you and all the members that I am not a mercenary and I do have a passion for Kent cricket." He acknowledges now that the backlash was inevitable, adding: "The county members regarded winning the County Championship to be the pinnacle, what the team should be judged upon. Success in the Sunday League was not rated highly by the committee or diehard supporters."

Mark Benson's immediate response was one of disappointment. "I've been to meetings in seasons when we haven't won anything and heard that we'd done OK," he said. "Then, when we finally do win something, we get loads of criticism." Steve Marsh also took a side-swipe at the hard-to-please members, saying: "If criticism comes from people I respect, like my captain, coach or other players, then I might take it to heart. But I don't take too much notice of outside comments. As far as I'm concerned the team has gone from strength to strength in the last four years. We've had one blip in the championship and people seem to want to crucify us for it."

The cricket committee appointed Benson captain for a sixth successive season, but he re-injured his knee during a pre-season game of five-a-side football and, despite prolonged recuperation, was ultimately forced to admit defeat. He retired after 290 games for the county, during which he scored 18,284 runs at an average of 40.27. He hit 48 hundreds and 98 half-centuries for the club – "it would have been nice to round up those figures," he admits – and still stands 11th on Kent's all-time leading run-scorers' list.

"With hindsight I probably captained too long because I felt it started to affect my own game," says Benson. "If you look at my own records, you'll see I always used to score stacks of runs at the beginning of a season but would then gradually, for one reason or another, tail off as the summer progressed. I'm quite a sensitive man and when you have to start leaving players out, they inevitably get grumpy with you and that used to affect my own performances. Unless you're very successful as a captain or coach I think three years is enough because people get fed up with hearing the same voice. It may well be that the committee felt there wasn't anyone ready to take over, but looking back I probably did it too long."

Marsh, who was officially installed as Benson's successor at the end of the summer, but captained the side throughout the 1995 season, pays this tribute: "Mark was the best player of quick bowling I've ever seen. Malcolm Marshall in his pomp thought Benny was the best and most frustrating opener he'd ever bowled at. He was brave, compact and unflappable, everything you want in a top player."

Although proud to become Kent's 27th club captain, Marsh hardly felt he had been welcomed into the post with open arms, and adds: "The club appointed me under sufferance really. I'd fallen into the job because of the injury to Benny and I'd done OK, so they had to give it me full time. It was obvious to me that they would get Jazzer [Matthew Fleming] in as soon as they could; I was just stalling them really."

Always one for a flutter, Marsh, having just banked £151,574 from his benefit year, still backed himself to be a success and quipped at the time: "At least I can pay off my account at Ladbrokes now." It was Marsh's gambler's instinct which helped engineer a 64-run win over Lancashire in Kent's championship curtain-raiser at Canterbury – their first win in their opening fixture for 23 years.

Contrivance between Marsh and his opposing captain, Mike Watkinson, left Lancashire the entire fourth day to chase 340. At 190 for two, they appeared the likelier winners until Martin McCague dismissed Neil Fairbrother, leaving Min Patel, with five for 28, to sweep Kent to victory. How Patel, a Manchester Polytechnic graduate, loved bowling against the Red Rose county. Starting with his seven for 75 in 1993, he improved his career-best figures three times against Lancashire.

Kent won by an innings over Essex at Chelmsford where, after hundreds from Marsh, Graham Cowdrey and Carl Hooper, Patel and Hooper bowled all bar 20 of the 198 overs needed to dismiss Essex twice. Patel returned match figures of 10 for 225, while Hooper was happy to be back in familiar surroundings after another year of Test underachievement with the West Indies. He had been fined after going absent without leave towards the end of the 1995 tour to England and team manager Wes Hall and coach Andy

Roberts were so exasperated by Hooper's failure to do himself justice that they advised him to seek counselling from Mike Brearley, the former England captain turned psychotherapist.

Marsh let his annoyance show when the game with Yorkshire at St Lawrence petered out in a dire draw on the spring Bank Holiday. Having had his suggestions for a run chase rebuffed by Yorkshire captain David Byas, Marsh unstrapped his wicketkeeping pads, marked out his run-up and joined the entire side in taking turns to bowl. Byas was unrepentant.

Without Benson at the top of his batting order Marsh, somewhat surprisingly, overlooked the selection claims of Neil Taylor, leaving him in the 2nd XI as captain. Clearly out of favour and surplus to requirements, Taylor later announced he would be joining Sussex. It was a sad end to an illustrious, if occasionally self-centred, 302-match career with Kent. He deserved a better send-off after scoring 17,721 runs at a tidy average of 39.82 and posting 42 hundreds for the county. Taylor, who had lost his first team place in July 1995, regretted that the "decision to leave was made for me, not by me". Obdurate to the end, Taylor marked his Sussex bow the following April with a century against Northamptonshire to become only the third batsman to post centuries on debut for two counties.

The opening batting berths remained a season-long problem for Kent, so much so that even the cavalier Fleming was asked to give it a try. Known universally as Jazzer, in reference to the 'Jazz hats' once worn by the boys at Fleming's old school, Eton College, he was a throwback to the amateur days when averages were regarded with disdain. Not surprisingly, his stint as makeshift opener proved a brief one.

On a seamers' pitch at The Nevill, Kent won a low-scoring match to move to the top of the championship table for the first time since 1988. Mark Ealham and Ben Phillips, on his debut, led the attack as Kent notched their first two-day victory in 17 seasons. With three victories under their belts by the end of May, Marsh's side had already matched their woeful win tally of 1995. Phillips, a strapping, likeable lad from Lewisham who played basketball out of season, quickly became a popular and ever-willing workhorse; a useful 'hit-the-deck' seamer and a capable late-order bat. But like Igglesden, the man he was meant to replace (and who failed to make an appearance all summer), Phillips proved frustratingly injury-prone early in his career.

After a brace of draws, Kent broke their Edgbaston bogey when Ealham outbowled Shaun Pollock to inspire a 36-run win over reigning champions Warwickshire. Ealham exploited muggy conditions superbly to return career-best figures of eight for 36 and both he and Patel were rewarded for their fine form with Test calls. Even without them, Kent managed an 83-run success over win-less Durham at The Mote, where Hooper again ruled supreme. After a first-innings 66, he stroked 105 from 78 balls for his third century in as many championship games in Maidstone.

I interviewed Hooper the following day while he watched a preview of the British Grand Prix on television. His obsession with Formula One was legendary. As Matthew Walker puts it: "If the game coincided with a grand prix, then you could forget about Hoops. He'd score a quick-fire fifty and get out so he could watch the race." A Michael Schumacher fanatic, Hooper offered me the entire field against the German driver for the Silverstone race. I readily accepted the £20 wager and, as it transpired, Schumacher retired three laps in, leaving Jacques Villeneuve to top the podium while I won the bet. On my next visit to Hooper's home he produced a crisp £20 note. But I declined, asking instead if he would give me one of his old bats some day.

It was on my recommendation of the new F1 game on Sony PlayStation that Hooper decided on a spur-of-the-moment spending spree. He sped to the Barretts Digital World store in Wincheap and paid in cash for a huge widescreen television, DVD and VHS players and a Dolby sound surround system. He spent so much that the manager agreed to throw in the PlayStation and games for free. The only problem was that the huge TV was too big to manoeuvre into his house, so he had to order a smaller set (which happened to be out of stock).

Back on the field, rain prevented Kent from securing a deserved win at Derby. On a sporting pitch, Hooper, Nigel Llong and Fleming all hit hundreds, but they lost Marsh with a broken left index finger after a blow from Devon Malcolm. Despite a career-best eight for 98 from Dean Headley, Derbyshire held out, though Kent still retained top spot. Headley also recorded what was to the first of a record-equalling three hat-tricks in a season. A few months earlier he had been denied another when the normally reliable Nick Knight dropped a slip catch on England A's tour of Pakistan.

Headley recalls of the Derby game: "I was having no-ball trouble and hated bowling at Kim Barnett. He'd walk all over the place as you approached and squared himself right up, but at the last second he just moved into line conventionally and would slap you for four. I sent down two no-balls and he hit me for two fours and after the first five balls of my opening over I'd conceded 12 runs. Marshy had chipped a finger, so I had Dave Fulton or 'Captain Peacock' as I called him then, behind the stumps. You could say things weren't looking good.

"Then I bowled one at Barnett that pitches on off stump and holds its line. He snicks off and Fulton, who could have caught it easily, decided to dive and catch it one-handed instead. Chris Adams got exactly the same ball: good length. he didn't know whether to play back or come forward, but it nipped away and went off the edge to Dave. That brought in Dean Jones, who asked Adams as they crossed, 'What's he doing with it?' He told him I was moving it away so, for my eighth ball of the over, I nipped one back in off the seam and trapped Jones leg before. So I'd bowled one over, three for 12!"

Once again, Kent's Cricket Week display, now with Hooper as acting captain, proved unsatisfactory as they slid to their first championship defeat of the season, a 192-run reverse against Worcestershire. Headley, dubbed 'Froggy' or 'Wide-Mouth Frog' because of his toothy grin, claimed a second championship hat-trick in successive games, but had nothing more to smile about as Alamgir Sheriyar skittled Kent for 108. Headley remembers: "The hat-trick was Tom Moody, to one that nipped back and bowled him; then in my next over, Reuben Spiring nicked an away-swinger to slip and I reversed one back into Vikram Solanki and took out his leg stump."

A deflated Hooper stood down from the captaincy after that reverse and defeat in the corresponding Sunday League game, Trevor Ward taking over as the fourth leader of the campaign. Ward took to the job surprisingly well as Kent landed an emphatic win at Wantage Road, where Northamptonshire capitulated in three days. Tim Wren, who now works as a plumber and central heating engineer, sparked the success with five for 45.

Ward skippered again on Kent's return to St Lawrence to take on Somerset in a game that went into the annals as Walker's match. Uncapped, recently restored to the side and aged just 22, Walker batted nine-and-half hours on a sublime pitch against a weak attack for his maiden double hundred. He plundered 41 fours in a magnificent unbeaten 275 out of Kent's total of 616 for seven, their highest on the ground. He broke the great Frank Woolley's ground-record score for a Kent player by five runs, but later that evening Walker confessed that he thought Ward's declaration had robbed him of a place in history.

He explained: "The boys said to me at lunch that 277 was the top score here, so when Trevor declared with me on 275 I thought, 'That's a bit bloody harsh.' It was only when they announced it over the public address that I realised what I'd actually done." He remained on the field for every ball of the match as Ward and Somerset captain Peter Bowler manufactured a target of 320 from 88 overs. Somerset were bowled out with eight overs remaining, giving Kent their sixth championship win of the season.

After the game, rumours began to circulate that press box doyen Jim Swanton had made an abortive attempt to keep Woolley's record intact.

Matthew Walker troops off with Dean Headley after his marathon innings against Somerset in 1996, still believing that Trevor Ward's declaration has denied him a record

Picture: Anthony Roberts

Walker says: "I've heard it from three different sources that Jim came up to our dressing room when I was on about 260 and confronted Trevor Ward. Apparently Swanton asked Trevor if he would declare soon. Wardy said, 'No,' and Swanton said, 'Well you do know he's getting close to Woolley's record, I think you should declare. We can't have a young player beating the great Woolley's record.'"

Ward is unable to confirm the story, but admits: "That's not to say it didn't happen. I have a head like a sieve when it comes to remembering most of my playing days." Walker believes that if Fleming, a player championed for the captaincy by Swanton well before he got the job in 1999, had been in charge the outcome might have been different. "Had Matthew been captain it probably would have happened; in my opinion Jazzer would have declared. With Swanton and the Band of Brothers in the background, it sometimes felt like we had a secret service out there controlling the club."

Marsh returned to the fold for the trip to Cardiff in late August, when rain and a fit of pique by Ottis Gibson frustrated Kent's tilt at an unlikely last-day victory. Kent's 323 for five declared was spread over the first three days of the game; Hooper top-scored with 77 to pass 1,000 runs for the season and also ensured, during one of the numerous breaks for drizzle, that I was presented with the autographed bat which I had asked for in lieu of cash payment for our Formula One wager at Maidstone. I have since loaned my most treasured item of cricketing memorabilia to the club for display in the Chiesman Pavilion trophy cabinets.

After a double forfeiture, only five hours remained and Marsh's initial run-chase deal with Matthew Maynard was thwarted by yet more rain. The skippers negotiated for a second time and, after Kent served up 50 quick runs, they shook hands on a second pact: Glamorgan would chase 110 from 13 overs on the understanding that they would see it through to the death. Neither captain had accounted for the reaction of Gibson, who had just discovered he was to be replaced by Waqar Younis. Armed with instructions to blast quick runs, Gibson stubbornly dug in and blocked everything. He was unbeaten on 12 when an exasperated Marsh shook hands on a draw.

With three games to go Kent remained on course for their first championship winners' pennant since 1978, but their limited-overs performances that year never reached the same levels of consistency. They lost eight times in a patchy defence of the AXA Equity and Law League title and could only finish 11th. Their one memorable performance came at Grace Road, where a head-to-head run-fest between Hooper and West Indies team-mate Phil Simmons resulted in a four-wicket win for Kent.

Simmons clubbed 139 from 105 balls in Leicestershire's 40-over total of 311 for four, then Hooper played a beautifully paced innings of 145, the then highest one-day score by a Kent player, to guarantee victory. One of his three sixes smashed a hole in the PVC weatherboarding beneath the roof of Leicestershire's indoor school, where it remains to this day. Hooper rated it as his finest limited-overs innings in terms of stroke play, but admitted that he was disappointed to get out with only three needed.

Walker remembers it as an extraordinary knock. "Carl and I added almost a hundred for the sixth wicket and I finished unbeaten with 18; that's how good he was. I spent the rest of the time open-mouthed, watching him from the other end. It was a serious innings and incredible to watch."

While performances of that ilk won Hooper many admirers, there were times when he let himself and the side down, be it through indifference to the team ethos or his poor time-keeping. Ahead of that season's Sunday League game with Essex at Ilford, Hooper contacted Foster to warn him that he had over-slept while visiting friends in London, but would do his best to get to the game on time.

Foster suggested that Hooper should arrive as surreptitiously as possible, so as not to alert Kent's supporters to his lateness. Meanwhile, Foster and Marsh asked the squad to vote on Hooper's inclusion. Almost to a man they wanted to select him, leaving Fulton, the sole objector, as 12th man. Hooper duly arrived 20 minutes into the game with his side already batting. Ignoring Foster's counsel, he paraded around the ground with kit bag slung over his shoulder and pads tucked under his arm and marched nonchalantly into the away dressing rooms. He went out to bat soon after at No 4, hit a sublime 73 from 57 balls and, in tandem with Fleming, who scored 112, added 91 inside 10 overs to help post a total that proved just beyond Essex's reach.

Kent went out of the B&H Cup to Northamptonshire in the quarter-finals and suffered a two-wicket defeat against Derbyshire in the second round of the NatWest Trophy. Going into September, Kent's sole focus was on winning the championship and their three-game run-in started well with a seven-wicket victory over Nottinghamshire at Tunbridge Wells that gave them a one-point lead at the top. On his return from injury, Ealham, an eleventh-hour inclusion when Phillips twisted his ankle warming up, took seven wickets in the game and player of the season McCague another eight.

Leicestershire were back in front after winning their game in hand, but Marsh was able to name a full-strength side for the final game at St Lawrence, where a stubborn Hampshire display almost put paid to Kent's title dream. Llong's career-best 130 helped Kent to an 87-run first-innings lead, but only

Dean Headley, David Fulton and Martin McCague stage a football-style routine to celebrate Headley's record-equalling third hat-trick in the 1996 season

Picture: Anthony Roberts

after Headley's record-equalling third hat-trick of the season had mopped up the Hampshire tail. "I got the first wicket quite unconventionally," Headley recalls. "We'd been peppering John Stephenson with short stuff and it looked as though he'd broken his hand, so I gave him another bouncer and he slashed it straight to third man. That exposed their ten and eleven, James Bovill and Simon Renshaw, who weren't the best batters you've ever seen. I'd got the ball reversing, felt on top of my game and, to top it all, I'd got umpire Ray Julian at my end looking to get into the record books for the most lbws in a season; there could only be one outcome. They both got full inswingers on the pads, up we went with the appeals and Ray raised his finger.

"Steve Marsh is a big Chelsea fan and he'd already come up with the idea of celebrating like Roberto Di Matteo if we took another hat-trick, so Pigsy [Martin McCague], Dave and I did exactly that."

Hampshire refused to wilt and Marsh was the only Kent batsman to reach fifty in their second innings, leaving a last-day target of 299. A broken wrist left

Stephenson incapacitated, yet Hampshire were still able to canter to 143 for one by 1.56pm on the Monday afternoon. In the next 42 action-packed minutes Kent took Hampshire's last eight wickets for seven runs to secure an astonishing 148-run triumph. McCague initiated the collapse with a 17-ball burst of five for three down the Nackington Road slope. Marsh was forced to stand four yards further back than normal as McCague bagged the first hat-trick of his Kent career. It was also the first instance of two hat-tricks in a match at St Lawrence.

Again the celebration was borrowed from the world of football. Fulton explains: "Macca celebrated his hat-trick like Fabrizio Ravanelli when he scored for Middlesbrough, pulling up his shirt and hooking it over the back of his head. For obvious reasons that soon became known as the 'Macca seven bellies'." McCague himself recalls: "The silly thing was, you can't see an awful lot when you pull your shirt up over your head and start running around. So the guys at mid-on and mid-off were in real danger once I started celebrating."

Fleming was left to polish off Hampshire with a golden-armed six-ball spell of three for nought. Having seen the side maintain their title chase in such spectacular fashion, Foster ran from the dressing rooms to congratulate his protégé McCague. From the other side of the ground, that year's president, Robin Baker White, galloped ruddy-faced from the hospitality units in the Les Ames Stand, clutching a bottle of champagne to toast Kent's remarkable turnaround. Baker White, a gentleman farmer and land owner whose palatial home lying off the Nackington Road overlooks Street End Cricket Club's quaint ground, hoisted the county flag to mark each of Kent's championship successes. With his beloved county 15 points behind the leaders going into the final round of games, he wanted nothing more than to raise it once more. Sadly, he did not have the opportunity.

Kent's title dream went unrealised when they crashed to a 10-wicket defeat inside three days at Bristol, effectively handing the champions' pennant to Leicestershire. In overcast conditions and on a seamer-friendly pitch, Kent struggled to cope with pace, bounce and an occasional shooter from the country's leading wicket-taker, Courtney Walsh, as they succumbed for 154 and 117 in their worst display of the summer. While Gloucestershire knocked off the 31 they needed, a distraught Hooper abandoned his fielding duties and disappeared into the dressing rooms to phone home and organise his flights out. Kent were restricted to four bonus points in suffering only their second defeat of the campaign and slipped to fourth in the final championship standings.

Recalling yet another near miss, Marsh says: "If you analyse the dressing room of that period we had quite a few fragile characters. When it came to a war, you couldn't quite depend on everyone turning up. Natural ability and talent is only 40 per cent of it, it's the determination in your heart and your head that makes up the other 60 per cent towards a winning team mentality. Too many people had a lack of self-belief."

Chris Penn, who had come even closer to winning the championship with Kent in 1988, was forced to retire from the game with so little to show for his haul of 296 first-class wickets over a 15-year career. A whole-hearted seam bowler and all-round good guy, Penn later underwent surgery to remove a rib in order to cure the circulatory problem to his right arm and shoulder that dogged his final seasons with Kent. He moved into coaching, firstly with the England and Wales Cricket Board and more recently at St Edmund's School in Canterbury.

1997

A new broom swept through St Lawrence following Kent's Jekyll and Hyde campaign of the previous summer; the appointment of Steve Marsh, as full-time captain, and New Zealander John Wright, as first team coach, followed in its wake. Although it was barely two years since Daryl Foster had led the county to their first title in 17 years, he had been cold-shouldered by a handful of the club's more vociferous supporters who refused to forgive him for overseeing Kent's first championship wooden spoon since 1895.

Clearly fed up with a lack of support from factions on the committee and fans alike, he chose to resign, despite being offered improved terms of £35,000 a year. He explains: "I had a year left on my contract and a further three-year option clause, so I asked the county to exercise that option and give me a further four years as coach. The committee only granted me a one-year option, in other words a further two years. By that stage I'd been coaching for 26 first-class seasons and even though I didn't recognise it at the time, it had been a long and tiring journey. There were other personal considerations as well. At home, my father's health had deteriorated and, as an only child, I felt I should be there. We also had grandchildren to enjoy." Foster became principal of the University of Western Australia's residential hall.

In explaining the committee room thinking of the day, Marsh adds: "The club made it known they didn't want Daryl back for 1997, even though I did. So Daryl left us, and I played a big part getting John in. Some big names like Kepler Wessels and Mike Gatting came up during discussions, but Wrighty was also on the shortlist. Once I spoke to him, I felt he was by far the best candidate and the guy for us. I'd played against him at the start of my career

Welcome to the club: Kent captain Steve Marsh with newly capped signings (left) Paul Strang and Alan Wells in 1997

Picture: Derek Stingemore, Kent Messenger, PD1673788

when he was finishing up at Derbyshire. I remembered he'd been a gutsy player who knew his own game and felt he had half a chance of being a decent coach. I did all the pre-season training that year and Wrighty pitched up with a couple of weeks to go. We'd done some team-building things, like go-carting and paint-balling, and the mood was good."

Mark Ealham was not the only player to be disappointed by Foster's departure. "It was Daryl who first came in and made a real impact," he says. "He was very influential on me starting to play well. Certain players in the side, and I was one of them, got a bit of stick for our shape and size, but Daryl brought a different approach and discipline to what we were doing. He used to stand about at training blowing his whistle and making us run our arses off. It was a tough time for a couple of years, but when you look back, we needed it and, in many ways, Daryl was ahead of his time. I was left thinking that maybe he left us a bit early."

Although it was not widely known at the time, Foster's successor already had ties to the county. Wright starred for Kent League side Holmesdale during the drought summer of 1976 and also made a handful of Kent 2nd XI appearances. Kent decided against making a contract offer, but he went on to spend 12 seasons with Derbyshire. He won 82 Test caps as a no-nonsense left-handed opener and though he retired from first-class cricket in 1992 he maintained his links with the game through radio commentary and media work. At the time of Kent's approach he was making an off-season crust as national sales manager for a Christchurch-based food manufacturers and bakers. Once described by Gerald Mortimer, the former cricket correspondent of the *Derby Evening Telegraph*, as "probably the nicest man in the world", Wright needed little persuasion to give up his day job and return to Kent as first team coach.

He proved a big hit that first season with his relaxed approach to coaching, but his laidback demeanour masked a fiercely determined personality. After all, this was a man who once glued a pair of gloves to his bat handle in order to perfect a new grip. Describing his coaching philosophy at the time, Wright said: "If you think you know it all at this game you're making your first big mistake. I'm still learning every day and there are always areas where the players can improve."

Marsh was keen to instil a no-blame culture into the dressing room for his first official season as captain. "I told the lads I wanted everyone to enjoy their cricket, to express themselves and that I'd give anyone a chance just as long as they were showing me some decent form. I didn't expect them back in their hotel rooms by 11pm. How could I? But what I did say was that if they couldn't perform the next day then it wouldn't be good for their careers. What I wanted to do was cut out all the excuses. If anyone messed up, it would be down to them, not me, and if they went wrong too often they'd be out of the side."

In the absence of Hooper through Test commitments, Marsh and Wright picked little-known Zimbabwean leg-spinner Paul Strang as their overseas professional. He proved a popular choice. Marsh explains: "There were a few names on the list, but Strang was the man I wanted. He was doing well for Zimbabwe and, being a leg-spinner, was something we hadn't ever had in our side during my time. He was something a bit different and we knew he was really enthusiastic about coming. It just seemed the ideal fit."

Recalling the day Strang first met the squad, Matthew Walker says: "When they announced the signing I didn't know much about him. But he arrived and came across to the nets wearing this big sun hat and went around the guys one by one, introducing himself. Straightaway he came across as a good bloke. He fitted in so well and united everyone. He was a real team man and a decent bowler. He chipped in with his runs and was fantastic in the field. Paul had a lot to do with how well we played that year. He wasn't the greatest overseas player we'd ever had by any stretch of the imagination, but he was so enthusiastic." Despite his reservations about Foster's departure, Ealham both welcomed the injection of fresh ideas from Wright and Strang's sociability.

Mark Benson's retirement, Hooper's absence and Neil Taylor's move to Hove left Kent with a huge chasm in their top-order batting and deposed Sussex captain Alan Wells was the man they signed to fill it. At 35, Wells was controversially lured to St Lawrence, after 16 years at Hove, with an unprecedented five-year contract. It was a move which annoyed a section of the membership and left some players feeling uneasy.

Trevor Ward remembers: "I rated Alan as one of the best players in county cricket. Every time we played against Sussex he scored hundreds against us for fun, so I was very much in favour of his signing. But I did think five years was a long contract given his age. If you spoke to Alan, he'd be honest and say he never found the form he had at Sussex with Kent."

David Fulton had yet to cement his place in the Kent side, but was still able to take a detached view of Wells's long-term contract. "It may have raised a few eyebrows that Alan got a five-year deal, but I was too young to worry about it. Good luck to him I said. But to me, that was part of the problem culturally at Kent. Too many people worried about everyone else and not themselves. Lots of people would be jumping around saying, 'Why has Wells got a five-year deal when I've only been given two?' To me, it didn't actually affect my life one jot if I'm in the team with a one-year deal, when Alan has five. If I delivered, I knew I'd get properly looked after; if I didn't then I'd be out on my ear. That's the nature of it."

Wells himself was just looking forward to a more peaceful existence. The publication of his diary of the 1994 season, *The Captain's Year*, had caused ructions at Hove, with its unswerving criticism of some of the senior players, and had led to his being stripped of the captaincy. Wells's upbeat note, when interviewed for the *Kent Messenger*, was: "Kent have always been an exciting team to watch and play against and I'm really looking forward to the move. I'm a Sussex man born and bred so I will be sad to leave, but I have my reasons. It wasn't the fact that four other players left that made my mind up to go; it was the way the club handled the change of captaincy that initiated all the upheaval."

In another unusual move that both peeved their supporters and flew in the face of a time-honoured St Lawrence tradition that 'Kent caps should be earned before they are awarded', the club handed county caps to Wells and Strang even before a ball had been bowled in anger.

The year started on a low note for Ealham when he arrived home from a pre-season holiday to find the basement of his cottage in Elham flooded by a burst water pipe, ruining his stock of cricket bats and equipment. Fortunately, the England all-rounder had just signed a new kit sponsorship deal with Gray-

Nicolls. It took yet more water, in the form of last-day rain showers over Canterbury, to prevent Derbyshire from securing a championship win in the opening round of games.

Over the four days Dean Headley and Fulton (the latter fractured a finger) both picked up injuries and, having sent down only three wicket-less overs in the match, Min Patel ruptured ligaments in his right knee later that week, playing for Bexley in a Kent League clash with Bromley. He underwent cruciate reconstruction surgery for the second time in his career and missed the rest of the season. During this era Kent's supporters became wearily accustomed to the weird and wonderful ways the players discovered to sustain injuries. Fulton, a junior England chess international who also represented the University of Kent at boxing and football, once missed Kent's pre-season when, following his introduction as a substitute for the UKC team, he broke his leg without even touching the ball after making an ill-advised challenge.

Despite their rash of injuries, Kent maintained an unbeaten run in all forms of cricket into May, only to slide to a final-day home defeat against Glamorgan. Struggling Sussex threatened to pull off a win at Horsham until Marsh and Ben Phillips joined forces in a 10th-wicket stand of 183 (then the sixth highest last-wicket partnership in championship history). Phillips hit an unbeaten 65, while Marsh's 142 was the highest score of his career. With Ealham and Headley missing on international duty and Strang unable to bowl with a chipped finger, Martin McCague stepped up to complete Kent's fightback with a match-winning haul of seven for 82.

Strang soon shook off his injury to score a vital 73 at Trent Bridge, where Kent won by an innings after he and Ealham (122) continued the trend of the wagging tail by adding 171 for the ninth wicket. Strang and Julian Thompson polished off Warwickshire at The Nevill, where a patient unbeaten 62 from Wells saw them home with six overs remaining and lifted Kent to second in the table. It also completed their third win over Warwickshire in the space of 13 days. The bogey had been laid once and for all.

Phillips was again the surprise batting star at Old Trafford, scoring his maiden first-class hundred as nightwatchman in a 58-run triumph over Lancashire. Marsh's men moved top after Strang, with match figures of 11 for 186, bowled them to victory with only seven balls to go. Poor batting in both innings led to a shock defeat to Durham at Chester-le-Street; then, with Igglesden back in the fold for the first time since 1995, Kent lost a rain-ruined game against Northamptonshire at The Mote by one wicket and dropped to fourth in the table.

After a stunning campaign for Cambridge University, Ed Smith was selected for his season's championship bow at Canterbury but was unable to prevent reigning champions Leicestershire from securing a six-wicket win. Although Ealham spent almost seven hours compiling 139 and Marsh unselfishly declared when unbeaten on 98 to set up a run chase, Kent ultimately slipped to a third successive defeat.

They broke the sequence, but only just, by beating Middlesex inside two-and-a-half days on a sporting pitch at Lord's. After the loss of 19 wickets on day one, Fulton batted for more than three hours with a broken left knuckle, making a priceless 45 as Middlesex were set 261 for victory. An unbeaten century from Mark Ramprakash took Middlesex to the cusp of victory before Strang had last man Phil Tufnell caught close in to wrap up a memorable four-run win two balls after lunch. The finish proved so tight that the lunchtime edition of that day's *Evening Standard* ran with the headline 'Ramprakash Steers Middlesex to Victory'. Fulton summed up the players' view of the pitch with the vivid description: "The ball would go up your nose on that."

Kent returned to the top following an innings win over Essex in Canterbury Week. Although Cambridge Blue Will House failed on his senior debut, Wells hit his maiden hundred for the club and Fleming a career-best 138 in Kent's total of 525 for nine declared. An intimidating four-wicket burst by McCague forced Essex to follow on and Strang polished them off with five for 119. Over the course of the season the Zimbabwean sent down 733 overs, twice the number of any other Kent bowler, taking 63 wickets at the modest rate of 30.62 runs apiece. He also completed the mini-double by passing 500 runs.

Fulton was struck by the contrast between the enigmatic Hooper and the ever-willing Strang. "I loved Hoops, he was brilliant for Kent," says Fulton. "But as a batting unit we relied too heavily upon him. He was head and shoulders above all of us, and subconsciously we probably felt that, no matter what the position, Hoops would get us out of the mire. He probably felt the pressure of that too. Strang was a breath of fresh air. He wasn't a superstar, just a guy who mucked in. All of a sudden, as a batting unit we felt that someone had to step up to the mark and score Hoops's runs."

Kent's next four-day game, at Taunton, ended in a memorable draw with the scores level after Marsh and Fleming, needing seven off the final over to beat Somerset, could only muster six. The match also lingered in the memory for Martin McCague's agonising attack of the yips. The Irishman cut his run-up yet lost his rhythm and self-belief to such an extent that he struggled even to let go of the ball. He sent down a series of wides, bumpers and beamers to concede 22 runs in 2.1 overs before a slow beamer to Rob Turner led umpire

Alan Whitehead to step in and force Marsh to withdraw McCague from the attack.

Describing the incident in his book *The Gloves are Off*, Marsh wrote: "Any umpire with an ounce of reason and compassion would have been able to understand the situation and show a bit of lenient common sense. Not Alan Whitehead. His usual domineering over-zealousness in stopping him bowling compounded Martin's loss of confidence and we basically lost our principal strike bowler for a season."

Despite securing five points for finishing level when batting fourth, Kent had missed the chance to go top and so travelled to Portsmouth trailing leaders Glamorgan by two points. Although Smith hit his maiden championship hundred, persistent rain ruined any chance of a result against Hampshire, but a thumping 272-run victory over Gloucestershire at St Lawrence took Kent into a 12-point lead at the start of September. The game had turned on the third day, when Wells and Ward posted a 193-run partnership inside 43 overs for Kent's third wicket. Wells reached his 1,000 runs for the summer, while Ward hit 15 fours in his first century in just over a year. Headley finished the job off with five for 92.

If Kent were to stifle the continued challenge of Glamorgan they needed to beat third-placed Yorkshire at Headingley, but once again their top-order batting frailties proved their undoing. Set to chase 240 at barely three an over Kent slumped to 48 for five, leaving Ealham and Fleming to bat out the final three hours for a draw. Going into the last round of games Kent trailed Glamorgan by only a point, but a dramatic opening day against Surrey all but put paid to their chances of claiming the title. Nineteen wickets fell on the opening day at St Lawrence as Surrey were shot out for 124, only for Kent to wobble to 217 for nine in reply and secure a single batting bonus point.

Umpires Trevor Jesty and Whitehead reported the pitch as 'poor', leaving ECB pitch inspector Harry Brind little choice but to hand the club a 10-point penalty, suspended for 12 months. The punishment represented a dreadfully unsatisfactory end to a distinguished 28-year career for head groundsman Brian Fitch, who had just announced his retirement. Kent rallied strongly through Fulton's maiden championship century to reach the 275 they needed for a five-wicket victory, but by then news of Glamorgan's win over Somerset had filtered through. It left Kent as championship runners-up for the third time in a decade. Graham Cowdrey's succinct verdict was: "I'm sick of second place. I just feel flat."

Wright managed to sound a defiant note, saying: "I don't regard Kent as a team of bottlers. They are a hard-working unit desperate for success, but I have always stressed the need for people to take responsibility for their own performances. We all have to learn to respond better in these pressure situations. If we crack it once, we will go on and win a stack of titles."

It was much the same story for Kent in one-day cricket that summer, when another exhilarating Benson and Hedges Cup run ended ignominiously with an eight-wicket drubbing by Surrey in the final. Kent suffered their sixth successive Lord's defeat after Marsh's gamble to bat first backfired. Having restricted Kent to 212 for nine, Surrey romped home on an easing pitch with five overs to spare, courtesy of Ben Hollioake's sumptuous 98. It was no coincidence, perhaps, that six of the Kent side, Fleming, Ward, Ealham, Cowdrey, Marsh and McCague, had also featured in the cup final defeats of 1992 and 1995.

Looking back, Marsh says: "I wouldn't dispute that we got something wrong to lose so many finals, but maybe we were a bit unlucky too. People seem to forget we were playing against sides with considerable quality. Look at that Surrey side: they had Alec Stewart, Graham Thorpe, the Hollioake brothers, Mark Butcher, Ali Brown, Chris Lewis, Saqlain Mushtaq and Martin Bicknell. On paper they were a better side than us." He remembers one of the national papers' cricket correspondents suggesting that Kent had developed a knack for 'bottling it' on the big occasion. "That never made sense to me. Surely if you're going to 'bottle it' you'd do that in the semi-final rather than at Lord's? I just think we under-performed on the day, possibly because our top players didn't come to the party often enough, or had character flaws."

Some of the Kent players had been convinced that Lancashire's professionalism off the pitch was critical to their victory in the 1995 final. This time they got too caught up in trying to look the part. Nigel Llong admits: "The way we prepared for that final was horrendous. We had team meetings galore about which hotel we should stay in, what we should wear to the ground and who should supply us with clothes, but at no point did we sit down and talk tactics or how we should bowl to Ali Brown and Mark Butcher. I think we went into the game under-prepared. We weren't going there to win, just to take part and, if I'm honest, I don't think Graham Cowdrey should have played. He went into it with a bad leg and passed himself fit on the morning, but couldn't really move."

Fulton also believes that Kent were guilty of taking their eye off the ball in the build-up to the game. "We all had matching blazers, yet they turned up looking like rag-bags and all rocked up at different times and still they spanked us. Suddenly people started to realise what matters most is what happens on the field of play during the match; that's all that really counts. You either seize the moment or you don't. What you wear to the ground, what transport you arrive in, is just a small component of your preparation. It's not the whole reason you win or lose."

Kent's interest in the NatWest Trophy ended with a first-round defeat by Middlesex, but they were confronted with another crunch match in the AXA Life Sunday League. With 12 wins from 16 starts Kent's destiny lay in their own hands as they travelled to Headingley for the final round of games but, once again, they saved their worst for last. Yorkshire were playing for pride alone, but Darren Lehmann's unbeaten 78 off 68 balls allowed them to romp to a seven-wicket win with 10 overs to spare. Kent's misery was compounded by a victory for Warwickshire over Gloucestershire which allowed them to steal the title.

Marsh reflects: "At the end Dean Headley came up to me and said thanks for the most enjoyable season he'd ever had. Although we didn't win anything, we'd taken great enjoyment out of revelling in each other's successes. That showed in our performances that year. When the top order failed, the bottom five battled away and helped the side to a decent score, but that's also the answer to why we kept finishing second. Had we scored more runs, we'd have probably won all three competitions." Marsh also believes that he and Wright complemented each other well. "Wrighty was brilliant that season. He was good cop to the team and I played bad cop, by giving them a rollicking if I had to, and it worked really well."

Although it was widely assumed that Hooper would return the following summer, Marsh lobbied for a different approach. "I felt we needed Paul, or a character like him, back for 1998 so that we could build on what we'd done that season. But the Kent committee refused to pay off Hoops in order to keep Paul, so that was that." Strang, who was recruited by Nottinghamshire the following season, was joined on Kent's released list by Tim Wren and Nick Preston.

1998

I was at St Lawrence conducting interviews for *Kent Messenger*'s pre-season cricket supplement when I witnessed the embarrassing final throes of the county's failed bid to lure Chris Adams to Canterbury. The Derbyshire batsman arrived at the ground inside a chauffeur-driven Rolls-Royce, sitting beside his agent Jonathan Barnett. John Wright and Steve Marsh were part of the welcoming party, but Barnett soon found himself backed into a corner by Kent's secretary, former brigadier Stuart Anderson. Once installed in the club offices, Anderson informed Barnett that he was not prepared to negotiate terms through an agent.

Recalling the day with a smile, Adams says: "The secretary was adamant he wouldn't conduct any dealings with Jonathan present, so with that, we just got up and walked out. If you wanted to attract a future player, then Kent went about it completely the wrong way that day." Adams and Barnett did eventually meet up with Wright and Marsh, to examine how any potential deal might be structured, but the damage had already been done. "I knew as we drove away from Canterbury that first time I wouldn't be joining them," says Adams. "We talked it through in the car and dismissed Kent. Not because it isn't a nice place to play, but simply because I felt that wasn't the right way to deal with people or go about your business."

Although their antiquated stance caused Kent to miss out on Adams – he figured, instead, in an era of unprecedented success for Sussex – at least it gave Wright an opportunity to blood the plethora of young batsmen coming through the ranks: Ed Smith, Chris Walsh, Matthew Banes, Jamie Ford, Will House, James Hockley and Rob Key. Incredibly, the first four had all been born at the same

Over and out: the life of the county cricketer finally lost its appeal for Graham Cowdrey
Picture: Ady Kerry, Kent Messenger, PD1673875

maternity unit in Penbury, near Tunbridge Wells, and went on to play at Tonbridge School under cricket master Chris Stone, whose fine work led him to succeed Alan Ealham as Kent's 2nd XI coach.

The influx of Kentish young guns effectively signalled the end of Graham

Cowdrey's career and he retired soon after announcing a club record benefit of £303,000 – some £100,000 more than the previous best for Richard Ellison. It also ended a 48-year connection between Kent and the Cowdrey family that began with the debut of 17-year-old Colin in 1950. Graham says that he knew as early as mid-June that he had had enough. "It was actually a second team game down at Taunton, where we were staying in a quite abysmal B&B. It was one of those where the landlady locked the door at about eight o'clock and got annoyed if you rang the doorbell any later. I just remember sitting in the dressing room and listening to the conversation; you realise you're not a 19-year-old with great ambition anymore and so excited about playing at Taunton. I just made the decision there and then."

He was left with the feeling that Kent had all the tools to be multiple winners in one-day competitions in the early and mid-Nineties. "For a period of time, probably about four years, I think we had the best one-day side in the country," he says. "Looking back, we should have won four or five one-day trophies in those years."

If nothing else, Cowdrey, especially when in tandem with his long-time room-mate Steve Marsh, left a substantial legacy of anecdotes and practical jokes. He admits: "Over the years I did a lot of winding people up, Matthew Fleming most of the time because it used to annoy him so much. He was easy prey. I remember we were playing at The Mote. I don't know why I did it, but I thought I'd just annoy him by putting his car keys in Min Patel's cricket shoes. Anyway, it was about half past eight when he finally got through to me at home and said, 'Van, where the effing hell are my car keys?' And I said, 'What's happened?' Of course Min had chucked his cricket gear in the boot of his car and gone home to Dartford, leaving Jazzer stuck at The Mote. He didn't talk to me for quite a while after that."

Fleming was the victim of another set-up in Birmingham, when Marsh and Cowdrey hired two escort girls over the phone using Fleming's credit card, which they had lifted from his wallet earlier in the evening. While the pranksters waited within earshot, the girls knocked on Fleming's hotel room door, only to be met with his incredulous response of, 'I think there's been some terrible mistake.' The pair confirmed that the credit card number matched Fleming's and I am told that the penny dropped with Fleming almost immediately. Forever the gentleman, he tipped the escorts for their wasted trip before plotting his own retribution on Marsh and Cowdrey.

Marsh, at least, got his comeuppance soon after when he returned to yet another city centre hotel bedroom to find Cowdrey fast asleep. Feeling frazzled and dehydrated, Marsh went to the bathroom, drank a glass of water and sloped off to his bed. He was woken the next morning by Cowdrey, asking, 'Marshy, what did you do with that glass of water I left in the bathroom last night?' A groggy Marsh replied, 'I drank it of course,' before being told that it had contained cleaning solution and both of Cowdrey's contact lenses.

Following Kent's three near misses of 1997, John Wright spent the winter studying the winning formulas of successful sporting sides from across the globe. He returned to St Lawrence with a locker-full of psychological ideas which he hoped would give Kent the winning edge so obviously lacking the previous summer. He even persuaded bowling consultant Graham Dilley to return to his old club in a bid to inspire the seamers during pre-season training.

Marsh was already aware that the players were responding less enthusiastically to his "up and at 'em" style of captaincy, and there was a further complication. "In '98 Wrighty came back a different person," he recalls. "He'd maybe got a little bit more confident after a year in the job and decided to take on my role. He came up with this idea for a mission statement, a 'corps covenant' that he wanted us all to buy into, which was fine, but surely you can't live or die by it?"

Nigel Llong could already sense, in Kent's build-up to the new season, that the players were not buying into Wright's vision. "I remember spending two-and-a-half days of pre-season over in Lucky's Bar going through this corps covenant John had introduced. We wasted time doing that while the sun shone, but then, once we went out to start netting, it rained. John very nearly strangled us; I remember Will House having to bat in the nets with the collar of his shirt in his mouth to help try and keep his head tucked in as John wanted. It meant Will couldn't move, was off balance, falling over and missing every ball. We all play a different way, so when John tried to make wholesale changes it blew up in his face.

"We went from being a bat-first-and-defend one-day side to being a side that chased. But we couldn't chase chickens, let alone runs. It was a terrible game plan for us. We didn't have grinders to get us over the line, we had a team of biffers and, with our attack, generally fancied our chances of defending anything. But Wrighty wanted to change all that."

The good cop, bad cop regime which had worked so well for Wright and Marsh the previous summer was now, in Marsh's words, "bad cop, bad cop". If the side were being asked to adopt an alien game plan in one-day cricket, they also felt straitjacketed in the four-day game. "In championship cricket John just wanted our openers to bat time," says Marsh. "They became frightened to play shots, whereas I just wanted them to use their brains and play it their way. Now, they all had excuses for failure.

"Our results as a team dipped quickly and problems started to appear in the dressing room. I knew some of it was coming from Jazzer; he was sowing the seeds for captaincy by murmuring about my 'off-the-field behaviour'. I called a squad meeting at Canterbury and gave them all an opportunity to fire me down and air the things they didn't like about me. It was 16 on to one potentially, but hardly a word was said. No one had the balls.

"By then, I knew what I had to say to the cricket committee wasn't counting for much and I became more and more disillusioned. I started to doubt myself, maybe my performances dropped a bit too, but for the first time I felt I couldn't be arsed with it all. By the end of the season Wrighty had become a trembling wreck. He wasn't inspiring us; if anything he was having the reverse effect."

The general unrest was reflected in the performances out in the middle, where Kent slid nine places down the championship table to finish 11th, with only five wins to their credit. Their tally of 18 batting bonus points was the second worst in the division. Only Carl Hooper posted 1,000 runs while vice-captain Trevor Ward, after suffering the embarrassment of being dropped for Canterbury Week, finished the summer with only 416 runs. Dean Headley was the lone bowler to take 50 wickets.

Highlights were few and far between, but opener Key made an impact with two centuries in his rookie season, including a maiden championship hundred in the innings win over Durham, only 10 days after his 19th birthday – making him the youngest player to score a hundred for Kent since Arthur Fagg in 1934 and the fourth youngest in the club's history. David Fulton's obdurate 207 against Yorkshire at The Mote was both Kent's first double hundred against the Tykes and, at 623 minutes, the longest ever innings by a Kent batsman. It also prevented defeat after Kent had followed on.

Despite Hooper's return to the fold Kent managed only eight AXA Life Sunday League victories to finish 14 points off the pace in fifth. They were dumped out of the NatWest Trophy by Warwickshire following an 167-run second-round drubbing at Edgbaston and lost by eight wickets to Leicestershire in a one-side Benson and Hedges Cup quarter-final at Grace Road.

Matthew Walker characterises Wright's period in charge as one of "endless meetings". One in particular sticks in his mind. "Three weeks from the end of the 1998 season we lost at home by an innings to Somerset. It was the match Andrew Caddick got his 100th wicket for the season, and we were hammered [the innings and 46-run reverse was Kent's heaviest defeat in three years]. We were all called together in the dressing room at around four o'clock and we were still there at 10 o'clock that night. I remember Chris Walsh was meant to be going up to London for an old boys' do. He had to nip out, make a quick call and send his apologies. It was madness: going round and round in circles.

> "Wrighty introduced this team-bonding idea that he'd nicked from the All Blacks. We wasted so much time on that, not just that year, but for the next five or six years. I reckon I lost days of my life sitting around dressing rooms and at pre-season camps working out what went in that bloody thing. Then he came up with an idea that we should mark each other out of 10 for honesty, work rate, discipline and two or three other things. Every fortnight or so we'd have a secret vote. You'd mark yourself and the team, then everyone else would mark you and you'd compare the results.
>
> "During a game at Lord's a few of the lads had enjoyed a late night and a couple of beers in London. At the next meeting they all got marked down to a six for poor discipline. That led to more arguments because they felt they still performed out on the pitch. Then, during a game of touch rugby in our warm-ups, Alan Wells broke through and scored a try and denied that I'd touched him. It was a laugh at the time, but at the next vote someone marked him down as a four for his lack of honesty. That's how ridiculous it got."

Although Hooper scored 1,999 runs in all forms of the game, at a healthy average of 46, even he knew his time with Kent was coming to an end. Having been persuaded to stay until the season's end by a cash-for-hundreds bonus deal, he signed off by scoring 62 in an hour to help Kent to a six-wicket home win over Somerset that clinched their place in the National League First Division for the following season.

After his farewell appearance, Hooper said: "I was really touched by the depth of feeling from everyone today. The ovation meant a lot to me. I may not be Kent born and bred and some would say I'm just an outsider, a professional playing for the cash, but after playing here for five seasons I do have a feeling for the club."

He describes his last year with Kent as his worst, "not in terms of performance, but because of the change of coach". He adds: "I thought Daryl was fantastic. Most times I'd arrive in England straight from a series in the Caribbean and he understood that I needed a couple of days' rest before starting up again for Kent. But that last year I arrived on the Thursday and there was a game about to start. I'd agreed over the phone with Wrighty to miss the first game and get on board for the next one. The following morning

I got a knock on my door early: it was Marshy and Wrighty and they wanted me to play there and then. That sort of set the tone for the rest of the season."

Hooper now lives in Adelaide, where he helps manage a chain of coffee shop bistros with his wife Connie and his two brothers-in-law (he also dabbles in currency trading). He believes that the county system continues to produce a "comfort zone", explaining: "You can play 10 to 15 years of county cricket, get a benefit, maybe a job for later on through one of your contacts and you're set up for life. You can't really blame Kent for that, though, that's the English system. But I think it's good to clean out the cabinet every so often and move players on; that didn't seem to happen much at Kent. Look how long Graham Cowdrey, Mark Ealham, Matthew Fleming and Trevor Ward all played for Kent without winning much. You need to let players know when they're coming in to the club that the minute their performances start petering out it'll be time to move on."

Hooper was, arguably, Kent's greatest overseas signing, yet he won nothing in his five seasons at the club. Those years brought him 6,714 first-class runs at an average of 50.48 – he is the only player in the county's history to finish with an average in excess of 50 after playing 25 games or more – as well as more than 4,000 one-day runs. If he was frustrated by the injuries which always seemed to afflict Kent's seamers when titles were up for grabs, team-mates found him both captivating and frustrating.

To Matthew Fleming he was a "flawed genius", adding: "When he was young and innocent and at his best, he was incredibly brilliant, but the time he should have being doing the most for Kent coincided with a time when he was all at sea personally. Hoops would admit that it was not a happy time in his life. Once he got over that initial, naive burst of brilliance and enthusiasm, he became the most cynical, money-minded, disruptive influence you could possibly have in the dressing room and a really tough man to captain.

"When he was good, he was very good, but when he was bad, he was equally very bad. When at his most positive he was a fantastic influence, but when he was being 'Bad Hoops' he could be appalling. We knew he had personal problems and I felt he found it very difficult to cope with the 'Brian Lara affect', how Brian got all the plaudits and the money while Hoops didn't."

With a fractured dressing room and on-field results moving in the wrong direction Kent reacted swiftly by sacking Marsh, not that he failed to see the axe falling. "People were phoning me up and saying stuff like, 'Don't you dare give up,' which was nice, but it was also a clear indication as to what was coming. Sure enough, I got a call from Derek Ufton [then chairman of cricket] to meet him and Wrighty. Derek spent 20 minutes talking pleasantries with me, chatting about Chelsea football and Charlton, but then I had to say, 'Hang on, Derek, let's talk about why we're really here.' He said there were a 'few elements' within the club who were talking about whether we needed a change of captain or not and that he wanted to get things settled. I said, 'Derek, let's be honest here, there is going to be change of captain isn't there? He finally said, 'Yes, there will be a change,' so I said, 'No problem, but now give me the reasons.'

"He went on to say I'd lost some important tosses, that some of the committee were at odds with my lifestyle and that they wanted to freshen things up, but other than that he never had much to hold against me. I put it to him that I felt Wrighty and I had worked really hard together. That we'd faced up to the players and the press hand-in-hand in order to try and get us through. I asked them both if they agreed with me. Derek and Wrighty both agreed 100 per cent. So I quickly responded, 'In that case, Derek, why am I getting the sack and John is keeping his job?' Strangely, neither of them could answer that one. So I said, 'Thanks very much,' and the meeting ended there and then."

Marsh's sacking led his father-in-law and former county opener, Bob Wilson, to resign from the Kent committee. In a comment piece for the *Kent Messenger* I wrote: "The truth is, Marsh has been made to pay for the under-achievement of fellow senior players at the club. It is they, as well as the committee, who should be hanging their heads in shame following this latest public relations disaster."

The worst-kept secret within the county was that Fleming aspired to the Kent captaincy, so it came as no surprise when the former Royal Green Jackets officer was appointed as Marsh's successor. Walker believes that there was a clear distinction between Fleming and his predecessors. "I think it was a huge personal thing for Jazzer. He wanted to become captain of Kent, whereas for Marshy and others since, it was a job they were simply invited to do." In Llong's view, "it was probably the right time for a change, but whether it was done the right way was questionable."

Fleming heard the news of his appointment in Bangladesh, where he was touring with England's one-day squad. He made it clear in his column for the *Cricketer International* magazine that he regarded it as rather more than a mere job. "It is an awesome responsibility, a source of enormous pride and the most exciting of all challenges. We must uphold the tradition, the integrity and the values of this great game. Yet, at the same time, we must not be fearful of taking bold and imaginative decisions to secure cricket's popularity and health well into the next millennium."

Mark Ealham, who was also on the Bangladesh trip, vividly remembers how he heard of Fleming's accession. "He called me and said, 'Ealy, can you come to my room please?' I thought, 'Certainly Lord Fleming!' I wondered at first if maybe someone had died back home. As I went into his room he was sat at his desk. Up to that moment he'd just been Jazzer, even to the point of taking snaps for his family album at England net sessions, which Bumble [then England coach David Lloyd] found hilarious.

"He summoned me to say, 'Ealy, I've been appointed captain of Kent and thought you should be the first to know.' I shook his hand, said congratulations and told him he'd have my backing. But the day he called me into that room was the day someone else came down, whipped out his character and threw another one in. Matthew came back from that tour a different bloke and that was the defining moment."

Recalling events in Bangladesh, Fleming says he was very much aware that Ealham was the other major contender for the post: "It was him or me, because I knew Wrighty had spoken to Mark about it. He was the only other obvious candidate. I felt that part of Ealy wanted the job, but in other areas he didn't really fancy it. After telling Ealy about the club's decision some idiot, I think it was Dougie Brown or Adam Hollioake, pinned up a sign on my hotel room door saying, 'Kent captain, please knock and wait for the butler'."

The 1998 season marked the end of the road for Alan Igglesden, who announced his retirement, at the age of 34, after completing his testimonial year. A modest, generous and likeable man, Igglesden could look back on a stop-start career in which he had taken 409 first-class wickets for the county at an average of 28.35 and won three Test caps. He quipped: "OK, I've had my injuries, but I don't think I've let anybody down in between times. In this game you've got to be able to smile at yourself and my doctors and specialists tell me that it's just the way I'm made – my discs slip out at a moment's notice and my knees are quite loosely jointed."

On a more sombre note, November marked the death of Doug Wright, leg-spin legend and king of hat-tricks, aged 84. The county also lost another loyal servant, the elegant right-handed batsman Arthur Phebey, who died at the age of 73.

EIGHT

1999-2001: To The Manor Born?

WITH A former Army officer as their newly installed captain, it seemed appropriate that Kent's St Lawrence headquarters, selected as England's training base for the 1999 World Cup, should look spick and span that spring. Matthew Fleming had made no secret of his leadership ambitions and admits that even when Mark Benson was given the job in 1991 "a very Band of Brothers based minority" had pushed his claims.

Although he enjoyed leading, he insisted that he could also be led without complaint. "I'd be very upset if anyone said I didn't give 100 per cent to whoever else was captain," he says, "even though there was always a part of me that thought I would have done things differently and wanted the chance to do things differently. I always used to look at our international players coming back into county cricket. You'd watched the intensity they'd played with at international level yet, when they came back to Kent, they visibly relaxed. Being made captain had the opposite effect on me."

The club also had a fresh face at the administrative helm following the appointment of Paul Millman as chief executive, though secretary Stuart Anderson remained on the pay-roll as a consultant through to the completion of the World Cup. Millman, who had played cricket for Gloucestershire 2nd XI and was a world-ranked squash player, joined Kent from Merrydown, the Sussex-based cider manufacturers. "I want Kent to be perceived as the benchmark county, the county who set the standards," was his stirring battle cry.

Even Kent's iconic St Lawrence lime looked resplendent that spring, despite a close-season pollarding and a bleak long-term prognosis that alluded to dry rot. After giving the 180-year-old specimen a life expectancy of no more than 10 years, Kent called in Jim Swanton, a past president, to plant a locum lime near the boundary. He noted: "The tradition of the lime tree is an admirable eccentricity and we ought to preserve it."

Although 'Gentleman Jim' had his detractors, I found him unfailingly helpful. He was always available for a quote, would offer a word of advice when needed and even sent me complimentary signed copies of his books. Having agreed to my request for an interview one summer he summoned me to his home, Delf House in Sandwich. I was ushered into an office crammed with weighty tomes and cricket memorabilia. The interview went well, even if at times it felt as though I was the one being interrogated, but everything ground to a halt at 11am. After first checking his watch, Jim rang the hand bell on his giant desk to summon the housemaid, Valerie, for his mid-morning 'freshener'. I had little choice in the matter. "I'll have my usual and I think the same for our guest," he pronounced. And so, for the first and only time, I was privileged to take pink gins with the formidable E. W. Swanton.

David Fulton soon detected a change of tone with Fleming in charge. "He tried to change the culture of the place He had seen that some people had been a bit selfish, so he started with team-building projects and we did pre-season training with the Army. There was a lot of resistance to it from the old school, but he wanted us to get to know the marketing department, the office staff, and the stewards even. Because Jazzer felt we were all part of the same Kent team."

Fulton adds: "I felt it was a shift in the right direction, and one which I looked to extend in my time as captain. I have to say, though, that I felt sorry for Marshy. It can't have been nice for him to carry on playing after being 'Goonered' from the captaincy as it were. In that regard, he conducted himself very professionally at all times. I never heard Marshy whinge." Marsh, then 38, later admitted that he even turned down an offer from Middlesex in order to finish his playing days with Kent.

Action man: Matthew Fleming puts heart and soul into his bowling for Kent

Picture: Ady Kerry, Kent Messenger, PD1673782

At the start of his tenure Fleming called me to one side to set out the ground rules for the working relationship between the captain and local media man. He explained: "Look, Mark, there's no way you'll agree with everything I do on the cricket field, and there's little chance of me agreeing with everything you write in your papers. So let's agree to disagree now, shake hands on it and get on with our jobs." And we did.

Within weeks, I commented in the *Kent Messenger* on a perceived lack of team spirit in the camp, adding: "Fleming must realise that you cannot run a cricket side like a battalion of the Royal Green Jackets. Perhaps a rethink on the man-management front is called for."

John Wright also appeared hell-bent on implementing change as the new season approached. The slow bowlers toiled away at net sessions with former England spinner Eddie Hemmings, and Richard Ellison was hired as a part-time coach to assist the seamers. Bobby Simpson, the former Australia captain, joined the squad in pre-season to improve slip fielding and work with the batsmen. "A lot of it's down to the mental approach," he told me. "The main thing is cricket's a great game – it's just played by idiots." Wright also invited Lord Cowdrey to give a lecture to the squad about the philosophy of batting, and employed a players' chef to introduce a new dietary regime. To strengthen the side's mental approach, he took on Peter Cohen, a respected sports psychologist.

On the playing side, left-arm swing bowler Kristian Adams, from Clee-thorpes, was drafted in after impressing at a pre-season trial and, to give the side a degree of all-round menace, Kent plumped for the Birmingham-born 'fair dinkum Aussie', Andrew Symonds, as their new overseas player. The 23-year-old had missed out on World Cup selection and had a point to prove. He also sounded a dismissive note in his first interview for the *Kent Messenger*, saying: "To be honest with you, county cricket isn't regarded with the same respect in Australia as Sheffield Shield cricket is, but filling my boots over here can do me no harm."

Kent even had to come up with a new name for the side who played in the CGU National League. They were the last county to reveal theirs, eventually opting for Spitfires. Cynics pointed out the apparent link between the name and a top-selling bottled-beer brand of Kent's principal sponsors, Shepherd Neame. Millman insisted that they had chosen Spitfires by way of tribute to the fighter squadrons stationed at a dozen Second World War airbases across Kent.

Sporting their bright blue, red and grey strip, complete with the Faversham brewery's Spitfire trademark, Kent went on to finish a creditable third in the National League's top flight, though still 14 points behind winners Lancashire. With no B&H Cup to contest that year, Kent posted a nervy opening-round win over Cheshire in the NatWest Trophy then survived a scare against Holland on a pudding of a pitch at Amstelveen to reach the quarter-finals. Their 12-game unbeaten run in all competitions ended with a poor bowling performance at Taunton, where Somerset cantered to a six-wicket win. St Lawrence was packed for World Cup warm-up games against England and South Africa, and in the competition itself a Canterbury crowd of 10,000 watched England despatch Kenya by nine wickets. Kent's dapper scorer, Jack Foley, was on England duty throughout the event.

In the PPP Healthcare County Championship, Kent's team in transition arguably punched above their weight in finishing fifth in a year dominated by Surrey. The high placing also guaranteed that Kent would be in the First Division when the competition was split the following season. Hampered once more by injuries to the seam attack, Fleming conjured only two appearances out of Martin Saggers, while Ben Phillips missed the entire campaign. Both were made to prove their fitness before securing contract extensions.

With only David Masters for pace back-up, Fleming signed giant rookies James Watson (6ft 7in) and James Golding (6ft 4in) as cover, but it was left to Julian Thompson to shoulder the main burden. He responded magnificently to head the averages with 64 scalps at an average of 19.77 and secure the player-of-the-season award. He was deservedly capped at The Nevill, his home club ground, and topped the year off by becoming a father for the first time. A fit-again Min Patel bagged 63 wickets at almost 25 apiece, but Martin McCague took a paltry 21 wickets in 10 appearances. Troubled by ankle pain, he underwent surgery at the end of the season.

Fleming was reminded in Kent's opening championship game, against Middlesex at Lord's, that the battles with team-mates would be almost as hard as the ones with opposing teams.

"There was a strong core of the team who didn't embrace the change-over and in my first game as captain there were four players, who I won't mention, but I'll never forgive. We'd had a long chat about the values which should underpin the team, yet I know they crawled back into the hotel at 3.30am. To this day, my one regret is that I didn't drop all four of them. But I didn't have enough proof and I would have had to rip the backbone out of the team. Yet still I wish I'd done it. I'm probably the only captain in the history of the club to fine somebody a four-figure sum for being fat, and I should have done something similar with those four. It was a big kick in the teeth. There was one crucial 15-minute spell in that game where we could have pushed on to win, but we dropped two catches in the slips. So all that rubbish about, 'It doesn't affect how I play,' didn't wash with me anymore. That's what led me to picking people like Julian Thompson. Apart from the fact he was a great bowler, he was also a better man. After that, if I had a 50-50 call to make on selection, I'd pick on moral grounds and if I knew someone didn't get pissed and go out shagging every night, I'd select him over the player who had, because I felt it made him the better man."

A last-day run chase at Stockton-on-Tees secured Kent's first four-day win of the summer in mid-May, but Fleming had to wait until 2 July for his next championship success – a victory over Warwickshire in a surprisingly low-scoring game at Maidstone, where Tim Munton took a hat-trick only to finish on the losing side. The pattern was identical in Kent's next match: Alamgir Sheriyar took three in three for Worcestershire at New Road, but also finished on the losing side as Fleming hit his first championship hundred for two years.

Thompson then claimed eight in the match against Nottinghamshire, and Kent landed a fourth straight win when they eased to a seven-wicket success over Canterbury Week visitors Essex. Symonds, in his final championship appearance, signed off with 132 after being dropped early on by Queensland team-mate Stuart Law. Kent ended August with an innings win over Northamptonshire, who were shot out for 69 and 86, but it was to be their last championship victory of the summer.

Kent mustered only 34 batting bonus points and the averages also told a sorry tale. Symonds topped the standings with 940 runs at 40.87 as no Kent player reached 1,000 first-class runs for the first time since 1919. Fleming admits: "Ealy, Marshy and I felt we were carrying the batting unit on our shoulders. Every game we'd be 40 for four and it was a standing joke between the three of us as we'd start putting our pads on at half eleven…if we were lucky. It was ridiculously embarrassing at times and it became a double-edged sword because the bowlers were never getting enough rest. Yet they still went out on the lash so, in the end, it all caught up with them."

After yet another disappointing season with the bat Matthew Walker was advised by his skipper to find some winter work. "Jazzer felt it would do me good to spend some time in the 'real world' as he put it, so he had a chat with his friend, Hugo Fenwick, who offered me a job at their Ricemans department store in Canterbury. I ended up working in the toy department. Father Christmas rang in sick one day, so when they asked for volunteers I thought, why not, and put my hand up. Standing in as Santa, wearing that white beard and the big red suit, has to be one of the most surreal moments of my life."

Recalling his frustration at Walker's continued underachievement, Fleming says: "When I took over as captain I had to go and pick Matt up from his house every morning and take him to training. He was drinking and his lifestyle wasn't the best and in those days we used to train at a small gym in Canterbury next to the *Kentish Gazette* offices. The first time we went there, I put Walks on a running machine and after 400 metres he got dizzy and had to come off. He then went the other way, became a lot keener on fitness, started running every day, but couldn't hit the ball off the square."

Despite the misgivings of some supporters and players, Kent agreed to extend Wright's contract as head coach for another year, heralding Trevor Ward's decision to quit the club in September. Fleming reflects: "Wardy and I grew up together playing cricket with Colin Page and were mates, but never anything more than mates. He ended up absolutely hating me and it must have been tough for him to keep seeing me. I think we're all right now, though. The tragedy is, he came so close to playing for England. His big mantra was, 'I'm not going to change, they'll have to pick me as I am.' We tried to tell him how close he was and if he just adapted his game a little he could play for England, but he wouldn't have it."

Ward, who made a modest £60,000 from his benefit season, went on to join Leicestershire, but was angered by the nature of his departure after 13 seasons with the county. He said: "I always thought leaving Kent would be the hardest decision I could ever have to make, but it's been made the easiest. Which is sad in many ways. I have no qualms with the chief executive, Paul Millman; in fact, I think Paul is the only one here who's been truthful with me."

He added: "The fact of the matter is, one player stayed in the side who had scored six single-figure scores on the bounce. I was then left out of the NatWest Trophy for a guy who was averaging six in one-day cricket. There was no cricketing logic to that; it had become personal." Ward concluded: "A lot of other players would go too if they had the choice." To a degree, he was right.

In November, with crass timing and scant regard for the player's feelings, the club sacked Nigel Llong, moments after he had finished hosting a St Lawrence coaching session for young players and only days after a limited-overs deal had been mooted by the county. He was convinced that Wright, rather than Fleming, had argued for his omission from the side. Will House left to join Sussex and Chris Walsh, Jamie Ford and Simon Willis all retired from playing. Walsh and Ford pursued jobs in the City, while Willis joined Kent's administration team.

2000

The threatened Millennium Bug failed to materialise, but the curse blighting Kent's pace attack surfaced once more, eventually forcing both Dean Headley and Julian Thompson to retire from cricket without bowling a ball in anger for the county all summer. Headley was sent home from England's tour of

South Africa after being diagnosed with a spinal stress fracture, only to be awarded an ECB central contract. He underwent surgery to insert two screws into his spine, but finally had to admit defeat in March 2001. Bugged by persistent knee troubles that required two operations, 'Doc' Thompson was also forced to end his cricket career prematurely and return to medicine. He became Kent's honorary medical adviser last year.

In the space of five January days, Kent lost two more club stalwarts. Jim Swanton died at the age of 92 and soon afterwards Chris Taylor, his co-curator and former head steward, died at 79. A mood of gloom seemed to be enveloping the club when Lord Cowdrey, newly installed as county president, issued a rallying cry at the annual meeting in March. Urging members to get behind Fleming and the team, Lord Cowdrey said: "The game is whingeing too much, but we at Kent have a lot to be proud of. We have three wonderful grounds and must fight to protect our game, our championship and our county from all that sully it."

The retirements of Headley and Thompson, coupled with Martin McCague's absence following an ankle operation, left Fleming's pace attack looking at best threadbare. Yet the department was further weakened as the season progressed. Shoulder and back injuries restricted Ben Phillips to three one-day starts, and later Mark Ealham (broken finger), Min Patel (shoulder) and Fleming himself (with a torn calf) all spent time out of the side. Contracts were offered to former Somerset right-armer Ben Trott and Danish-born teenager Amjad Khan, who had been discovered playing club cricket in Copenhagen by Wright's ex-Derbyshire team-mate and then Denmark coach, Ole Mortensen. With so many bowlers absent or injured, it came as a surprise when Fleming turned to India's cultured batsman, Rahul Dravid, as his overseas player.

As if to draw a line under Marsh's first team involvement, Kent invited him to captain the county's second string and remain on the staff solely as a batsman. After luring understudy wicketkeeper Geraint Jones away from Wales, where he was working as an apprentice pharmacist, they enticed experienced gloveman and fitness fanatic Paul Nixon to join from Leicestershire – the signs pointing towards the St Lawrence exit doors could not have been painted larger for Marsh. Having won two championships at Grace Road, Nixon hoped to instil the same winning mentality at Kent.

There were changes in the committee room, too, where Derek Ufton stood down after a decade as chairman of cricket. He was replaced by Mike Denness, who reflects: "Derek was a bit upset with how the change [from Marsh to Fleming] all unfolded, but as far as I was concerned there needed to be a change." Denness had ended his playing career at Kent in 1976 after unsuccessfully suggesting that Graham Johnson should replace him as captain. This time he could feel more confident that his proposal would be accepted when he earmarked Johnson as the next chairman of cricket.

Following the introduction of a two-divisional championship, Fleming was keen for the side to hit the ground running, but rain and poor form soon dashed that hope. Three of their first four B&H Cup ties were called off and the other ended with a two-run defeat to Essex. Kent at least won their final tie, by 77 runs against Middlesex, but could only finish fourth in the southern group. Kent's NatWest Trophy campaign proved equally brief as they went down to a five-wicket defeat in a rain-delayed fourth-round game against Glamorgan.

Two of Kent's opening four Norwich Union League games were also wiped out by bad weather and though they opened their win account with a seven-wicket success over Northamptonshire, Kent lost their next four. More by luck than judgment, Kent broke their run of defeats with a three-run success at Hove. With Sussex only three wickets down and needing five for victory from the last six balls, Fleming was forced to think quickly on his feet. Having miscalculated his bowling allocation, he called on Matthew Walker to bowl the final over – it was Walker's seventh over in 76 league appearances – yet it proved a masterstroke. Will House patted two back and then nudged a single from the third, leaving Australian Michael Bevan to finish off. Well set, Bevan inexplicably drove the fourth and fifth deliveries to fielders and clipped the last straight to David Fulton at deep midwicket.

Kent's good fortune soon abandoned them as they lost their next two league starts to slide deeper into the relegation mire. Three successive wins eased the threat, but it was only thanks to wins over Yorkshire and Worcestershire that Kent avoided the drop.

Persistent rain had led to three draws at the start of the four-day campaign, but Kent moved off the foot of the championship table with an 190-run success over Durham in a game of 16 lbws at The Nevill. Fleming's three-and-a-half hour vigil for 39 proved pivotal in the context of a low-scoring game. Andrew Caddick performed wonders with bat and ball as Somerset sneaked a two-wicket win at Bath, and Kent also tasted defeat on a seamer-friendly Headingley pitch.

Kent's first championship hundred of the season, by Fulton on 1 July, inspired a last-day fightback for a draw against Somerset at The Mote, then Min Patel's six for 77 on a poor Derby pitch helped secure an eight-wicket win. Dravid dislocated a finger but, thankfully for those fortunate enough to witness the following game against Hampshire, he was fit for what proved to be a captivating duel against Shane Warne. After an 112-year association it was to be Hampshire's last game at the United Services Ground; the heaviest of heavy rollers, 'Hercules', had worked overtime to create a slow, dry turner.

Warne had already struck twice in Kent's first innings when Dravid came to the crease at 15 for two. Combining nimble footwork with rapid, yet impeccable assessment of length, and with a technique later adopted by Kevin Pietersen, Dravid defended on the front foot with his bat a foot or so in front of his left pad, thus reducing the risk of bat-pad nicks to close fielders. If not right forward, he would rock back deep into his crease, leaving his strokes impossibly late. It was a batting master class.

Clearly frustrated, Warne went through his full repertoire: the flipper, the googly, the 'zooter', both over and round the wicket. He even tried the occasional bouncer, but Dravid reigned supreme for six hours on his way to a maiden championship hundred; he reached the milestone of 10,000 first-class career runs in the process. A part-time leg-spinner, Giles White, achieved what the great Warne could not by claiming Dravid's wicket, though by then he had made 137. Patel came to the fore in Hampshire's second innings, taking five for 46, and Kent were left with a tricky target of 205. Again Dravid excelled with an unbeaten 73 which steered Kent to a six-wicket win and lifted them out of the bottom three at Hampshire's expense. Warne marvelled in the *Wisden Cricketer*: "When you see him display that kind of lightness on his feet, you wonder whether he could have been a ballroom dancer."

Kent effectively sealed Hampshire's fate, and ensured their own survival, with a tense 15-run win in the return fixture at St Lawrence. Alan Wells was acting captain as Paul Nixon's unbeaten 134, his highest score for the county, laid the foundations and McCague's five for 52 completed the job. Defeat by Yorkshire in their last game left Kent fifth out of nine. The lack of reliable batting back-up for Dravid, who averaged 55, was shown by the fact that Nixon, in 72nd place, was the next Kent player to feature in the national averages. Seamers Martin Saggers and David Masters, with 57 and 48 wickets respectively, shared the club's player-of-the-season award.

The bond which Dravid forged with John Wright strongly influenced his departure at the end of the season to become India's coach. Fleming believes that Wright had already been told by Kent that he would not be offered a new contract, so the parting seemed to suit both sides. "In the end it was either Wrighty or the batsmen. John was saying, get rid of them all, he was posing the question, 'Key, Fulton, Walker and, to a degree, Smith. Why keep them?' Yet to me, it had become apparent that, in among his greatest strengths, perhaps John's real weakness was that he coached people to be the image of himself and didn't enable players to go out and make the most of their talents. It was interesting, but really unfair on Wrighty, that when Inverarity came along the next season and unlocked the door, they all got runs. In every other way Wrighty was fantastic and it's why he went on, I think, to become such a good coach of India. You can't tell much to Sachin Tendulkar, Rahul Dravid or Virender Sehwag; you've just got to help them to be better."

Wright admitted at the time: "The biggest frustration is that I was not able to solve the batting problems. We've been too dependent on overseas players. I don't know how I'll be remembered, but I don't think we did badly when you consider all the factors like injuries, pitch preparation and even little things, like losing the toss at vital times."

Rob Key believes it was too easy for batsmen who failed under Wright to transfer the blame to him. "He wanted success for you almost as much as you did for yourself. The problem was, he couldn't hide his disappointment. He'd scored a lot of runs as a player, so he just couldn't understand why Dave Fulton kept nicking off to the keeper and I kept going leg before. Wardy and Wells weren't playing as well as they had in previous years and the youngsters kept making the same mistakes, which Wrighty found hard to relate to. With that, he became more intense. We probably drove him around the bend and, to this day, I feel we were all a bit to blame for his change of tack as a coach."

Fulton was struck by the contrast between the upbeat character who took over as coach in 1997 and the man who had run out of solutions (and patience) by the end of the 2000 season. "During his honeymoon period in 1997 all he really did was tell us how good we were," Fulton recalls. "His stock saying was, 'If you were a Kiwi you'd have played 50 Tests by now.' He used to say to me, 'Fults, you've got so much time. You play the quicks so well and you're the best fielder I've ever seen at bat-pad.' You were on cloud nine and you really wanted to go out and play for this bloke. By contrast, we went down to Taunton in 2000 and on a night out Wrighty got his guitar out and made up a song about the team members. One by one, he went round making up lyrics to a set tune. When he got to me, he paused and couldn't think of anything positive to sing, and came up with, 'Dave Fulton is a great short-lego.' So from being the best thing since sliced bread when he first turned up, I'd become a half-decent short leg and that was about it."

Richard Clinton and James Watson, neither of whom had featured all season, were released in 2000, while off-spinner Darren Scott retired after only seven senior appearances. The season's end also marked the retirement of former captain Steve Marsh. After an emotional farewell appearance at St Lawrence, playing solely as a batsman in Spitfires' league victory against Yorkshire, he retained his place for the final round of games. Hitting 38 in Kent's eight-wicket win over Worcestershire at New Road, Marsh neutralised the threat of Glenn McGrath before signing off with his last scoring shot, a straight six off Matt Rawnsley.

Marsh, who ended his 291-match career with 749 dismissals, putting him fourth on Kent's all-time wicketkeeping list, admits: "The big disappointment came in my last year when they brought in Paul Nixon. He had it written into his contract that he had to keep wicket for the first team when fit, so I had no chance to compete with him on a level playing field."

He is critical of both Wright and Fleming. "I think John Wright soon realised he'd made the wrong decision because he found out he couldn't work with Jazzer as he had with me. What disappointed me most was how Jazzer changed. If you look at his batting record whenever anyone else was captain, it wasn't any great shakes. But once he took over, he became determined and sensible, a player who would look at the game situation before going for his shots. That just made me realise he'd let the team down and hadn't really put it all in for me.'

Not surprisingly, Fleming has a different take on events. "There is something, possibly it's subconscious, but with some people when they take the step up to captaincy and embrace the added responsibility that comes with it, they also step up their performances. Perhaps that added responsibility was what I needed rather than people like Daryl Foster saying, 'Oh you're un-coachable.' I can sympathise with Marshy for saying what he did, but there was never a conscious moment when I felt I could give more as a player. I sometimes look back on my younger days and maybe wish I'd done things differently. But I genuinely didn't care about averages, genuinely didn't care about bowling uphill into the wind, or fielding wherever, but I know now if I'd been a bit smarter, I could have been better."

On 4 December 2000, only 10 months into his year's term as club president, Lord Cowdrey of Tonbridge died, having suffered a stroke days earlier. He was 67. Television commentator Richie Benaud, who played against him, said: "You hear a lot of people classed as being lovers of cricket, well Colin was, with a passion."

2001

It was optimistic in the extreme to believe that Kent's decision to award their wealthy captain a benefit season in 2001 would not ruffle a few feathers. After all, the club did announce their decision on the very day that Fleming's family's business, the Robert Fleming Investment Bank, changed hands for £4.8 billion.

The unfortunate timing was not lost on or appreciated by Fleming who, with his usual candour, said: "One or two people have expressed their surprise that I've taken a benefit, but if I had as much money as some people think then I wouldn't have accepted Kent's offer. I had a very small shareholding in the bank and yes, I'm lucky to be a Fleming and fortunate that the sale came during my lifetime, but it certainly wasn't like winning *Who Wants To Be A Millionaire?* It hasn't changed my life, I still need to earn a living and I still want to be a cricketer. A benefit is awarded for hard work and long-term commitment and I would like to think I deserve one on those grounds." Fleming made sure that local charities also benefited.

Early that year I interviewed Fleming at his home, at Lyminge near Folkestone. The country nest was littered with Kent cricketing ephemera. Even during a trip to the downstairs toilet I spotted a framed letter on Kent County Cricket Club notepaper. Dated 26 September 1988, it was Fleming's first contract offer, signed by club secretary David Dalby and 2nd XI coach Alan Ealham, revealing the princely starting salary of £3,500 plus bonuses and incentives. It riles Fleming to this day that the secretary initially spelled his surname incorrectly and had to Tipp-Ex over the error before re-typing it.

Fleming made a determined if ultimately futile attempt to bolster his fragile top order for 2001 by signing Mark Ramprakash, who became the latest star name to spurn Kent's advances when he joined reigning champions Surrey. Fleming was at least able to wring a little PR mileage out of the approach, saying: "Our members and players would be disappointed to be involved with a club that was not ambitious enough to try and sign someone like Ramprakash. He was never going to leave the south east, which is why we thought we had a chance, but Surrey's late bid won the day." He warned that Surrey were becoming "the Manchester United of cricket".

In a less high-profile effort to strengthen resources Fleming attempted to sign Middlesex seamer Jamie Hewitt but was later ordered to pay £400 costs for an ECB hearing after being found guilty of making an illegal approach. Kent were also warned as to their future conduct. Fleming eventually got his man the following season but Hewitt made just one appearance before retiring from the game through injury.

At least Fleming's close-season advice to David Fulton bore fruit as he, Rob Key and the Kent top order went on to enjoy a vintage summer. Under the quiet, watchful leadership of part-time coaching adviser John Inverarity, Kent's young batsmen finally came of age. Inverarity, who had galvanised Kent under Chris Cowdrey's captaincy in 1988, agreed to join the club for 14 weeks in an advisory capacity during his summer holidays from the Hale School near Perth. He outlined his philosophy: "My greatest role as a teacher is to get the chemistry right within the school so that the whole enterprise runs well. So my aim at Kent is to do the man-management role as well as I can and create an environment in which the players want to play well. That may not necessarily mean we win trophies, but I'd be happy if I can see 10 or 11 Kent players have good seasons, rather than just five or six."

Having signed the South African Daryll Cullinan to give the batting more steel, Inverarity used his quirky methods to nurture the rest; six Kent batsmen eased past 500 runs for the summer. The batting unit was led magnificently by openers Fulton, with a career-best tally of 1,729 runs averaging 78.59, and Key, who made 1,073 runs at 41.17. It was the first time either had passed 1,000 runs in a season. Key hit three hundreds and Fulton eight, including a record championship sequence of 509 runs without being dismissed. The run-fest also proved expensive for Fleming, who promised a bottle of champagne to every player who scored a hundred or took five wickets in an innings that year. "To my annoyance," Fleming says, "Alan Wells kept playing for the second team and scoring hundred after hundred."

Ed Smith cashed in with three centuries, only to miss out on his 1,000 by 53 runs, but he and Key both received their county caps from the Duke of Kent, the club's patron, during Canterbury Week. Martin Saggers and Cullinan were also capped during the summer.

Recalling the build-up to his extraordinary season, Fulton says: "I knew it was my last chance because Jazzer had told me as much. He came out of the winter contract meeting and said, 'You've got this new contract by the skin of your teeth. We need to see the real Dave Fulton in 2001.' It wasn't rocket science, but to hear this was my last chance certainly focused the mind." He was also given "a taste of the real world", working on the sports desk at the *Kent Messenger*'s Chatham office.

"I spent hours sat down with Chris Stone in the coach's room at the back of the Frank Woolley Stand going through my batting videos and deciding what type of player I wanted to be. Two things in my technique needed overhauling, but in terms of my approach to batting, this was the end of the 'Tav' [he had earned the nickname after being asked to play an anchor role]. I wanted to go back to how I'd been at the start of my career, putting bat to ball with more flair and freedom. We noticed that my pre-movements, before the ball arrived, had got so bad that my feet were going in all the wrong places. For two months

Chris ran in and threw balls at me while I worked on moving my feet. I didn't even hold a bat; I just pretended I had one. After that my feet were moving exactly where I wanted them to. It meant that once I re-introduced a bat, my hands were closer to my body, I could swing the blade down straight, my balance was good and I was no longer nicking off."

With Inverarity's arrivals came the 'Inver drills', which Fulton describes as "a checkpoint for your technique, a way of aligning everything. Like getting an MoT for your batting every day." Key and Smith also felt the benefit of the drills, and Fulton stresses: "You can't underestimate the role Invers played that year. Wrighty had been very intense sometimes, then Invers pitched up and you could almost hear people start to breathe again. Wrighty laid the foundations, if you like, and Invers capitalised on them."

Key admits that the club were close to saying, 'Goodbye, you're all crap,' after the 2000 season. He, too, was given a gee-up speech by Fleming and worked on his game in Australia before returning to feel the liberating effect of Inverarity's coaching methods. "I was 21 by the time Invers arrived and that bit more experienced. Thanks to Wrighty I had a defensive game, so when Invers said, 'Go out there and express yourself,' it was like the shackles coming off. His first speech revolved around, 'Look, if you get out playing a hook shot, but 95 per cent of the time you get runs from it, then you'll never hear me saying don't play that shot. I'll say keep playing it, but play it better.'

"He liked us to dominate if we could, especially against spin. I remember a game against Cambridge University when Ed and I both came off at the interval with fifties and we were feeling quite pleased with ourselves. Invers said, 'I don't know about you, but I thought that was pretty crap. The bloke can't bowl, he's not spinning it and you're only scoring at two an over. It's embarrassing.'"

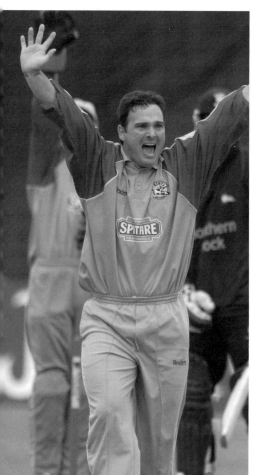

Mark Ealham appeals successfully for a leg-before decision

Picture: Matthew Walker, Kent Messenger, PD1673796

Key also recalls that there were "a few wacky ideas" in addition to the 'Inver drills'. "During the warm-ups one day he was getting us to practise how we walked out to bat. He got us doing this jaunty stride; I can only describe it as a 'monkey walk'. I felt a complete tit doing it, but he had so many good ideas to offer that you didn't mind the occasional stupid thing."

Fulton felt that he had "brought some time in the team" after opening the season with hundreds against Cambridge and Surrey, but Kent's plans were thrown off course when Cullinan tore knee ligaments in only his third championship appearance. To his credit, he stayed in Canterbury through to September, coaching the county's age-group sides, leaving Fleming to call on Andrew Symonds as his back-up overseas player from the first week of July. The Australian arrived on an 18-month deal.

Although championship runs were more plentiful, wins were still hard to come by and Kent's disappointing return of four victories left them third in the final Cricinfo Championship table – 44 points behind winners Yorkshire. They had to wait until Tunbridge Wells in May for their first success, a three-day innings win over Essex inspired by Fulton's 179, his fourth century in nine knocks, and 124 from Walker. Ben Trott, having been advised by Inverarity to alter his run-up, claimed match figures of 11 for 78 in only his eighth game.

Two months went by before Kent's next championship success, an emphatic 268-run win over Leicestershire at Canterbury where, on 4 July, Fulton became the first player to 1,000 first-class runs for the season. The side then completed their first championship double with a thumping innings victory over bottom-of-the-table Essex at Southend. Key's hundred was followed by five-wicket returns for Mark Ealham and Trott.

Nixon returned to his old stomping ground at Grace Road to clatter 16 from the final over and secure a thrilling three-wicket win over Leicestershire. In a match of seven centuries – Walker, Symonds and Smith all passed three figures for Kent – Nixon hit twos from Darren Maddy's first four balls then worked the last two deliveries to the square-leg ropes as Kent successfully chased 400 plus for only the second time in their history.

The game marked a championship debut for 19-year-old off-spinner James Tredwell. After winning his call-up at 11am, when Min Patel failed a fitness test on a ricked neck, Tredwell set off from Arundel, where England Under-19s were based prior to a one-day international against the West Indies at Hove. After two train journeys and a brace of taxi rides he got to Grace Road at four o'clock. Within 15 minutes of taking the field, Fleming called him up to bowl and Tredwell was able to celebrate his maiden championship scalp, that of former England batsman Aftab Habib for 153, with his 15th ball.

Fulton nominates his performance in the Canterbury Week draw against Somerset as his personal highlight of an outstanding season. "I scored 208 not out, then 104 not out at a run a ball to set up the declaration. I spent every minute of the game on the field and took seven catches. The only gutting thing was we didn't win the game. You don't get too many matches like that; I was playing so well and felt in such good form that when I got to 20 I kind of knew I'd get to three figures. I then hit two more big hundreds in the space of three weeks and, unbeknown to me at the time, was picked by Nasser [Hussain] for the Headingley Test. Then they [the selectors] did a U-turn and stuck with Mark Butcher instead." Fulton still took great pride from being chosen as the Professional Cricketers' Association's player of the year.

Kent showed improvement in one-day cricket in 2001, though it was not necessarily borne out by their results. Defeats to Middlesex and Sussex saw them go out in the group stages of the Benson and Hedges Cup, and big-match nerves again got the better of them at Taunton, where a poor bowling display allowed Somerset to coast to a 52-run quarter-final victory. Once again, Kent were gunning for silverware on a single front and, by the time Inverarity returned to Australia in July, handing over the coaching reins to Stone, Spitfires had already racked up four Norwich Union League wins (they also tied with Somerset).

An eight-match unbeaten run ended with back-to-back defeats to leaders Leicestershire in August, but it was Kent rather than Leicestershire who drew inspiration from the result at Canterbury. Fleming reflects: "I didn't think we could win the title until Leicestershire beat us at Canterbury and were singing, *We Are the Champions* in their dressing room. I knew then we were going to do it because I knew they were gone. They weren't the gritty Leicestershire anymore; their previous side had real focus, but now they'd become cocky. They lost their next couple of games and I remember being in the car with Ealy when he rang up Trevor Ward. I'm not sure if he knew I was there with Ealy, but Wardy said, 'We don't know how to win anymore; I don't think we'll win another game this season.'"

Kent responded brilliantly with victories over Surrey, Gloucestershire, Yorkshire and Northamptonshire that moved them level on points with Leicestershire going into the final round of matches. As fate would have it, Kent were pitted against Warwickshire at Edgbaston for their final league game, but this time their Birmingham bogey was nowhere to be seen. James Hockley's watchful 90 and a stunning 35-ball fifty from Key made light of a rain-affected pitch as Kent posted 216 for six from their reduced allocation of

40 overs. Though the Bears made a good start and were favourites to win at 158 for three, Symonds was having none of it.

At a team huddle following Ian Bell's dismissal, Symonds gave the Kent side full blast. Coming on to bowl seam-up as sixth change soon after, he turned the game irrevocably Kent's way with a spell of five for 18 and capped that by diving full length to stop David Hemp's blazing drive before returning to Nixon to complete the run-out. Spitfires edged home by nine runs for their fifth Sunday League title and, with only two defeats to their names, had set a club record for fewest losses in a league season.

Remembering Symonds's contribution, Fulton says: "When you look at our mid-Nineties side, on paper it was fantastic, but you had guys who would go missing at key times, others who had very good averages but who didn't really know how to win, and guys who maybe every now and then looked after themselves a little bit. There was a big difference in 2001: we had a real belief. We also had a bloke, in Symmo, who didn't care about the things out of his control. All that mattered to him was that it was bat against ball and a game to be won."

Leicestershire, who had known that they would still claim the title on run rate if they won their final game against Nottinghamshire, completed their fall from grace with a five-wicket defeat. As Kent began to celebrate, Fleming told me that a strong wind and short boundary had left Symonds with no option but to bowl seam rather than spin. "He was possibly our quickest bowler. When the force is with Symmo, as it was today, and when he's in that form, you just let him get on with it." Elton John's *Candle in the Wind* boomed out of the CD player as Kent celebrated in their Edgbaston dressing room. The Kent players taunted Leicestershire as they bellowed out the line: "The candle burned out long before the legend ever did."

Fleming contacted the Copthorne Hotel in Birmingham to organise an impromptu celebratory dinner in their banqueting suite; I felt incredibly proud when he extended an invitation to me. No sooner had the soup bowls been cleared than 12th man Martin McCague took to the tables to lead the sing-song. The silver Norwich Union Trophy, a stylised sculpture of a batsman playing a hook shot, also did the rounds but came home in two pieces after the boisterous Irishman fell on it. "I was so hammered I don't remember," he admits, "but rumour has it that I sat on the trophy or dropped it. Either way, it ended up broken, but it could have been anyone, we were all over the shop that night. To my mind, we won it as a team and broke it as a team."

Inverarity's oft-repeated advice to players – "just effing do it" – inspired one of a wild evening's more memorable moments. Fleming recalls: "Smudge [Ed

Smith] got quite pissed and decided he would ring John Inverarity, who was fast asleep somewhere in Perth. All Ed said was, 'Invers, we just effing did it,' and with that he hung up." Fleming also remembers that, with McCague out cold, "the lads shaved his nether regions for his troubles".

In the sober light of day Fleming decided the time was right to step down as captain. "Not only was there another phase of team transition to go through, I also realised there were only a handful of people that I really wanted to play cricket with for Kent. You can see that on the DVD, by the reaction of our players at the end. The people you hug are those you really want to be with, and then there are the others. I knew I didn't have the time to go through the process of getting rid of the people I didn't want to be with, so it was time for a new man. It dawns on you eventually when you walk into the changing room that in 15 years' time those seats will be filled by other players whom supporters will love or hate, applaud or boo, and in the bigger picture that's what happens. We are just there for the then and now, so Kent, the club, should always come first and that's why I stopped when I did."

It was a typical Fleming touch that he should want to mark the success in style. "I'd seen a pair of presentation cufflinks in the glass cabinets at St Lawrence that had been awarded to Frank Woolley and the Kent side by Lord Harris after they'd won the championship in 1906. So I decided I'd have a pair of cufflinks made for every member of the squad, with their initials and the Kent horse on one side, and 'Norwich Union League winners 2001' on the other. I was trying to recreate something, but clearly it was something they weren't ready for. I don't think I got a single thank-you letter; maybe they didn't realise the cufflinks were from me. I don't know."

The trophy was later repaired by a Canterbury silversmith, but the divisions within Kent's dressing room were never truly repaired. Indeed, within months they would be fully exposed. Having played no part in the trophy success, Wells retired from the game at the end of his five-year deal, while the luckless Ben Phillips, together with fringe players Paul Lazenbury and Kristian Adams, was released.

NINE

2002-05: Tav Takes The Baton

KENT'S TIMING, in trying to lure John Inverarity away full-time from his head teacher's position in Perth, was about as masterly as an Alan Igglesden on-drive. So, in what many Kent followers interpreted as a stop-gap measure, Inverarity recommended his former Western Australia team-mate, Ian Brayshaw. Ironically, once Inverarity did decide to retire from teaching, Kent were unceremoniously gazumped by a rival bid from Warwickshire.

The hugely likeable Brayshaw was the county's first director of cricket, with a brief to oversee development of the game from grass roots, through county age group levels and the planned Kent Academy, right up to the first team. A wily and slippery seam bowler – and one of the exclusive club to take 10 wickets in an innings – he admitted to me that he faced a steep learning curve. Over the winter he watched videos of Kent's players and sought advice from Inverarity, Dennis Lillee and Rod Marsh.

Mindful of his own experience when taking over from Steve Marsh, club captain Matthew Fleming offered the four-day leadership for 2002 to David Fulton, while retaining control of the club's limited-overs fortunes himself. Fulton takes up the story: "I'd never seriously been considered as a captain because I'd never scored enough runs, but Jazzer was coming to an end and maybe saw me as someone who cared about the players and the club. He told me his plans as we were driving to a golf day. He was talking about maybe splitting the captaincy and at no stage in the conversation did I imagine he would be splitting it with me, until he said, 'How would you feel about doing the four-day stuff?' All I could say was, 'Yes, that would be quite nice.' It was a neat handover; it was like being handed the baton while still on the move. I think that's how Kent should be looking to work it now in the takeover from Keysie.

"For Jazzer and me, that style of handover worked well. There was a perception that he was still calling all the shots, but actually he let me have free rein on team selection in four-day cricket. I felt there were no issues at all. As to whether it worked for the other guys, you'd have to ask them, but Jazzer is very comfortable in his own skin. He doesn't have the insecurities that blight a lot of sporting leaders."

Fleming believes that the arrangement worked well, though Kent hardly shone under him as they tried to defend the Norwich Union National League, losing half their matches. Generally preferring James Tredwell to Min Patel as their one-day spin option, Kent won only two of their five Benson and Hedges Cup group games and crashed out of the C&G Trophy by five runs following a dramatic semi-final collapse against Somerset at Taunton.

Chasing Somerset's imposing 50-over total of 344 for five, a 48-ball innings of 63 by pinch-hitter Fleming at least gave Kent a flying start. Following a seventh-wicket stand of 74 between Mark Ealham and Paul Nixon, they needed nine from 15 balls to reach Lord's once more. Nixon, backing up, and James Golding, chancing a single to the substitute fielder, were then run out, and David Masters yorked, so, with an over remaining and Ealham on strike, Kent only required six. Heaving at Steffan Jones's first delivery, a slow full toss, Ealham miscued low to midwicket and sloped off, crestfallen.

After watching his side lose their last four wickets for three runs, a dejected Fleming said: "Anyone who tells you it's not the winning or losing that counts – it's the taking part – has never lost a semi-final like that. I'm not happy with the way we bowled or fielded, but I'm proud of the way we got into a position where we should have won the game."

Although Kent won seven of their Frizzell County Championship games, three more than the previous summer, they could not improve on their third-place spot of 2001 and finished 47 points behind title-winning Surrey. The campaign started with a high-scoring draw against Hampshire on a St Lawrence belter which, by a quirk in the fixture list, preceded Kent's first trip to the Rose Bowl, where they followed on to lose by eight wickets. In only his third championship appearance, Amjad Khan bagged six for 52 and eight in the game to secure the side's opening win, ending a sequence of five successive defeats by Yorkshire. Martin Saggers followed suit in ideal swing-bowling conditions at a near waterlogged Nevill ground, taking six for 39 in a four-wicket success over Sussex.

Martin Bicknell masterminded Surrey's nine-wicket victory at the Oval, but Kent travelled to Aigburth, one of the leafier suburbs of Liverpool, to record a six-wicket win over Lancashire, Fulton and Andrew Symonds both hitting centuries as they chased down a target of 360. Kent's inability to bowl sides out was apparent in draws against Warwickshire and Sussex, games that included hundreds for Fulton and Ed Smith and another six-wicket return from Khan, but then Surrey completed the double over Kent in a game which was painful in more ways than one for Fulton.

Kent dominated the first three days, despite an extraordinary hundred from Surrey's captain, Adam Hollioake. Needing 410 to win, Surrey were apparently sunk on 208 for seven before tailenders Saqlain Mushtaq and Jimmy

Ormond gave opener Ian Ward such stout support that they edged to a two-wicket win. Fulton describes it as "one of the lowest moments in my time as captain. I watched from the balcony with a busted finger. It was horrendous seeing it unfold."

In Fulton's absence, Patel oversaw Kent's six-wicket win at Leicester, where Rob Key hit his third hundred of the summer and Saggers took nine wickets. Key was rewarded the following month with a Test debut against India; Saggers, despite finishing as the joint leading wicket-taker in the country, with 83 victims, had to wait longer for his call-up.

Fulton returned to the fold to take six catches and lead by example with a battling 89 in a 153-run victory over Somerset in Canterbury Week. Three games without a win put paid to Kent's vague title aspirations, but they sustained interest by announcing the capture of Australia's legendary Test captain, Steve Waugh, for the final month as overseas locum for Symonds, who had been called away by Australia A.

Waugh's debut, in a Norwich Union League match against Leicestershire, inflated the St Lawrence crowd to 7,000. He did not disappoint, an unbeaten 59 guiding Kent to victory with two balls to spare. Championship form was more elusive, but he signed off with a determined 146 on a tricky Headingley pitch which inspired Kent to an eight-wicket win over Yorkshire. He described his short-term colleagues as "a good bunch", but admitted: "I have found the travelling in county cricket difficult. The miles up and down the motorway aren't easy and you have to respect these guys for doing that all year and still playing good cricket in between."

Recalling his brief stint in his autobiography, *Out of My Comfort Zone*, Waugh revealed that Kent's players were able to pass on a trick or two to the battle-hardened international. "On my first day in the field I got a whiff of the mentality of some of the guys when I was offered some extra-strong mints from a team-mate, which I thought was a nice gesture to make me feel welcome. Seconds later, as I crunched into a chalky, coin-sized lozenge, a startled voice said, 'What the hell are you doing? Don't chew the mints!' 'Why not? They taste pretty good, pal.' 'You're wasting them. You're supposed to suck 'em and then use the saliva to polish the ball. It's the best ball-shiner available.' 'Piss off, mate, I'm eating mine,' I said."

Fulton's stock was certainly on the up, particularly after Waugh, in a column for the *Sunday Times*, had mentioned him as a potential England captain. Fulton clearly relished Waugh's involvement, writing in *The Captains' Tales*: "What struck me about him, as soon as he hit his first throw-down, was the intensity he poured into every shot. Waugh would hit throw-downs like they

A guard of honour for Australia's captain, Steve Waugh, as he makes his debut against Leicestershire in 2002

Picture: Derek Stingemore, Kent Messenger, PD1673797

were the last few balls he was ever going to face in Test cricket. In his short time at Kent part of his mystique evaporated. Underneath his tag of 'best in the world' existed a really good guy, who made everyone feel comfortable around him."

Fulton also admits that when Waugh began taking fielding drills Brayshaw was made to look "all at sea". In his four-week stay Waugh also helped to set up a coaching exchange scheme between Kent and New South Wales and encouraged the county to honour their capped players by awarding each with a boxed commemorative, numbered cap as the Australian Test side had done with their famous baggy greens.

Although I had felt privileged to report on Waugh's only Kent hundred, the game at Headingley was forever tainted by the shabby treatment of Paul Nixon. I was sitting in the press box, watching the opening overs, when Nixon emerged from the players' balcony and pulled up a chair next to mine. I greeted him with a hearty, "Morning Nikko, good to see you." On turning to look him in the eye, I instantly spotted something was amiss.

He looked ashen-faced, a little dazed if anything. Glibly, I responded: "What's up, mate? You look like you've been given the boot." Without a flicker, Nixon replied: "The thing is, Marko, you're right. They've sacked me." He had not missed a championship game in the three seasons since Kent tempted him away from Leicestershire, yet the club left it to their new four-day skipper, Fulton, to break the news.

Nixon was livid at how the county had manipulated his departure in favour of promising rookie Geraint Jones. By refusing to offer Nixon a contract unless he agreed to a substantial wage cut, they had put him in a near impossible position. Nixon seethed: "Sadly, good man management and cricket don't always go together. I'm disappointed in the way the club captain [Fleming], the chairman [Carl Openshaw] and the chief executive [Paul Millman] couldn't tell me the news, when they were the ones who had really pushed for me to come here in the first place. I've got nothing but respect for David, because he told me the news as soon as he knew."

He continued: "The response I've had from the lads has been fantastic and it just goes to show how little the hirers and firers at the club understand how a team works and what makes Kent tick. Dropping a bombshell like this affects everyone. If they're prepared to cut a guy who's playing good cricket and giving his all to the side, then what sort of message are they sending out to everyone else?"

Fleming's version of events is: "If I remember the timing correctly, someone's girlfriend said something they shouldn't have and it all got out before it should have. The committee were left with an almost impossible decision; the heartbeat of the club earning almost £75,000 with one or two more years left in him, or the future in Geraint on £30,000. It was a really tough call. Inevitably, I wish it could have been handled differently. I've learned since that sometimes when decisions are made to look bad, or crass, the process behind making those decisions made sense to the decision-makers at the time. I hated getting rid of Nikko, but it was a case of Kent or Nikko."

Fulton calls it "the toughest decision of his career". He explains: "Technically, we were still challenging for second place and some of the committee thought it best not to tell him until after Headingley. I said I was not prepared to stand next to someone I cared about and pretend everything was OK. The guy had a right to know, so I called him to my hotel room the night before the game, told him the bad news, and that I had been involved in the decision. It was not a time for any cowardly passing of the buck. To his credit, Nixon couldn't have handled the situation any better and [at breakfast the next day] he told me he'd play, but that he wanted to address the guys before the start. He told them what had happened, but that he wanted to finish at Kent on a winning note. There were tears in the eyes of quite a few players and they were charged up to win."

Although Nixon's clumsily handled exit was the summer's most high-profile axing, Kent also released seamer David Masters, who has served Leicestershire and Essex with distinction since. However, it was the low-key exodus of fringe players James Hockley, Matt Banes and James Golding that really annoyed Martin McCague. Although the trio had played their part in Kent's 2nd XI securing a championship and one-day double, Banes and Hockley had been largely overlooked by the first team; Golding, with 18 wickets at a cost of 18 apiece, topped Spitfires' National League averages.

McCague fumed: "I think these are the first steps in a big stride backwards for English cricket. The players voted overwhelmingly against the change to two overseas stars next year and asked for restrictions on European passport holders. But the counties voted for two [overseas professionals], and it is the young players who are paying for it with their jobs. Golding and Hockley have never been given an extended opportunity to show us what they are even capable of."

Having been told of his departure on the same day that Kent awarded him his 2nd XI cap, Banes enjoyed a promising close season playing Australian grade cricket. Kent reinstated him on a summer contract, only to release him for a second time at the end of 2003. As for McCague, his rant in defence of the three youngsters proved to be his last and, after missing out on first team action all year, he was sacked after 12 years with the club.

He recalls: "It was my benefit year and I'd also been taken on the pre-season trip to South Africa, so things were looking quite good at the start there. A lot of the bowlers were injured over in Port Elizabeth, but I worked my nuts off trying to get back to somewhere near where I'd been with my bowling. I was named in the squad for our first championship game but, once we got back home, the others miraculously got off the treatment table and played while I got made 12th man. Because most of them had hardly bowled in pre-season we got spanked for 670 by Hampshire, and I got fobbed off to go and play a Club and Ground game in Folkestone. I bowled seven overs, smacked a half-century and never played for the first team again.

"I wanted to announce my retirement mid-season but was asked to hold off. A couple of weeks later, the club announced Matthew Fleming's retirement and said virtually nothing about me. Then, for the final home game of the season, Matthew got presented with a nice big silver salver but my send-off was being asked to conduct the toss for him. I felt like telling them to shove it, but thought better of it and went out to the middle one last time and did it. I didn't need a salver and it may sound like sour grapes now, but at least I remained true to myself."

Having masterminded the terms of his own retirement, Fleming, who had successfully applied to become a prospective parliamentary candidate for the Conservatives, enjoyed his last hurrah in front of an appreciative St Lawrence crowd of almost 6,000 for Kent's penultimate National League fixture against Glamorgan.

Farewell banners adorned the players' balcony as Openshaw presented the outgoing captain with his salver. "I was left feeling a complete emotional wreck by the end," said a tearful Fleming. "I knew there was going to be a presentation during the interval, but I wasn't expecting to see so many Kent fans in front of the balcony. Although I wanted to say thank you, I couldn't get anything out. I had to go and sit in the corner and get myself together in time to bat."

The bare statistics point to an unremarkable Kent career – a first-class batting average of 30 and almost 36 with the ball – but it is more fitting to remember Fleming for his showmanship and flashes of brilliance: the four direct-hit run-outs against Surrey in a National League game in 2001, or his fastest league fifty off 16 balls against Yorkshire at St Lawrence in 1996. Even in his swansong summer, Jazzer collected the Walter Lawrence Trophy for the fastest first-class hundred of the year, a 66-ball century against Sri Lanka.

Although Fleming played in 11 one-day internationals, he insists: "Captaining Kent in Canterbury Week were always my best days of the year, better even than playing for England. I would have loved to have won the championship there, I had a real affinity for the week; it was everything I thought cricket should be, with the balance of tradition with all the marquees. I never set out trying to play for England. I only ever wanted to play for, and captain, Kent. Playing for England was just something that happened."

He adds: "There were some fantastic people who played for Kent in that period. Paul Strang and Julian Thompson and our physiotherapist Martyn Sigley were fantastic men. Martyn was a key component to us eventually winning something. I tried to tell him so, but was never sure I got the message across. Min Patel was a properly good guy as well, but you never knew which Min was going to turn up or if he might go in the neck and blame the hotel pillows again. Yet you had the other group, with Hoops playing up, Fulton underachieving; Walks, a lovely guy and hugely talented, but a baby on occasions. Even Keysie at times. I hope he looks back now that he's a captain and realises what a pain in the arse he was as a stroppy teenager. We had too many people with too many distractions, who didn't mature at that same time or understand the game sufficiently for us to have fulfilled our potential over a longer period of time.

"I was a huge believer that only a part of a captain's responsibility lay on the pitch, so I really gave it my all for three years, off the pitch as well as on, and felt I left the club a much happier and united place with a staff who had a greater sense of belonging. There were things I might have done better and yes, we could have been more successful. But I hope people thought it was better when I left than when I started. No one else at Kent captained Rahul Dravid and Steve Waugh, but I did. So pop that in your pipe and smoke it!"

2003

If 1992 was the Royal Family's *annus horribilis*, Kent's year of wall-to-wall gloom was 2003. David Fulton, now in sole charge as captain, was intent on creating squad strength in depth as well as competition for places, but even before the season had begun his own career was in the balance. Fulton suffered a freak accident while practising pull shots in the nets on 11 April.

Moments after tapping away a stray ball as it rolled back onto the artificial surface, Fulton resumed his stance and had barely started to turn and face the bowling machine (operated by Simon Willis) when the next bouncer, catching him unawares, smashed into the side of his helmet. Fired out by the machine at almost 90mph, the plastic practice ball reared off the pitch and slid between the peak and grille of Fulton's helmet, catching him flush on the right eye. The sickening blow ripped out his tear duct and left him in fear of losing the sight in his eye.

Speaking a fortnight later, Fulton told the *Kent Messenger*: "When a ball hits you in the eye with such force it burns like hell, and you do tend to fear the worst. I was lucky that our physiotherapist, Martyn Sigley, was on hand and treated me with cold, damp towels and ice within two minutes. After that, it was straight round to A&E and then over to hospital in Ashford." A two-hour operation to reconstruct his right eye and lachrymal gland left Fulton sporting a scarred eye-socket and 30 stitches. He was sounding an over-optimistic note when he said: "I really don't think I'll have any problems when it comes to batting against quick bowlers again."

As the season got under way Kent were missing not just Fulton, but also his opening partner, Rob Key, who was unavailable at the behest of England coach Duncan Fletcher. In their absence, interest centred on the form of Fulton's close-season signings: Somerset's livewire all-rounder Peter Trego, Surrey's promising but untried left-handed batsman Michael Carberry and Worcestershire's hot-blooded, left-arm swing bowler Alamgir Sheriyar. Fulton described Sheriyar, who had been the leading wicket-taker in the country in

1999, as the "final piece in the jigsaw". He was also hoping that 2nd XI batsman Alex Loudon, South African-born all-rounder Matt Dennington and left-arm spinner Rob Ferley would press for places as the season wore on. In the event, none of the new recruits made a concerted impact, and the young players failed to progress as hoped.

The side lurched from one bad result to another, prompting Fulton to make a premature, possibly ill-advised, return to championship cricket on 30 May – barely six weeks after his accident. He could not prevent Lancashire's win at Canterbury; moreover, his bad luck continued when a rearing delivery left him nursing a cracked right thumb. More worryingly still, it became apparent that the blow to his eye had left Fulton with a blind spot. A slip chance which before he would have snaffled with nonchalant ease crashed into his chest almost before he had moved his hands in reaction. With head bowed, Fulton moved himself out of the cordon and rarely went back thereafter. To his eternal credit, Fulton showed immense bravery during a fighting return to first-class cricket that season and even went on to grind his way to eight more championship centuries. But the injury undoubtedly reduced his peripheral vision, stripped him of confidence and greatly reduced his range of stroke play.

Vice-captain and beneficiary Mark Ealham was promoted to lead the side during Fulton's early recuperation, but selection policy seemed to change by the hour. Only three players, Ealham, Geraint Jones and Matthew Walker, appeared in all 16 championship matches and, early on at least, results were abysmal. The change to regulations covering overseas players also muddied the waters, allowing Kent to field two at any one time and bring in replacements as cover for injury or international duty. The revolving-door policy led to Greg Blewett, Andrew Symonds, Mohammad Sami and Muttiah Muralitharan each taking his turn with varying degrees of success in what Ed Smith later described as an "expensive circus".

Blewett averaged a modest 31 from seven championship starts, while Pakistan strike bowler Sami managed only three mid-season appearances before sustaining an ankle injury. He at least departed on a spectacular note: his match figures of 15 for 114 in Kent's opening four-day win, over Nottinghamshire at The Mote, were the finest at the county-town ground and Kent's best anywhere since Doug Wright's haul of 16 for 80 against Somerset in 1939.

The combination of Symonds and Muralitharan was the most effective overseas pairing in what proved to be a season of two halves. Kent mustered only 67 points as they failed to win any of their opening eight matches, then, with a partially sighted Fulton back at the helm, they went to collect 131 points from the last eight games, picking up all six of their victories in the process to finish fourth.

With Min Patel sidelined by injury, Muralitharan was the key to Kent's huge improvement in the second half of the summer, taking 33 wickets at a miserly average of 13.54 in only five games. He was as affable off the field as he was successful on it. Walker recalls: "He had ants in his pants. When he was in the dressing room he could never sit still or stop talking. He was fantastic to have around. If you went out for a meal he never gave you chance to pay. I remember one night, just after our starters, I asked the waiter to take my credit card in order to pay the bill at the end. He said, 'It's OK, sir, Mr Muralitharan's already taken care of it.' "

Muttiah Muralitharan weaves his magic in a National League match against Worcestershire

Picture: Derek Stingemore, Kent Messenger, PD1673798

The consistent Martin Saggers, who finally won England recognition with a call-up for the winter tour of Bangladesh, was again Kent's leading wicket-taker with 58, while Sheriyar and Ealham could be reasonably content with 38 apiece.

Once Fulton returned to open, Kent's batting also proved more reliable, with Smith leading the way. He scored 1,447 runs for the county at an average of 60, was the first batsman in the country to pass 1,000 runs and became only the third Kent player, after Wally Hardinge and Frank Woolley, to hit hundreds in four successive innings (he also recorded five hundreds and three ducks in a bizarre eight-innings sequence).

With his average approaching three figures Smith made his Test debut against South Africa at Trent Bridge. He had captained Kent against the touring side a week earlier, foreshadowing future problems when he became embroiled in an ugly difference of opinion with Saggers over who should set his field. The South Africans took one international innings to work out Smith's front-foot bias and, after three Tests, he was jettisoned by England.

Ealham reached 900 runs, as did Geraint Jones in his first full season, the highlight of which was a maiden championship century against Leicestershire, the day after Paul Nixon had made an unbeaten 113. It was the first time since 1928 that both wicketkeepers had scored a century in the same game at Canterbury. Excellent form with bat and gloves was enough to win Jones a place on England's winter tour of the West Indies. New boy Carberry posted a respectable 824 runs, while Walker, with 1,051, passed 1,000 for the first time since his debut a decade earlier.

On the limited-overs front, supporters had a new competition and a new venue to enjoy, with the loudly trumpeted introduction of the Twenty20 Cup and Kent's return to the refurbished county ground at Beckenham for the first time since 1954. Kent's apathetic approach was reflected in defeats in four of their five zonal games and they also crashed out of the C&G Trophy in the early rounds when a disappointing batting display allowed Gloucestershire to progress. Kent proved equally inconsistent in the National Cricket League, where they mustered only seven wins to finish a disappointing sixth.

Fulton admits that none of the new signings met his expectations. He was well aware of the risk factor in recruiting Trego and feels that his own absence from the side was critical. "By the time I got back he'd let himself down quite badly and the rest of the lads had made their minds up about him. He and Sheriyar had become big mates and were doing their own thing. Within the year Trego had gone."

As for Sheriyar, Fulton says the club were partially to blame for his dramatic dip in form. "I felt Sheriyar could bowl and, being a left-armer, gave us something different. As a captain you're judged on your results, where you finish in the tables. The question I had back then was, how do coaches get judged? I'm not pointing the finger, just asking the question. Look at the facts: Sheriyar ran up and bowled big hooping in-swingers one year; suddenly he came to us and lost that. Something technically wasn't quite happening for him, but we didn't seem to know as a coaching unit how to put it right."

Kent's tendency to play hard ball during player-contract negotiations came back to bite them hard at the end of the season when Fulton's attempts to re-ignite Mark Ealham's career backfired to such an extent that he left the club. It remains one of the most controversial chapters in Kent's lengthy catalogue of contractual blunders. "I was unwilling to compromise when Mark demanded a two-year contract," explains Fulton. "He had enjoyed a good season and we got on well, but I thought the fact his contract was up had played a part in his high levels of motivation. I therefore wanted to keep his contract short and remunerate him well to keep him fully energised. Ealy was an experienced cricketer with an old-school mindset. He would do his job on the field, but wouldn't always embrace elements of new thinking off it. Winter fitness-testing and ice baths to aid recuperation were snubbed, and he was at times quite vocal with his opinions, which made our job with other players harder.

"Come contract meeting time I didn't like the way he tried to force our hand and I was happy that we didn't budge on our position. Looking back, it was a mistake because he was a home-grown lad and a top performer and I should have trusted him more. Our loss was Nottinghamshire's gain."

Ealham, recently retired after winning the championship during his six seasons with Nottinghamshire, admits now that there was fault on both sides. "I got a tip-off from an agent as early as July that the club had put me on the list for potential release at the end of the summer; I couldn't believe it. The weird thing was, I'd had a great season under Fults. I scored 900 runs and took 40 odd wickets, which for an all-rounder was right up there with the best. As the season drew to a close, and possibly because I'd had such a good year, Kent maybe started to think they couldn't release me because the public would go nuts. So I approached the club to ask what was happening.

"I had a heart-to-heart with Paul Millman and finally had to put him over a barrel and say, 'I want to know where my future lies.' We held a final meeting in the committee room, with me, Mike Denness, Fulton and the chief executive. They wanted to drag it out, but I instantly asked had they got any more than a one-year contract on offer. They ummed and ahhed but said no. So I jumped to my feet, shook their hands and walked out. That was the end of my Kent career. I was gutted, I couldn't believe what had just happened. I sat in the car feeling very glum. It was a horrible feeling because I'd been with the club since I was 16. It's old hat now, but I think the supporters, who'd given me great backing in my benefit year incidentally, understood my reasons for holding out for a longer contract and then for ultimately going."

Ealham, who won eight Test caps and played in 64 one-day internationals while with Kent, is now able to view the episode more objectively. "I can start to see Kent's point, because they were looking at me as maybe someone who'd been disgruntled for a couple of seasons. Maybe they were right to say we'll give you a year and see how you go? But I wanted a bit more security than that. For me it was all down to Kirsty and I starting a family and making sure we kept paying the mortgage. Three years on offer at Trent Bridge was better than one at Kent. I can't put all the blame on Kent, because there were times I shouldn't have behaved as I did. But I'm glad now they did it because I went on to have a fantastic time at Nottinghamshire and can still look back and feel that overall I had a good time with Kent too."

Matthew Fleming is equally convinced that the parting, in hindsight, was right for both player and club. "One of the reasons we all got so frustrated with him was that we were all so jealous of Mark. He had so much talent and if he'd had a bit more oomph about him he could have achieved so much more. He'd reached the stage at Kent where he was becoming a grumpy old pro who just wanted to keep ticking over. Maybe without realising it, he'd become quite subversive. I remember having to leave him out of a floodlit one-day game because he'd walked out on practice the previous day. I'm really glad he went to Nottinghamshire so that when people write his cricketing epitaph it will end on a really positive note. Kent would have been a much stronger side with Ealy firing on all cylinders, but he wasn't. I don't think he could do that for Kent anymore."

Once the dust had settled on Ealham's departure, the county's management team found time for some soul-searching. Fulton, recalling the moment when he and Ian Brayshaw agreed a change was necessary, says: "He and I went for a swim in my mother-in-law's pool and Ian asked me, 'What do you think?' and I said, 'I don't honestly think you and I are the dream team.' I count Sticks as a friend, one of the nicest men in cricket, and it would have been very tempting to recommend him again but, hand on heart, I didn't feel we were getting the best out of the guys."

Brayshaw duly tendered his resignation but, prior to his departure, he and Fulton were invited to formulate a coaching blueprint and make recommendations to the committee as to who should take over the head coach's role. They proposed a Kentish triumvirate of Simon Willis, Paul Farbrace and Chris Stone for 2004. Some members saw it as a fudge, others viewed it as a pragmatic, budget-conscious option. What worried me was how the players might respond to having three bosses, four if you added Fulton into the mix. Which of the quartet would a player ultimately answer to? It seemed to me that confusion would ultimately reign and, in the fullness of time, it did.

To anyone involved with Kent on a day-to-day basis, 2003 ended tragically with the death of Richard Davis on 29 December

The much-travelled Richard 'Dickie' Davis, who died in 2003, aged only 37

following his two-year battle against a brain tumour. He was only 37. Each of his five counties was represented at an intensely moving funeral; the tiny village of Blean came to a virtual standstill on 9 January as cricket said goodbye to the kindly man they all knew as Dickie.

On my drive home to Whitstable on that stormy winter's day a dazzling rainbow formed over the estuary, causing me to marvel at mother nature and then at the courage shown that day by Dickie's widow Samantha and his sister-in-law Claudine, the wife of David Fulton. In paying tribute to their bravery, I wrote: "I imagined the rainbow to be Dickie's vehicle to heaven. Where, even now, he is weighing up which end would be best for bowling left-arm spin."

2004

Kent's players were presented with an unwelcome reminder of 2003's traumas when Ed Smith's diary of the season was published barely a month into the new campaign. The idea had been planted by Steve Waugh, who urged Smith to "tell the truth as much as you can". The author was soon made aware that the truth can hurt. Although *On and Off the Field* was frank, insightful and an engaging read, team-mates were wounded; David Fulton even sought solicitors' advice over the content. Whether Smith realised it at the time or not, he had landed the first blows of what was to become a season of acrimony.

The greatest crime was that the in-house quarrelling only served to damage team spirit and detract from the side's prime objective: to win the County Championship. The one certainty is, had Kent pulled together and batted better at the start of their four-day games they would have become worthy champions. As it was, they finished second, 16 points adrift, despite winning seven games, the most in the division and two more than title-winning Warwickshire. Kent were the only county to boast four batsmen, Fulton, Rob Key, Smith and Matthew Walker, with over 1,000 runs, yet they mustered only 43 batting points, 22 fewer than Warwickshire. It proved beyond question that poor first-innings batting was responsible for their tossing away the best chance of winning the championship since 1978.

Initially, Fulton re-engaged Symonds and Mohammad Sami as his overseas recruits, but as the season progressed injuries led Kent to engage New Zealander Ian Butler, Pakistan's master-blaster Shahid Afridi and Australian batsman Michael Bevan. For varied reasons, all three proved ineffective. The county gave a development contract to paceman Simon Cusden and then beat off a reported 10 counter-bids to sign Cusden's England Under-19 new ball partner, David Stiff, from Yorkshire. Anticipating Geraint Jones's absence on

Test duty, Fulton also took on 22-year-old Irishman Niall O'Brien as understudy.

Despite prolonged spells of rain, everything appeared rosy in Kent's camp throughout April, when Fulton's willingness to barter in the opening four-day match led to a run-chase win in Bristol. Only 55 overs were bowled on the opening three days, but Fulton and Chris Taylor struck a deal for Kent to chase 302, which they did for the loss of three wickets, courtesy of unbeaten hundreds from Key and Michael Carberry, his maiden championship century. Then, chasing an unlikely target of 429 to beat Worcestershire at St Lawrence, Kent were inspired by a career-best 64 from nightwatchman Martin Saggers and romped home, scoring 112 in the final hour with hundreds from player of the season Walker and Carberry, whose 112 was to remain his championship best for Kent. It was their first Canterbury win over Worcestershire since 1914, their then highest ever fourth-innings total and biggest successful run chase. It was also the first time the county had won their two opening championship matches since 1964.

After a rain-ruined draw with Gloucestershire, Kent's insistence that Jones should gain batting practice by playing against New Zealand was vindicated by his hundred in Kent's nine-wicket win. Beneficiary Min Patel then returned to the fold for the first time since September 2002 after recuperating from surgery to fuse together two vertebrae. Patel's six wickets backed up Sami's match return of 10 for 138 in the 145-run win over Northamptonshire that took Kent top in mid-May. The game also featured hundreds from Fulton, his first since his eye injury a year earlier, Key and Symonds. Despite his centuries in both of Kent's previous victories, Carberry was inexplicably dropped to No 6 and became disenchanted thereafter.

Key maintained his excellent form, scoring 86 and 199 at the Oval, where Surrey recovered from a dreadful start to land a 75-run win. Key, the first Kent player to be dismissed for 199, followed up with an innings of 180 against Lancashire at Tunbridge Wells which took him past 1,000 runs for the season on 2 June. It was the earliest any player had reached the landmark since Graeme Hick in 1988 and he was also the third Kent batsman in four years to win the race to 1,000 (all in matches against Lancashire). No Kent player had ever achieved the feat in as few as 11 innings. Almost submerged by the statistics – Kent's first-innings total of 615 remains a ground record – was a seven-wicket victory.

This game, and the corresponding Totesport National League fixture, showcased Symonds's dynamic versatility as an all-rounder. He took an astonishing catch in Lancashire's first innings, then held together Kent's threadbare attack with a marathon, match-winning spell of off-spin. On the following day he made a blistering 146 off 110 balls which is still the highest score by a Kent player in one-day cricket. "He was incredible in those games," recalls Fulton. "It wasn't until later that I found out he'd been drinking till three in the morning." He adds: "He had been at Kent long enough to be quite familiar in the dressing room. The problem was, he didn't know that there were one or two people around who would load the gun and let Symmo fire it. The more he played for us the more his standards slipped in other areas and there were times you would wonder how on earth you would deal with it."

Fulton himself bruised a knuckle in the league game against Lancashire and, having appointed Smith as his four-day vice-captain and Key as limited-overs deputy at the season's start, he duly handed over the reins to Smith for the trip to Worcester. Either through injury or international absence, Kent were missing Jones, Martin Saggers, Sami and Patel, as well as Fulton, and Smith was forced to give a debut to Cusden. It soon became clear that he went into the game without the full support of his team.

With increasing tension in the dressing room following the release of Smith's diary, Fulton anticipated problems. "The night before I took Symmo, Keysie and Walks out for dinner and a drink. I could tell, from some of the conversations, where things were going and I wanted to sort it out. I told them I couldn't play, that Ed was acting captain and I wanted them to give him 100 per cent support. Whatever they thought of him, I asked them to back him up and try and win the match. Ed had a lot of qualities: he is very intelligent, he's a student of the game and tactically he had some really good ideas. His weakness was that he wasn't everyone's cup of tea and couldn't guarantee that everyone would follow him."

After losing the toss, Kent appeared lethargic and flat in the field. On several occasions senior players meandered off to the dressing room to be replaced by the 12th man, seemingly without consulting Smith first. With Worcester-shire coasting towards 300 with only four wickets down Fulton, who had travelled to New Road to assist first-season coach Simon Willis, realised something was amiss and took matters into his own hands by going on as 12th man. "The big mistake I made," he now admits, "rather than pulling them all in and telling them to get their heads down and get on with it, was to go out into the middle.

"I was moving a few fielders around when George Sharp [the umpire] told me I couldn't do that as 12th man. I didn't know it was against the laws and afterwards felt I hadn't helped the situation. But what I had seen was

Kent's Twenty20 captain, Andrew Symonds, plotting with Shahid Afridi in 2004
Picture: Ady Kerry

disgraceful. Not walking in to celebrate when you took a wicket, not wanting to do as the captain says; there was almost a mutiny situation going on. For me, we had a championship to win, Ed was the acting captain, they should do as he said. It was as simple as that. Clearly it wasn't so simple to the protagonists. From the sidelines you couldn't hear what was being said, but Ed has told me subsequently, and it was bang out of order. The body language was poor and wasn't acceptable, but to be fair to Ed, he didn't come off and bleat about it.

"There was obviously an issue, and it was childish. I didn't know the full extent of some of the stuff that happened out there and wish now that I'd handled it differently, but at the time I was so close to things that I thought that by reclaiming the captaincy I could sort it out. It was a mistake, I undermined Ed by doing it, and I hold my hand up to that now."

Mike Denness, the chairman of cricket, was summoned to Worcester that afternoon in an attempt to stem the revolt and, in order to get to the heart of the unsavoury events, he interviewed Smith, Willis and Fulton, as well as the alleged dissenters, Symonds and Key. Denness recalls: "In conversation to me Andrew said, 'Smith doesn't understand cricket. He couldn't captain anything and I'd do the same thing again' So I posed him the question, 'You've just got in the Australia side, would you speak to Steve Waugh the same way?' He couldn't answer it, but of course he would never have spoken to Steve in such a manner."

Denness adds: "Put aside Andrew's record for Kent for a second, look at his record for Australia; look at the indiscipline that appears to surround this lad. Then look at the facts of what happened to Kent cricket at Worcester. He didn't think he'd done anything wrong, but it was diabolical what he did."

Despite the unrest, and to his great credit at the time, Symonds went on to score Kent's only century of the match, but only dogged 10th-wicket resistance from O'Brien and Alamgir Sheriyar, who batted out the final 31 balls, allowed Kent to escape with a draw. They pocketed 12 points, but the general sense of unease lingered for the rest of the season.

Fulton returned to the helm at Beckenham, where an unbeaten 156 from Symonds and torrential rain on the final day saved Kent from a probable defeat against Warwickshire. In Sami's absence on international duty, Kent signed Butler as a low-budget replacement and were made to pay the price with an innings and 45-run defeat to Sussex at Hove. Fulton scored Kent's sole hundred of the game, while Butler returned one for 100 as Sussex recorded their first championship win that summer. After making 506 runs at an average of 72.25 in his five championship starts, Symonds departed for treatment on a persistent Achilles problem, leaving Kent to sign Bevan as his locum.

The left-hander marked his debut with a half-century at Southgate, but could not prevent Middlesex from landing an 119-run win to leapfrog Kent in the chase for the title. Fulton top-scored with 121, Patel bagged his 500th first-class wicket and occasional off-spinner Alex Loudon revealed his doosra for the first time to claim five for 53. Kent then avenged their early-season defeat at Hove with a 236-run Canterbury Week drubbing of Sussex. Walker hit centuries in each innings and Smith made 166 and 93 against a weakened attack.

Successive draws against Warwickshire, Surrey and Lancashire left Kent 40 points behind Warwickshire with only two matches remaining. Key, back from England duty, hit 131 and Smith made 156 as Kent wrapped up an 194-run win over relegation-bound Northamptonshire and, despite an innings win over Middlesex in their last match, they finished as runners-up for the 11th time. Smith bowed out with an innings of 189, against the side he was soon to join, and Key became the first Kent batsman since Colin Cowdrey in 1965 to top the national averages. There were no feats to match on the bowling side: for the first time since 1883 no Kent bowler took 50 first-class wickets.

It was a season of one-day disappointments as the Spitfires, wearing a new, all-black limited-overs strip that Fulton believed would give them greater presence, suffered National League relegation for the first time. They lost heavily in the third round of the C&G Trophy, to the inevitable Warwickshire, while the Twenty20 Cup campaign plumbed new depths. Bad went to worse after the appointment of Symonds as acting captain. He started off well enough, with an amazing 43-ball innings of 112 that eased Kent to a seven-wicket win over Middlesex at Maidstone, but Symonds's pre-match decision to drop Smith, who had just made successive one-day fifties, re-opened the wounds of antagonism between the two.

Fulton justifies his high-risk decision to appoint Symonds like this: "I felt Symmo could win us the competition, captaincy would give him some responsibility and because the game's over inside a couple of hours, there weren't too many nuances to man management to worry about. I felt the best call was for me not to play and Symmo to captain, so I let the cricket committee know. They and the coaches backed my reasoning.

"The night before that first game I went around to Symmo's house for dinner because I'd found out that he didn't want Ed in the side. Ed had just scored 80 off 50 balls against Warwickshire at Beckenham, so Mike Denness and the cricket committee said to me there should be good cricketing reasons for dropping him. If there were, he was prepared to back Symmo. I asked him his reasons. After a few choice words, he said it was because he [Smith] was 'a selfish, one-paced player and that he wasn't good in the field'. I took those to be cricketing reasons, even if I didn't agree with them all and, having wanted Symmo as captain, I now needed to back him.

"I planned to go to Maidstone the next day to manage the situation but I picked up the worst vomiting and diarrhoea bug and spent much of the next 24 hours running to the bathroom. To make matters worse, Symmo went for a scan on his Achilles on the morning of the game and turned up late. Wilco and Farbie [coaches Willis and Farbrace] felt Symmo should tell the players that day's team, but when he rocked up late he said something to the effect, 'Right guys, Dennington and Smith you're not playing. Let's go and win.' By all accounts it was a complete fiasco. Eddie couldn't believe it, he phoned the chief executive and went ballistic. Looking back, he probably didn't get it quite right in terms of how he reacted, but after this and the incident at Worcester, I had some sympathy for him. Symmo went out, smacked a hundred, won it and told me later that everything would be all right."

Fulton was commentating for Radio Kent as the game against Essex proved the opposite. "We had Shahid Afridi playing and I said to Symmo that I felt we had plenty of firepower at the top with him alone, and that he should maybe hold himself back in reserve. He said no, he wanted to go 'all guns blazing', so

End of the road: an emotional Ed Smith walks off after making 189 in what proved to be his final innings for Kent

Picture: Ady Kerry

again, I'd made the call to make him captain and had to back him. We were 50 for three and ended up scoring 125. In the field the plans were rubbish, the bowling was rubbish, the whole thing was a shambles and we just got picked apart as Essex won in about 15 overs. It was embarrassing. The Essex boys came in and started singing. Symmo got stuck into a beer and said something like, 'What are they shouting about? It's only a game of Twenty20.' Fulton continues:

> "I remember driving home afterwards with my wife Claudine and saying, 'What have I done?' We had played abysmally and our captain's reaction was to neck a bottle of beer and say, 'It's only a game of Twenty20,' when it was fast becoming the most important competition for us. It had meant so much to me that I'd left myself out hoping that we could win the bloody thing. I pulled up at some traffic lights on the Maidstone ring road and remember punching the sun visor in my car out of anger and frustration. I knocked it clean off. I then heard a horn hooting to one side. I looked across and it was [Essex players] Ronnie Irani and James Middlebrook sitting in the car next to me asking if I was all right. That was just the lowest moment."

By the time Kent got around to disciplining the principal New Road mutineers, Symonds had left the country and Key, having been the only one to apologise, was back in the England side. Exasperated by the club's painfully slow disciplinary procedures, Denness resigned as chairman of cricket and offered the role to his former team-mate, Graham Johnson. Unable to agree the wording of the press release announcing his departure, Denness gave me a *Kent Messenger* exclusive. To this day, Denness remains livid over the affair and how the club chose to handle it: "I know that what happened to Ed was a disgrace," he says. "This person [Symonds] is under contract to the club at the end of the day. The club should have disciplined him in no uncertain terms, in the same way Australia have done since.

"The meeting I had over at the chairman's place [Carl Openshaw's home in Tunbridge Wells] was not very successful, so I took a back seat on it and left it to the chairman to deal with. I believed he was going to speak to certain people, rather than have me go through it all again, but I don't know what happened, if anything. I decided that if that was to be the procedure, then it would be far better if I wasn't around. I asked myself, 'Do I really need this aggravation, or to be treated in this way?' The answer was no, I didn't. I had been, and was prepared to stand and be counted by what happened cricket-wise, but not to be judged by a chief executive or anyone else.

"Kent wouldn't agree on the press release that was going to go out. I said to them, 'You've got to tell the truth on this, you've got to be open.' I told them, 'If you don't agree, then I'm open to talking to the press.' So they put out their press release. It was diabolical, almost like going back to the old days. Although the Band of Brothers weren't involved this time, here they [club officers] were whispering, 'We can't do that.'"

Denness still stands by his decision, explaining: "I've never had an ego, never wanted one, and non first-class cricketers cannot afford to have an ego when it comes to cricket. The fact that it even happened was a tragedy and, in hindsight, it's hard to believe that individuals conducted themselves as they did. Even the umpires were taken aback by what went on, which, to my mind, was quite atrocious. Happily for the player and the club Rob Key apologised and matured thereafter, but I think that history shows that Symonds never did."

Perhaps the most depressing element of all is that Smith left for Middlesex at the end of the season and his close friend, Alex Loudon, moved to Warwickshire, despite the offer of captaincy in the future. The hugely promising Loudon, who was to retire from cricket in 2007, cited a "lack of faith and confidence in the Kent coaching structure" as his major reason for leaving; Smith was more pointed. "The idea that I would leave Kent, the team that I have always supported and the place I was born, because of an argument with an overseas pro is not credible," he said. "Much more of a factor is a series of decisions by Kent that sadly left me with diminished trust in the leadership of the club."

Graham Johnson's first task as newly appointed chairman of cricket was to quell a members' close-season revolt and resist sustained calls for an extraordinary general meeting. His second was to appoint former South Africa Test coach Graham Ford as Kent's new director of cricket to sort out the mess.

2005

A savage overnight storm that wreaked havoc across east Kent on 9 January also brought a cricketing icon crashing to its knees as the county lost their famous St Lawrence lime tree. The ailing 180-year-old specimen buckled and finally shattered, some seven feet from its broad base. As news of the tree's demise spread, a small crowd gathered to pay their last respects to a tree which had presided over every Kent match since 1847. The lime had come to represent all that was good and wholesome about cricket in Kent. It proffered shade for supporters, a leafy backdrop to marching bands gracing Canterbury

Fallen idol: the famous Canterbury lime after being struck down by a storm in January 2005
Picture: Ady Kerry

Week, and even a resting place for members whose final wish was to have their ashes scattered around the gnarled base.

The understudy appeared little more than a sapling when former president Bobby Neame conducted the planting ceremony to establish the young pretender inside the boundary ropes. The old lime lives on, however. A number of grafts eventually took root and were planted at Kent's outgrounds in Tunbridge Wells and Beckenham, while the few remaining hunks of sound timber were turned into wooden trinkets for sale in the club shop to help pay, in part, for the clear-up operation.

Soon afterwards, on 1 March, Kent lost another legend when Brian Luckhurst died from cancer of the oesophagus at his home in Alkham, near Dover. He was 66. At his funeral in mid-April, held on the very day Luckhurst's year of presidency was due to end, a packed congregation at the Church of St Anthony and Parmiers, which overlooked Lucky's home, stood in appreciation.

Another much-admired past president, Don Beney, also died that summer at the age of 90. A founder member of the Kent County Cricket Supporters' Club, he became universally known as 'Uncle Don' for his tireless fund-raising for club causes and Kent beneficiaries alike. Despite the long journey from his home in West Wickham, Beney took great pride in his record of never having missed a meeting during his 18-year stint on the county's general committee.

It all made for a grim backdrop to the start of Graham Ford's tenure as director of cricket but, prior to his arrival, Kent had at least set about much-needed squad strengthening as the departure of Ed Smith and Alex Loudon, at the end of the 2004 season, was followed by the release, a year later, of Michael Carberry, Ben Trott and Alamgir Sheriyar. Carberry has flourished since at Hampshire and complained earlier this year that he had been "messed about for three years" by Kent.

To fill the vacancies, Kent captured 28-year-old batsman and serial under-achiever Darren Stevens from Leicestershire, and the quietly effective Middlesex seamer, Simon Cook. Whitstable-raised teenager Joe Denly was taken onto the staff as one for the future, but Kent were forced to admit defeat in their audacious attempt to sign Kevin Pietersen from Nottinghamshire. Chairman Carl Openshaw said: "It's fair to say that the sorts of salary figures being bandied about are outside our existing wage structure. We would have made a competitive bid, but heard all along that he would join Hampshire. We never had an opportunity to put a figure on the table."

Kent capitalised on Ford's links by bringing in former Test batsman Martin van Jaarsveld as the club's first Kolpak signing and another South African, all-rounder Andrew Hall, joined as overseas professional in late May. Having already performed capably for Northamptonshire and Worcestershire respectively, both players were known to Kent supporters and, in general, their arrival met with a favourable response from a membership who had grown tired of expensive imports disappearing after a handful of games. Van Jaarsveld and Hall felt even more at home when Kent signed another South African, Justin Kemp. Neil Dexter, a Johannesburg-born batsman with a British passport, came with a glowing recommendation from his former school-mate, Matt Dennington. After scoring two stylish, late-season fifties Dexter was offered a two-year deal.

Kent signed local league wicketkeeper Paul Dixey as further cover for Jones and O'Brien, but said farewell to batting guru and age-group coach Chris Stone, who went to work in South Africa, leaving Ford and Simon Willis to run first team affairs. Ford, quiet and unassuming to the point of appearing dour, won the instant respect of Kent's players and, though it rarely showed, he was genuinely excited by the challenges.

With Jones on Ashes duty for much of the season and with so many new players to bed in, Kent inevitably took time to settle. Of the side picked for the opening championship fixture only four, Fulton, Rob Key, Matthew Walker and Amjad Khan, had played in the equivalent game a year earlier. At least Van Jaarsveld wasted no time in making a good impression, becoming

History in the making: Martin van Jaarsveld, in 2005, on his way to becoming the first Kent player to score a century in both innings on debut

Picture: Barry Goodwin, Kent Messenger, PD1673799

the first Kent batsman to score a century in both innings on championship debut.

Hall arrived from international duty three weeks into May, just in time for Kent's first win of the four-day campaign, over Nottinghamshire. It was no coincidence that all six of Kent's victories came during Hall's abridged stay, yet he had limited say in the outcome at Trent Bridge. After bagging a pair on debut, he bowled effectively on the final day to take four for 42.

The new-look side had the makings of a useful championship outfit. Yet their one-day cricket in 2005 was woeful. They finished eighth with only six wins from their first season in the Totesport National League's Second Division. Fulton, averaging only 23, voiced concerns over his own continued selection in the one-day team and chose to canvass the team's opinion. Their negative response left him with little option but to stand down from the side to face Warwickshire in a C&G Trophy quarter-final at Edgbaston. Grudgingly, it seemed, Walker agreed to take charge of the one-day side as Kent crashed out by five wickets. Fulton had effectively signed his own captaincy death warrant and the ramifications of his decision rumbled through to September.

Walker remained at the helm throughout a pitiful Twenty20 campaign. Spitfires suffered six straight defeats and a no result before breaking their duck with a five-run success over Essex. Even so, Kent, with the worst record of any county, finished bottom of their qualifying group.

Returning to the championship, Key scored a brace of centuries in the draw against Surrey at The Nevill, where he and Van Jaarsveld posted a third-wicket stand of 323, a county record. Kent arrived in Maidstone to play Gloucestershire two days after heavy rain left the county town awash and caught The Mote's ground staff unawares. As a result, the game was played out on a seamer-friendly surface and completed in just over two-and-half days. Denly, drafted in at the eleventh hour for his championship debut, made four and 10, and though Kent won by seven wickets an ECB pitch panel, chaired by Tony Pigott, declared the wicket unfit for first-class cricket.

They were docked eight points, the same punishment meted out to Surrey for ball-tampering that summer. Both club officials and members believed that the county had been harshly treated, but an appeal proved futile. Disappointingly, for supporters in central and west Kent, the county have not played a first-class fixture in Maidstone since.

The players, still feeling aggrieved, took out their frustrations on Glamorgan; Van Jaarsveld made a career-best 262 not out in Kent's 10-wicket victory at Cardiff. Fulton's side then moved top of the Frizzell Championship table on 18 June, following their innings and 154-run win over Warwickshire at Edgbaston, where Min Patel bagged six for 53 to complement hundreds from Walker and Stevens, his first for the club. In their first championship match at St Lawrence for almost two months, Kent surprisingly lost to lowly Sussex. Not for the last time Mushtaq Ahmed was the architect of Kent's demise.

The title seemed to be slipping from their grasp at Guildford, until a dramatic last-day turnaround converted an inevitable draw into a dramatic four-wicket win for Kent. Fulton calls it the "the most incredible victory of my career". Surrey collapsed, inexplicably, from 240 for two to 350 all out on the last day, leaving Kent a target of 231 from 35 overs. Several Kent players, the captain included, wondered initially if the run chase was feasible, but history changed Fulton's mind for him. He says: "A couple of years earlier I'd agreed a run chase with Mark Butcher which we ended up losing. It sent us bottom or second bottom and became an even more significant moment to me because I got some dodgy messages on my phone from members asking why I'd agreed to the deal. After that, I got the players together and told them if I had my time again I would still agree to that chase because I felt we were good enough, and believed we could have won. So when the opportunity arose at Guildford, I ended up thinking, let's play positive cricket, and play to win."

Kemp, who had been sceptical about Kent's chances, forgot his doubts to make an unbeaten 47 off 37 balls which settled the outcome with five balls remaining. Jimmy Ormond, the Surrey pace bowler, was so upset by his side's capitulation that he punched the dressing-room door and broke his hand.

Kent enthralled a sizeable Canterbury Week crowd, but annoyed the club's marketing department, by beating struggling Glamorgan by an innings and 124 runs inside three days. Stevens hit the first double hundred of his career in Kent's total of 587, and Andrew Hall followed up an innings of 133, his first century for the county, with four wickets in Glamorgan's second innings. Seamers Hall, Cook and Khan, plus leading wicket-taker Patel, nigh-on carried the Kent attack all summer as Martin Saggers suffered through injury and Simon Cusden, David Stiff and Robbie Joseph were plagued by poor form and no-ball issues.

Stevens maintained his excellent run with centuries in draws against Hampshire and Middlesex, but when Kent also drew their return fixture with Middlesex, at Lord's, they slipped further behind in the championship race. Slim hopes became non-existent when they went into their game against leaders Nottinghamshire without both Hall and Kemp after South Africa's new coach, Mickey Arthur, demanded their immediate return home to take part in two benefit games for Jacques Kallis, a round of book signings and a team-bonding camp. Kent were rightly aggrieved but powerless to reverse the decision.

Despite a classy unbeaten 79 from Dexter on debut, Nottinghamshire took control. The equivalent of a day's play was lost to rain and on the final morning Fulton took the biggest gamble of his career by brokering a one-sided run-chase deal with his opposite number, Stephen Fleming. Kent were left with just 70 overs to pursue an improbable target of 420 for a win that might just have kept the championship race alive until its concluding week. Kent's embarrassing pursuit ended virtually before it began and they capitulated to 205 all out. As if to make a point, Mark Ealham claimed the winning catch at gully as Nottinghamshire clinched their first championship in 14 years.

Hampshire captain Shane Warne, whose side might have overhauled Nottinghamshire had Kent held them to a draw, accused Fulton of 'gifting' the winners' pennant to Fleming, and added: "It was one of the dumbest things I've seen in my life." Five years on, Fulton believes he had no choice but to gamble in order to keep Kent's fading title dream alive. He says: "Some members could see my point, others didn't, and we received nasty mail, a couple of dodgy phone calls and some threats. It wasn't nice, but Kent fans are passionate about their cricket. I'd rather that than indifference."

The following week, crestfallen at their umpteenth near miss in the championship, Kent slipped, almost without murmur, to an eight-wicket defeat against Sussex at Hove. Although it was only their third reverse that summer they finished fifth and out of the prize money. The following day, in a revealing letter sent to every member of the county club's staff, Fulton announced his resignation as captain with immediate effect.

He wrote: "I am standing down as captain because I cannot take us where I want to go. It is not a fight I am winning on the field, where I am having less and less influence, nor off it, where we need to meet some huge challenges. At the start of the season we talked about 'creating and sustaining a winning environment'. In truth, we are still some way short of achieving this. I wanted us to be fearless and share in a vision; let the bitching, moaning and complaining be for other clubs. We have a choice: accept our lot and settle for middle-of-the-road mediocrity, or pursue our goals with greater vigour and clarity of purpose." Fulton vowed his support to "whoever picks up the reins" and went on to play 15 more first-class games the following season before retiring from the game.

A day or so after Fulton's resignation, Ford rang and asked to meet me in the Bat and Ball. Incredibly to me, he wanted to gauge my opinion on who should succeed Fulton. Flattered in the extreme that the coach even considered my views to be marginally valuable, we enjoyed a half-hour chat over a couple of pints when Ford asked outright whom I would appoint.

Although I respected Patel's contributions and would have loved to have seen him enjoy a shot at leadership, I felt his age and fitness record ruled him out. I also admired Van Jaarsveld, not just for his batting ability, world-class slip-catching and experience at the highest level, but also for his sound work ethic. I felt he was a man players would be prepared to follow into a war, but I also knew that Van Jaarsveld himself felt he was not quite ready for the job.

Walker's stint as one-day captain had proved unsuccessful, Jones already had enough on his plate and, like Hall, might miss games through international commitments; Kemp and Stevens were still not certain of a starting place.

So, by process of elimination, there was only one candidate: Beckenham's finest, Robert Key. To my relief, Ford almost immediately agreed with my reasoning and Key's appointment was rubber-stamped just before Christmas. The general committee also acted swiftly in order to settle dressing-room concerns. Having already held tentative talks with Warwickshire over potential moves to Edgbaston, both Saggers and Patel chose to play on under Key. Perhaps these were the first indications of a positive new era for Kent cricket.

TEN

2006-09: Birthday Present

DESPITE GLOOMY financial forecasts, Kent jetted off to the sunshine of La Manga for their pre-season training camp, where a slim-line Rob Key, back to his fittest after undergoing shoulder surgery during the winter, led the players for the first time. Much of the side's focus during their stay at the Spanish resort centred around improving their performance levels in one-day cricket without jeopardising their proud record of being the only county not to have sampled life in the County Championship's Second Division.

Director of cricket Graham Ford and his right-hand man Simon Willis were determined to repair Kent's reputation as one-day whipping boys and their policy worked to a degree when the county qualified for the knockout stages of the Twenty20 Cup for the first time. Overall, however, the season degenerated into one of mid-table mediocrity as Kent finished fifth in both the championship and the Second Division of the Pro40 National League.

That spring chief executive Paul Millman unveiled grand redevelopment plans for the St Lawrence Ground which promised fully refurbished stands, corporate hospitality suites, permanent floodlights, a conference centre, new club offices, cricket museum and a three-star hotel. 'All very grand,' mused Kent's more sceptical supporters, 'but who pays for all this?'

The management board's plan revolved around the sale of three pockets of land: the Bat and Ball field, which they use largely as a car park, the committee car parking area and, more controversially, the players' practice area near to St Lawrence Forstal.

The county embarked on the costly process of sourcing preferred business partners and seeking planning permission but, by the time both elements were in place, the UK economy had started its downturn. Kent's initial development partners, Persimmon Homes (South-East), were forced to pull out of the scheme and, as I write four years on, the first sod has still to be turned. In my review for that season's *Wisden Cricketers' Almanack*, I wrote that there was "an underlying sense of treading water rather than progress".

The expression *déjà vu* came to mind in describing Kent's woeful bowling performances in 2006. Almost before the season had begun, the list of injured bowlers stretched to Saggers, Cook, Khan, Patel and Joseph. South Africa's crass mid-season decision to recall first Justin Kemp, and then Andrew Hall, either side of the Twenty20 qualifiers and for the second successive summer, only made matters worse.

The first indication of Key's willingness to experiment as a captain came on a poor wicket at Stockton-on-Tees. With his side freefalling towards defeat in their second innings, Key promoted James Tredwell to pinch-hit a rapid 47 at No 5 in the order, leaving Kemp and Darren Stevens to flay a shellshocked Durham attack and post a match-winning total of 411.

If you looked hard enough, there were other slivers of light and hope emerging from the all-enveloping murk. At Fenner's, Kent Academy player James Iles, at the age of 16 years and 95 days, became Kent's youngest first-class player when he took to the field against Cambridge University. The right-arm seamer was given leave of absence from Maidstone Grammar School in order to break Wally Hardinge's record from 1902 by 16 days. Showing no sign of nerves, Iles began with four successive maidens.

Soon after, Kent's St Lawrence headquarters made its bow as a pop-concert venue when, on 3 June, Sir Elton John arrived by helicopter to play to a crowd of 16,000. Although selling tickets had proved tougher than expected, the event still brought in £40,000. In another effort to balance the books, the club auctioned Albert Chevallier Tayler's famous oil of Kent in the field against Lancashire in 1906, the year of their maiden championship success.

Unable to cover the insurance premiums, Kent had already loaned the painting for display at Lord's, and chairman Carl Openshaw greeted the news that the buyer at Sotheby's was a charitable trust, ensuring that it remained on display, as the "ideal outcome". After deductions, the better-than-expected price of £680,000 was reduced to £492,000, money which members felt should be ring-fenced for a suitable project like the planned Kent cricket museum. The reality, it seems, is that it was simply swallowed up by the club's deepening well of debt.

Back on the field, the little-known South African, Tyron Henderson, was the player unearthed by Ford to replace Kemp and he made an immediate impact on his Twenty20 debut against Essex at Beckenham. After losing his kit-bag on the flight over, the all-rounder borrowed boots and bat to take a wicket with his first ball and hit a six from the second delivery he faced. Henderson collected the man-of-the-match award after Kent's 39-run win, and his sunny disposition also helped secure a contract for the remainder of the season. Spitfires qualified from their group with five wins from eight starts, but they were outmanoeuvred by Leicestershire in a one-sided quarter-final at Grace Road. Kent also failed to make much impression in the new-look C&G Trophy, mustering only four wins in the south conference.

With the notable exception of the final day against Hampshire, when he and David Fulton batted all day to thwart Shane Warne, Key struggled to blend the responsibilities of leadership with batting form. The batting generally misfired in the championship; Walker and Van Jaarsveld were the only players to pass 1,000 runs and slip specialist Van Jaarsveld also pocketed 36 catches, the most by an outfielder since Chris Tavaré in 1978.

Kent's bowling department was largely shambolic; Amjad Khan's tally of 34 wickets was the lowest for Kent's leading wicket-taker since George Hearne in 1875. Martin Saggers made just two appearances in the championship because of ankle and heel injuries and, after playing only eight first-class games in three years, a homesick David Stiff left the club to join Leicestershire. Fellow seamers Simon Cusden and Matt Dennington also left the club.

Kent appeared to have pulled off a coup by signing the talented West Indies all-rounder Dwayne Bravo as their mid-term locum for Hall, but the Trinidadian clearly joined with a brief to improve his batting and generally abstain from bowling. He scored one championship fifty on debut, took eight wickets costing almost 55 apiece and left by mutual consent after only five, hugely disappointing appearances. Left-arm spinner Rob Ferley turned down Kent's offer of a one-year deal in order to join Nottinghamshire.

Behind the stumps, Niall O'Brien shared duties with Geraint Jones, who returned to the county a near broken man after losing his England Test berth amid much criticism. It made matters worse that O'Brien, who was himself struggling for form, also laboured to contain his fiery temperament. He too, was released and joined Northamptonshire.

Beneficiary David Fulton just failed in his quest to score 1,000 runs in his final season, but he was at least allowed to stage-manage his Canterbury farewell, ending his 15-year association with the club by scoring 155 against Middlesex in his 200th and last first-class appearance for Kent. He retired to become a presenter with Sky Sports and, rather more significantly for Kent, agent for the likes of Walker, Dexter and Joe Denly. At the season's end, Ford signed a two-year contract extension and moved swiftly to engage Pakistan all-rounder Yasir Arafat as the first of Kent's overseas professionals for 2007.

Everyone involved with the county, as well as the wider cricketing world, was shaken to the core by Bob Woolmer's death in the West Indies, just a month before the start of the 2007 season.

2007

David Fulton's retirement and the release of four bowlers left Rob Key with no option but to strengthen the Kent squad. Key and Graham Ford conducted their business extremely well; apart from bringing a fresh dynamism to the side, the new recruits also played a big part in maintaining Kent's Division One status in the championship and winning the county's first knockout title for 29 years.

Promising Harrow School batsman Sam Northeast and Durham UCCE keeper Paul Dixey joined the staff, but Kent's most astute signing (as a Kolpak player) was South African all-rounder Ryan McLaren. Primarily a skilful right-

Former Kent batsman Michael Carberry edges Andrew Hall to Geraint Jones in the Friends Provident Trophy at Tunbridge Wells in 2007

Picture: Matthew Walker, Kent Messenger, PD1673790

arm pace bowler, he also turned out to be a useful left-handed batsman and the most athletic of fielders. Encouragingly for Kent, the move was also endorsed by McLaren's mentor, former Test bowler Allan Donald. "Allan was very enthusiastic," said McLaren, "and thinks that 24 is the ideal age for me to give county cricket my best shot."

And 'give it his best shot' he did. Taking 44 first-class wickets at 24 (the most by a Kent bowler), McLaren became so integral to the team's success that he played the last two championship games with a fractured thumb and earned a three-year contract after Key described him as a "seriously serious cricketer".

With Yasir Arafat and Andrew Hall already on board as their overseas options and Martin Saggers seemingly on the mend, Key felt positively bullish. "We've tried to create a staff based on quality rather than quantity this year," he said, "and I think we've achieved that. There's no one at the club now that I wouldn't be happy going into a game of cricket with. Last year was very different to that. There were times, and I know this sounds hard, when I had to throw the ball to a couple of our bowlers not knowing what they might do with it."

Key already knew by then that Amjad Khan would miss the entire season after breaking down on the England A tour of Bangladesh and undergoing surgery to reconstruct his right cruciate knee ligament. Min Patel played in the opening championship game against Sussex, but a Kent career featuring 673 wickets (589 first-class) ended in abrupt retirement after he lost his battle against persistent back and neck problems.

Ford predicted that off-spinner James Tredwell would start to flourish and that Joe Denly would step up to fill David Fulton's boots at the top of the batting order. Ford also believed that the regular presence in the side of Geraint Jones "could be massively important". Jones later admitted that he had emerged from the constant scrutiny of international cricket "feeling something like a zombie", but was soon revelling in the comfort zone of county cricket.

Arafat's home championship debut was against his former county, Sussex, and his contribution with bat and ball enabled Kent to avenge their heavy defeat in the opening round of games. Arafat top-scored with 122 then bagged four for 36 as Sussex were shot out for 102; Simon Cook completed the innings victory with excellent figures of six for 35. Key made 169 in a defeat at Chester-le-Street and was one of three Kent century-makers in a high-scoring draw against Hampshire.

Jones's lusty century turned the game against Surrey at Whitgift School, leading to an innings win, and James Tredwell's maiden championship hundred helped secure a draw with Yorkshire at The Nevill. A predictable defeat at Old Trafford was followed by an abortive trip to Worcester, where summer floods had left the New Road square and outfield unplayable.

Worcestershire's chief executive, Mark Newton, had balked at calls to move the game to Kidderminster, insisting that conditions would eventually be fit for play. When the players arrived, however, they discovered a pudding pitch and khaki-coloured outfield, encrusted with river effluent and an all-pervading stench. On the scheduled first morning umpires Richard Kettleborough and Martin Bodenham reported to Lord's that prospects for any play were bleak and at noon on the third day the game was duly abandoned.

The ECB commented that Newton had acted "in good faith, although highly optimistically". To rub salt into Kentish wounds, the board rescinded their initial suggestion to re-schedule the match, then Warwickshire, Yorkshire, Durham and Lancashire vetoed a compromise offer to award Kent nine points for the abandonment rather than the customary four. Kent's acute sense of grievance only softened when they managed to avoid relegation.

Saggers returned from a successful loan spell with Essex to bring added firepower to the attack, but rain robbed Key's side of a probable home win over Warwickshire after Arafat had become the first Kent player to score a hundred batting at No 9. Bad weather led to another stalemate at Scarborough, after which the largely ineffective Sri Lankan, Lasith Malinga, replaced Andrew Hall. Malinga sent down only seven expensive overs as Kent lost inside two days to Surrey on a sporting Canterbury Week pitch. No matter where they played, bad weather continued to blight Kent progress and persistent rain back at St Lawrence washed out the opening three days of an inevitable draw with Worcestershire.

A high-scoring draw with title-chasing Lancashire at Canterbury was of marginally more use to Kent than it was to Lancashire, but relegation still threatened at the start of September. It took a stunning century in difficult conditions by Martin van Jaarsveld at the Rose Bowl to end that threat as Kent landed their maiden first-class win at Hampshire's headquarters. Ford admitted after the 10-wicket victory: "I was so relieved and happy that I really couldn't sleep."

Ford also referred to the "energy" in the Kent dressing room, and his conviction that the side was bursting with promise led him to turn down mid-season overtures from the Indian Cricket Board. He explained to the *Kent Messenger*: "I've made the decision and there's no point going around wondering what if? There would have been some marvellous aspects to taking a job like that, but there would have been tough times too."

Kent finished the championship season with only three wins from 16 starts and there were times when their one-day returns that summer were equally bleak. They tinkered with the batting order throughout their Friends Provident Trophy campaign and failed to qualify despite recording five wins. The NatWest Pro40 League served as little more than a distraction from more important challenges.

Against a generally gloomy backdrop, Kent somehow emerged as the surprise package of the Twenty20 jamboree in 2007. The first signs of their transition from hit-and-giggle no-hopers to cool-headed title contenders came during the qualifying stages, where a tie against Hampshire coupled with four wins – generally when batting first – took Kent through to the knockout stages for the second successive year. Incredibly, Kent lost seven successive tosses during their run to the final, but they proved equally adept at defending a score and chasing one. Key, improvising to his heart's delight at the top of the order, and Denly both scored almost 300 runs in that season's competition.

Tigerish fielding, accurate pace bowling from South African locum Morne Morkel, McLaren and Arafat, coupled with subtle, mid-innings strangulation

Darren Stevens, who made the winning hit, and Yasir Arafat are jubilant after Kent's Twenty20 Cup triumph in 2007

Picture: Barry Goodwin, Kent Messenger, PD1673792

from Darren Stevens, Cook and the wily Tredwell, were all vital to the winning formula. By the time Kent travelled to Trent Bridge for their rain-delayed quarter-final in mid-July, they were so comfortable with the format and their own form that they thrashed Nottinghamshire by nine wickets despite having to bat second. A record stand of 96 between Key and Denly was instrumental in Kent reaching finals' day for the first time. Although the pundits thought they were long-priced outsiders to lift the cup, to me, at least, the omens for Kent glory felt good as I arrived at Edgbaston early on my 47th birthday.

For one thing, Kent had overwhelmed their semi-final opponents, Sussex, in the Friends Provident Trophy earlier in the season, and they seemed well placed to progress after restricting Sussex to 140. Malinga was flattered by his figures of three for 30 and the most telling spell came from Stevens, who conceded only 13 runs in his four overs. With Key to the fore, making an unbeaten 68, Kent sailed through to the final with five wickets and four balls intact. During the interval Kent Academy assistant Andy 'Bomber' Bennett romped to victory in the mascots' race, wearing the county's Spitfire-styled costume.

Key backed his hunch to field first in the final against Gloucestershire, but the plan was in danger of misfiring after New Zealander Hamish Marshall cracked a quick 65. McLaren, who had earlier run out Chris Adams with an audacious, mid-air, backhand flick in the semi-final, had the force still with him to produce the first Twenty20 final hat-trick. Marshall chopped on, Steve Adshead missed an off-cutter then McLaren trapped left-hander Ian Fisher leg before with a swinging yorker to bring Spitfires supporters to their feet.

The first signs of anxiety surfaced, early in Kent's reply, when Key's clip to wide mid-on was snaffled low down by Marshall. Key moped off, questioning whether the ball had carried, only to be censured later by the ECB for his fit of pique. Matthew Walker, however, chose the best occasion to end a run of poor scores. His chip-and-chase innings of 45 from 35 balls settled the nerves until he departed at 109 for four. Despite some 'stand-and-deliver' drives from Stevens, Kent still needed 13 off the final over.

After some debate, Gloucestershire's most expensive bowler, Carl Greenidge, was entrusted with the responsibility: that he delivered only three balls tells its own story. Stevens, a previous winner of the competition with Leicestershire, displayed steely nerves in steering Kent to victory. He helped the first ball for four to midwicket, let the next go by for a leg-side wide and scampered a single to leave Arafat on strike.

A blistering straight drive was palmed by Greenidge for a single, leaving Stevens on strike and six needed off three balls. He cover-drove the next delivery, a low full toss, towards the extra-cover boundary and set off. By the time he arrived at the non-striker's end the ball had reached the ropes; only then did it dawn on Stevens that umpire Peter Willey was signalling a no-ball. The title was Kent's.

Stevens explained afterwards: "I didn't know it was a no-ball, but then I saw Yasir jumping up and down shouting, 'It's game over, it was a no-ball.' Even Peter Willey wasn't sure but once Neil Mallender [the other umpire] started walking over we all started celebrating." Stevens added: "It's the best day of my career, a great day all-round. To come out on top means I'll remember this day, this occasion and the feeling for a long time."

My birthday was made when Stevens presented me with his champagne-sodden match shirt in the dressing room afterwards, where Kent, understandably celebrated their third one-day win in 13 years with rather more than a few beers. Canterbury City Council later hosted a joint civic reception to mark the county's Twenty20 Cup success and that of the Kent Ladies team who, for the second season running, had proved invincible in their championship. Key, who scored 2,000 runs in all forms of the game that year to be voted player of the season, called the cup triumph "the biggest day of my Kent career", but felt his side's overall courage in avoiding championship relegation against the odds ranked almost as highly.

The season's end marked the departure of Paul Farbrace, who left his post as Kent Academy director to become right-hand man to Trevor Bayliss, the newly appointed Sri Lanka coach. He was replaced at St Lawrence by Phil Relf.

In September a special general meeting of club members voted to approve the club's redevelopment scheme and, in the belief that the county were on course for a brighter future, Carl Openshaw stood down after nine years as chairman. Former president George Kennedy, a businessman and ex rugby league player, was elected unanimously as his successor. Kennedy had already served on the club's committee since 2002 and was also the driving force behind the project steering group set up to implement the ground improvement scheme.

2008

The danger of focusing attention on limited-overs glory at the expense of the bread-and-butter grind of the County Championship first became apparent to Kent in 1995. Although they claimed that year's Sunday League title, captain Mark Benson and coach Daryl Foster faced a members' rebellion for finishing bottom in the championship. Thirteen years later, Rob Key and Graham Ford were to face a similar reaction.

In many ways the 2008 campaign resembled 1997's 'nearly season'. Kent reached two one-day finals and blew a glorious chance to win promotion in the National League, only to suffer the indignity of championship relegation on the final day of the season – making for a wholly unsatisfactory end to my tenure as the Kent Messenger Group's cricket correspondent.

Rewind six months to pre-season, however, and the mood appeared buoyant at Kent's training camp. The club had silverware to display for the first time since 2001 and, though head coach Ford and assistant Simon Willis were working within a salary cap, they felt Kent had strengthened their hand. With Ryan McLaren, Justin Kemp and Martin van Jaarsveld forming the steadfast South African spine to their existing team, the coaches added a little spice to the one-day mix by signing Pakistan all-rounder Azhar Mahmood from Surrey.

Putting on the style: Joe Denly drives through the off side

Picture: Anthony Roberts

Amjad Khan's return to full fitness enabled him to partner Robbie Joseph with the new ball, leaving Yasir Arafat and McLaren as formidable back-up. There was also Simon Cook, Martin Saggers and Kemp in support. Off-spinner James Tredwell continued to mature and batsman Neil Dexter was pushing for a first team slot. Willis thought the omens looked good but sounded a note of caution: "On paper, it all looks encouraging, but, as the cliché goes, trophies aren't won on paper."

Kent's main problem was that Willis's metaphorical sheet of paper was just too short: they used 17 players in 2008 and two of those made only a couple of one-day appearances. Ultimately, their strenuous, four-pronged title assault took so much out of the small squad that their mid-summer rollercoaster ride turned into a September train wreck.

A thoughtful Graham Ford watches the action unfold at Canterbury in 2008
Picture: Barry Goodwin, Kent Messenger, PD1673793

At the start of the season Kent revelled in their status as Twenty20 champions and carried their title-winning form into the longer one-day formats. They topped the South East Division in the Friends Provident Trophy, then beat Somerset in a quarter-final transferred from a sodden St Lawrence to Beckenham, thanks in no small part to a battling century from Dexter. Only selected when the in-form Van Jaarsveld rushed off to be with his wife, Jill, for the birth of their first child, Dexter was named man of the match, before being unceremoniously dumped as Van Jaarsveld returned for the semi-final against Durham at Chester-le-Street. Hundreds from Joe Denly and Van Jaarsveld, his fourth of the campaign, helped ease Kent into the final.

Before that, Kent had their Twenty 20 title to defend, and they did so with great honour. Six wins earned them a quarter-final trip to Edgbaston, where Darren Stevens mastered a slow pitch to make 69 off 32 balls and book Kent's place at finals' day. At the Rose Bowl they eliminated the Essex Eagles with a thoroughly professional, yet unmemorable 14-run win during which Denly became leading run scorer in that season's competition.

Arafat was the only Kent bowler to escape severe punishment against Middlesex in the final as man of the match Owais Shah hit five sixes in a sublime 75. Key led the riposte with a 30-ball half-century, but Kent needed 16 from the final over, which would be bowled by their former team-mate, Tyron Henderson. Given that he had leaked 46 from his first three overs, Henderson showed remarkable composure at the death. With two balls remaining Kent

The disappointment shows on Kent faces after the Friends Provident Trophy final in 2008
Picture: Graham Morris

needed three to tie the scores – sufficient to win the title on fewer wickets lost
– but a change of bat for Kemp led to a dramatic change in fortunes for Kent.
He missed Henderson's next delivery, a slower ball then, in trying to straight-
drive a near yorker, he could only pick out the bowler, who gleefully completed
a run-out as Kemp attempted to gallop through..

Barely three weeks later, Kent returned to the big stage in the Friends
Provident Trophy final at Lord's. Team selection played a big part in their five-
wicket defeat to Essex. Kemp, who lost form and confidence after the Rose
Bowl trauma, still kept his place ahead of Dexter. Key also continued to back
his out-of-sorts senior pro, Mahmood, who was preferred to front-line bowlers
Cook, Khan and Saggers.

Kent made a poor start to post a disappointing 214, despite fifties from Van
Jaarsveld and McLaren. They were possibly 50 short of a working total, and
though Joseph jolted Essex by removing England pair Ravi Bopara and Alastair
Cook in the space of five runs, Grant Flower's calm unbeaten 70 put them back
on track for a five-wicket win. Kent contributed to their downfall with a below-
par display in the field, including 11 wides and two no-balls. Essex went on to
beat Kent in the sides' final NatWest Pro40 League game, denying Kent a play-
off place in the process.

There was a similar tale of promise unfulfilled in the Liverpool Victoria County Championship. Kent already had three draws under the belts when McLaren's best return for the county, six for 75, decided a low-scoring game at Trent Bridge. Kent's second win came courtesy of an extraordinary all-round effort from Van Jaarsveld, who scored two unbeaten hundreds and took five for 33 in Surrey's second innings at the Oval.

In a summer of poor batting returns, only Van Jaarsveld reached 1,000 runs. Joseph led the wicket-takers with 55 and McLaren took a respectable 50 to catch the eye of South Africa's selectors. They tested his resolve by inviting him to join their one-day squad, but Kent quickly pointed out his contractual obligations as a Kolpak player and effectively stalled his departure for a further 18 months.

Kent's championship prognosis still appeared good when they outpointed Yorkshire by three wickets at St Lawrence, helped by 157 from Key, his only championship hundred of the summer, and six for 55 from Mahmood. At that stage Kent were only two points off the top of the table, but the one-day setbacks knocked the stuffing out of Key's side and they won only one of their last eight championship games, against Lancashire.

The reality was that Kent's under-manned squad were beginning to unravel and the sense that the world was against them surfaced in a show of exasperation from Key as they lost in two-and-a-half days to Durham at Chester-le-Street. He said the playing surface was "absolutely ridiculous" and dubbed the ECB pitch panel as "a bit of a Muppet Show" for taking no action. He was later fined £1,250 by the ECB and went on to admit the remarks were "inappropriate".

Despite their growing sense of frustration Kent would have gone top if they had removed Yorkshire's last-wicket pair at Scarborough and, with two games remaining they still had an outside chance of winning the title. They travelled to Liverpool fully rested and led by 126 on first innings after bowling out Lancashire for 107 on a damp pitch. Kent hardly helped their cause by conceding 76 extras in a low-scoring game and were shot out for 92 after an inspired spell of seam bowling from Glen Chapple (six for 40).

Suddenly, relegation was a possibility, though Kent knew that a high-scoring draw would enable them to survive. Unfortunately their opponents, Durham, had a different kind of motivation: a clearcut victory could earn them their first championship crown. The writing was on the wall for Kent after they had been bowled out for 225 and their despair was only matched by Durham's elation as they completed an innings victory. Kent's proud record as the only county to have played exclusively in Division One of the championship was at an end.

Ford reflected: "I look at other counties and the long list of players they have fielded in this competition compared to our 15 and it made me realise how much more man-power they have. We put in some truly outstanding performances, but unfortunately it all came to a hugely disappointing end." He reasoned that the side had simply "run out of gas".

While Ford delighted Kent officials by ruling himself out of the running to replace Peter Moores as England coach, the fans were unhappy to lose that season's beneficiary, Matthew Walker, to Essex, and Dexter to Middlesex. Dexter confirmed his departure through David Fulton, former Kent captain turned players' agent, and described his final two seasons at Kent as "incredibly frustrating". Kent's chairman of cricket, Graham Johnson, voiced his frustrations for contrasting reasons, saying: "We offered him a three-year contract that would have provided him with an outstanding opportunity to make the most of his undoubted talent. It is a great pity that he does not feel able to take advantage of this opportunity."

News of Dexter's departure came only three days after Kent had announced that Walker would be released. Although Key fully expected to lose one batsman, he never believed that both would leave. He explained: "The big problem for me about this was the timings, which worked out badly for us. We had verbal assurances from Neil that he wanted to stay at Kent and we'd said to Walks that, if Neil were to say, there wouldn't be anything for him, I was honest with both players all along."

After confirming that he had been knocked back after making initial approaches to Middlesex batsman Ed Joyce and Worcestershire's Ben Smith, Key added: "We must move forward from this. There's no point dwelling on it now, the decisions have been made whether we like them or not. I'd like to think we can turn this into a positive. Yes we've lost two players, but who's to say that in eight months' time we won't be stronger for it?"

With one year now under his belt at Essex, Walker recalls the "negative attitude" of the Kent dressing room, but remains convinced that the mid-Nineties side should have been more successful. "When we had Headley, McCague, Ealham, Fleming, Patel and Hooper's off-spin as your front-line bowling attack, it seems extraordinary and disappointing that we didn't win more that we did. Three titles in my 15 years at the club just wasn't enough."

To add to the autumnal gloom, the economic downturn evolved into a full-blown recession, ensuring that Kent's redevelopment scheme was put firmly on hold. Indeed, the only ground work at Canterbury during those winter months led to the re-laying of three wickets in the middle of the ageing square.

The recession also led to redundancies at the club, when seven ground staff, office workers and maintenance staff lost their jobs.

By the end of October, I joined the list of economic victims when *Kent Messenger* announced their raft of departures. All in all, it was a season to remember, but for all the wrong reasons.

2009

Spring 2009 became belt-tightening time at St Lawrence once the county declared record pre-tax operating losses of £706,536 in February. Blaming the recession, delays to the redevelopment scheme, the loss of expected sponsorship deals with development partners, and rain (Kent lost 14 home days of cricket to bad weather in 2008), the club also revealed they had spent £1 million on "architects and other professional fees" relating to the plan.

Far from helping to balance the books, June concerts by the Sugababes and James Morrison produced a shortfall of £190,000 which chairman George Kennedy described as "embarrassing". The overall deficit for the year ending 31 October 2009 was more than £800,000. On the playing side Kent re-engaged James Hockley, who had been teaching at Marlborough House School in Cranbrook, and Rob Ferley, from Nottinghamshire.

The prime objective was to win immediate promotion back to the championship's top flight. The goal was achieved when Kent beat Middlesex at Uxbridge, despite two centuries in the match from Neil Dexter, and the title was secured on 17 September by a second batting bonus point against Leicestershire. "I'm really chuffed the boys have got the reward for their work because it really has been a hard slog," said Graham Ford. "The guys can be really proud of the fact that they've achieved this with a small squad and with only minimal contribution from an overseas pro."

Although relieved to have won promotion, captain Rob Key hardly looked like a man who had just picked up a cheque for £115,000 (£90,000 players' prize money and £25,000 county performance bonus). "I look at the banner and it says Division Two winners, so it won't go down as one of the great moments in my career," he admitted. "It's £90,000 for finishing 10th in my eyes."

With eight wins, two more than any other county in the division, Kent were worthy winners, yet there was powerful evidence of the gulf in class between the two divisions. In 2008 only Van Jaarsveld reached 1,000 first-class runs, but the following year he was joined by Darren Stevens, Key and player of the

Rob Key leads his side in after a Twenty20 victory at Tunbridge Wells in 2009
Picture: Matthew Walker, Kent Messenger, PD1673795

season Geraint Jones, who won promotion from No 6 to No 3 to canter past four figures for the first time in his career. The gap was even more noticeable in the field, where Kent continued to bowl teams out twice despite rarely being able to select their first-choice attack. Wayne Parnell made only five championship appearances and long-term injuries to Joseph and McLaren restricted them to a handful of matches.

Kent were indebted to James Tredwell, whose 69 wickets were comfortably the best return of his career (his 24 championship wickets in 2008 had cost him 51 apiece). Although Amjad Khan claimed 36 victims he never appeared quite back to his best. In his benefit year Martin Saggers managed only 10 wickets from four championship appearances before a knee problem forced him to announce his retirement. He will stay within the game, however, after being accepted onto the reserve list of the ECB's first-class umpires' panel.

While achieving their main target, Kent also went close to winning one-day silverware. Their experimental NatWest Pro40 League side performed wonders to secure third place and, after three successive Friends Provident Trophy wins, the side ultimately flagged to finish fourth in Group B. Once again, the Twenty20 Cup proved Spitfires' favourite format as they reached finals' day for the third straight year, only to under-perform woefully in their semi-final when they crashed out to a Marcus Trescothick inspired Somerset at Edgbaston.

As the season drew to a close, Van Jaarsveld and Key signed contract extensions, having both been linked with moves to Surrey, then Joe Denly, Jones, Stevens and Robbie Joseph also committed their long-term futures to Kent. Director of cricket Graham Ford was unable to follow suit, however. Having already accepted a first team coaching role with the Natal Dolphins for the English close season, Ford could not commit to Kent for the entire summer of 2010, so his six-year stint ended by mutual consent a week before the end of the season.

Summing up Ford's tenure, Matthew Walker says he was highly respected by some, but not every player's cup of tea. "I found it really hard to talk to Fordy," concedes Walker: "A bit like Chris Stone, it was as though he had nothing else in his life other than cricket, so I found it tough to break through to him and just have a chat like mates do. There was no human touch to him, he was always so guarded. The South African lads and Rob Key all thought the world of him, but he never had the oomph for me."

Ford's departure led to the return of Paul Farbrace who, after two years with Sri Lanka, made an emotional homecoming as coaching director. The 42-year-old confirmed that the lure of the top job at Kent had persuaded him to turn down a new three-year deal and his decision was in no way swayed by the terrorist attack on the Sri Lankan team bus at Lahore in March 2009 that left him nursing a shrapnel injury to his right arm.

In explaining the coaching ethos he will bring to St Lawrence, Farbrace said: "It's a bit like the strict teacher most of us had during our school days. You probably didn't really take to them at the time, but when you look back in later life you realise they were actually quite good for you. It's the same for me with coaching. It's not all about being a friend; it's about helping, supporting and showing the players you care about their successes. Those are the values I like to think I've taken from Colin Page, Bob Woolmer and the other coaches I've been lucky enough to work with."

The departure of chief executive Paul Millman, "with immediate effect", was confirmed in a terse, pre-Christmas press release. During Millman's 10-year term in office Kent spent all bar one season in the championship First Division, won the National League and Twenty20 titles and secured planning permission for their redevelopment scheme, but he was now being made the scapegoat for continued financial losses and the delayed ground improvements. Soon afterwards, Kent announced they would be looking to boost gate receipts for 2010 by switching their home Twenty20 qualifier against Essex to the Brit Oval.

Early in the new year Kent announced Australian seamer Stuart Clark (later ruled out) and Sri Lanka wrist spinner Malinga Bandara as their overseas players for 2010, while 16-year-old Kent Academy scholar and England Under-19 bowler Adam Ball was handed a three-year county contract. James Tredwell became the latest Kent player to win international honours when he made his England one-day international debut in the series win over Bangladesh.

And so, we arrive at the stage of the game where I take up the crystal ball from the Nackington Road end and attempt a short spell of prognostication. On the field, Kent appear to be approaching the 2010 season in good heart: with a new coaching set-up, fresh faces from overseas and a raft of senior players who have all bought into the long-term vision as sold by Key and Farbrace.

It is off the field where I foresee potential pitfalls. Although some Kent members have yet to fully embrace the prospect of ground redevelopment, the reality is that revitalising facilities and adding income streams represent Kent's only realistic hope of competing on a level playing field with the Test-hosting counties. I say realistic, because the alternative option of selling St Lawrence in its entirety for housing and moving the county club to a green-field site in Ashford or west Kent is far too horrific to contemplate. Yet, like many supporters, I also agonise over Kent's capacity to see the scheme through. My overriding fears are three-fold: firstly, that the hotel complex detracts from the leafy beauty of the St Lawrence Ground. Then, that the hotel and proposed conference centre become white elephants. And lastly, that the club struggle to service the additional borrowing they require to complete the project and members are left with an unfinished symphony.

If Kent are to pull the rabbit out of the redevelopment hat a strong character is required at the administrative helm. Not only to nip institutionalised lethargy in the bud, but also to drive the club forward with new marketing strategies. Most importantly – and however implausible it may sound – the redevelopment has to be completed within budget.

Whoever Kent appoint as their new chief executive there is no doubting the enormity of the tasks lying ahead. Managing a near destitute club with diminishing assets could quickly become a lonely, thankless task, especially if budget cuts and salary caps meant the team were unable to compete effectively in the championship's top flight.

So, if nothing else, I wish the new chief executive a good deal more luck than his predecessors have enjoyed in these past three decades. Perhaps the successful applicant would do well to remember the words of John Arlott, who once wrote: "Cricket is a game of the most terrifying stresses, with more luck about it than any other game I know. They call it a team game, but in fact it is the loneliest game of all."

The Best of Kent: 1967-2009

ELLIS'S XI

Brian Luckhurst
Rob Key
Chris Tavaré
Colin Cowdrey (Capt)
Martin van Jaarsveld
Bob Woolmer
Alan Knott
John Shepherd
Graham Dilley
Derek Underwood
Norman Graham

PENNELL'S XI

Mark Benson
Rob Key
Martin van Jaarsveld
Bob Woolmer
Trevor Ward
Steve Waugh (Capt)
Mark Ealham
Alan Knott
Dean Headley
Martin Saggers
Derek Underwood

*Only one overseas player permitted (Van Jaarsveld now classes as England-qualified)

On purist principle, I'm reluctant to select Martin van Jaarsveld but, as he's now England-qualified, merit wins over morals. It's tempting to choose another bowling all-rounder (in the Mark Ealham mould), but this side needs an injection of pace so step forward Graham Dilley. The overseas berth goes to John Shepherd, but only just (his smile wins him the casting vote in any 50-50 call). It seems a crime to leave out Asif Iqbal, while Terry Alderman was, arguably, Kent's most skilful new-ball bowler of the era. It would be heretical to give the captaincy to anyone other than Colin Cowdrey. A final plea to the legislators: bring back uncovered pitches so that Derek Underwood (with Norman Graham in harness) can give this side a fighting chance against any opposition.

Although he never skippered during his month with Kent, Steve Waugh's credentials as one of the foremost captains in Test history cannot be denied. He therefore ousts both Carl Hooper, as my overseas choice, and Mark Benson, from the captaincy. With solid left/right-hand openers, the top four offer consistency and durability to complement Trevor Ward's attacking flair. Alan Knott, and the support seamers, Waugh, Mark Ealham and Bob Woolmer, will provide attractive mid-order runs and occasional pyrotechnics. With a fully fit Dean Headley and Martin Saggers offering new-ball variety (one to hit the deck, the other, more slippery swing), what my attack lacks in searing pace it gains with Deadly's spin, speared down towards who else but the impish Knott. They'd take some beating.

KENT IN THE COUNTY CHAMPIONSHIP 1967-2009

	P	W	L	D	Tie	Ab	Pos	Most runs	Most wickets
1967	28	11	3	13	–	1	2	Cowdrey 1101	Underwood 111
1968	28	12	5	11	–	–	2	Denness 1299	Underwood 91
1969	24	4	6	14	–	–	10	Luckhurst 1593	Graham 77
1970	24	9	5	10	–	–	1	Denness 1445	Shepherd 84
1971	24	7	6	11	–	–	4	Denness 1391	Underwood 97
1972	20	7	4	9	–	–	2	Luckhurst 1345	Underwood 52
1973	20	4	3	13	–	–	4	Johnson 1175	Shepherd 78
1974	20	5	8	7	–	–	10	Luckhurst 1035	Woolmer 54
1975	20	8	4	8	–	–	5	Asif Iqbal 1262	Underwood 57
1976	20	5	7	8	–	–	14	Woolmer 1222	Shep/Under 48
1977	22	9	2	10	–	1	1=	Asif Iqbal 1224	Shepherd 87
1978	22	13	3	6	–	–	1	Tavaré 1335	Undewood 110
1979	22	6	3	13	–	–	5	Tavaré 1239	Underwood 104
1980	22	2	8	12	–	–	16	Tavaré 1050	Underwood 60
1981	22	5	7	10	–	–	9	Tavaré 1502	Jarvis 79
1982	22	3	4	15	–	–	13	Taylor 1083	Underwood 78
1983	24	7	4	13	–	–	7	Aslett 1437	Underwood 105
1984	24	8	3	11	2	–	5	Aslett 1231	Underwood 77
1985	24	4	5	15	–	–	9	Benson 1446	Underwood 64
1986	24	5	7	12	–	–	8	Benson 1242	Alderman 98
1987	24	2	7	15	–	–	14	Benson 1619	Baptiste 51
1988	22	10	5	7	–	–	2	Tavaré 1292	Penn 80
1989	22	3	8	11	–	–	15	Taylor 1495	Igglesden 53
1990	22	3	6	13	–	–	16	Taylor 1752	Davis 65
1991	22	6	3	12	1	–	6	Taylor 1647	Merrick 58
1992	22	9	3	10	–	–	2	Ward 1648	Davis 67
1993	17	6	4	7	–	–	8	Hooper 1304	Igglesden 50
1994	17	6	7	4	–	–	9	Hooper 1579	Patel 79
1995	17	3	10	4	–	–	18	De Silva 1661	Patel 51
1996	17	9	2	6	–	–	4	Hooper 1287	McCague 75
1997	17	8	4	5	–	–	2	Wells 1055	Strang 61
1998	17	5	5	7	–	–	11	Hooper 1215	Headley 52
1999	17	6	4	7	–	–	5	Symonds 829	Thompson 64
2000	16	4	4	8	–	–	6/1	Dravid 1039	Saggers 57
2001	16	4	3	9	–	–	3/1	Fulton 1729	Saggers 63
2002	16	7	4	5	–	–	3/1	Smith 1233	Saggers 79
2003	16	6	5	5	–	–	4/1	Smith 1352	Saggers 54
2004	16	7	3	6	–	–	2/1	Key 1274	Patel 41
2005	16	6	3	7	–	–	5/1	Key 1556	Patel 59
2006	16	4	4	8	–	–	5/1	Walker 1419	Khan 34
2007	16	3	5	7	–	1	7/1	Key 1250	McLaren 44
2008	16	4	6	6	–	–	8/1	Jaarsveld 1150	Joseph 55
2009	16	8	3	5	–	–	1/2	Jaarsveld 1475	Tredwell 69

KENT IN ONE-DAY COMPETITIONS 1967-2009

	Gillette Cup	B&H Cup	Twenty20	Sunday League						
				P	W	L	T	NR	Pts	Pos
1967	WINNERS	–	–							
1968	2nd rd	–	–							
1969	2nd rd	–	–	16	9	6	1	0	38	4
1970	Qtr-final	–	–	16	12	4	0	0	48	2
1971	Runners-up	–	–	16	8	8	0	0	32	8
1972	Semi-final	Group (3rd)	–	16	11	4	0	1	45	1
1973	Qtr-final	WINNERS	–	16	12	2	0	2	50	1
1974	WINNERS	Qtr-final	–	16	10	4	0	2	44	3
1975	2nd rd	Group (4th)	–	16	12	4	0	0	48	3
1976	2nd rd	WINNERS	–	16	10	6	0	0	40	1
1977	1st rd	Runners-up	–	16	7	6	0	3	34	6=
1978	Qtr-final	WINNERS	–	16	6	8	0	2	28	10=
1979	Qtr-final	Group (4th)	–	16	11	3	0	2	48	2
1980	2nd rd	Group (4th)	–	16	6	8	1	1	28	11=
1981	2nd rd	Semi-final	–	16	7	7	1	1	32	7=
1982	2nd rd	Qtr-final	–	16	9	7	0	0	36	4
1983	Runners-up	Semi-final	–	16	8	3	0	5	42	3
1984	Runners-up	Group (3rd)	–	16	6	8	0	2	28	9=
1985	Qtr-final	Semi-final	–	16	6	7	0	3	30	10=
1986	2nd rd	Final	–	16	7	5	1	3	36	6=
1987	2nd rd	Semi-final	–	16	8	5	0	3	38	6
1988	Qtr-final	Group (3rd)	–	16	7	6	0	3	34	7
1989	2nd rd	Semi-final	–	16	7	9	0	0	28	11=
1990	2nd rd	Group (3rd)	–	16	7	8	0	1	30	10=
1991	2nd rd	Qtr-final	–	16	6	8	1	1	28	10
1992	Qtr-final	Runners-up	–	17	8	5	0	4	40	5=
1993	2nd rd	Prelim rd	–	17	12	3	0	2	52	2
1994	Semi-final	Qtr-final	–	17	12	5	0	0	48	3
1995	2nd rd	Runners-up	–	17	12	4	0	1	50	1
1996	2nd rd	Qtr-final	–	17	8	8	1	0	34	10
1997	1st rd	Runners-up	–	17	12	4	0	1	50	2
1998	2nd rd	Qtr-final	–	17	8	6	0	3	38	5
1999	Qtr-final	–	–	16	8	6	0	2	36	3/1
2000	4th rd	Group (4th)	–	16	7	7	0	2	32	5/1
2001	Qtr-final	Group (4th)	–	16	11	2	1	2	50	1/1
2002	Semi-final	Group (3rd)	–	16	7	8	1	0	30	5/1
2003	4th rd	–	Group (3rd)	16	7	8	1	0	30	6/1
2004	3rd rd	–	Group (4th)	16	5	9	0	2	24	8/1
2005	Qtr-final	–	Group (6th)	18	6	10	0	2	28	8/2
2006	Group (7th)	–	Qtr-final	8	5	3	0	0	10	5/2
2007	Group (4th)	–	WINNERS	8	5	3	0	0	10	5/2
2008	Runners-up	–	Runners-up	8	4	2	0	2	10	4/2
2009	Group (4th)	–	Semi-final	8	4	3	0	1	9	3/2

Notes and Sources

Quoted material, apart from where indicated in the text or referenced in the notes below, is taken from conversations with the authors between September 2009 and February 2010. Clive Ellis and Mark Pennell are immensely grateful to the following for their willingness to give a frank account of their time with Kent (the list is purely alphabetical):

Asif Iqbal, Mark Benson, Chris Cowdrey, Graham Cowdrey, Mike Denness, Fanie de Villiers, Alan Dixon, Alan Ealham, Mark Ealham, Matthew Fleming, Daryl Foster, David Fulton, Norman Graham, James Graham-Brown, Dean Headley, Carl Hooper, Kevin Jarvis, Graham Johnson, Nick Kemp, Rob Key, Nigel Llong, Martin McCague, Steve Marsh, Chris Penn, John Shepherd, Chris Tavaré, Neil Taylor, Derek Underwood, Matthew Walker, Trevor Ward, Vince Wells, Jim Woodhouse, John Wright. Chris Adams, who might have played for Kent (see p.204), is also thanked.

INTRODUCTION
p.8 "beef and beer" *A History of County Cricket: Kent*
p.9 "he could make music…" *A History of County Cricket: Kent*
p.11 "a few pet bees…" *The Daily Telegraph*
p.16 "softened up the gloves…" *Good Enough?*
p.20 "on his best days…" *The Daily Telegraph*

1957-66
p.20 "We're all behind you… The fact that Les…" *M.C.C.*
p.24 "ample revenge… *Beating the Bat*
p.28 "was a tremendous…" *I Declare*
p.31 "Nice wicket that…" *Beating the Bat*

ONE
p.35 "defray the cost" *Kent committee minutes*
p.43 "both highly disappointing…" *Boot Boy to President*
p.44 "both prepared…" *M.C.C.*
p.49 "I may be overstating…" *M.C.C.*
p.50 "What a tragedy…" *M.C.C.*
p.51 "the most incredible…" *Beating the Bat*
p.52 "the stuff of legend… must rank alongside…" *Boot Boy to President*

p.53 "It says a lot…" *Beating the Bat*

p.54 "awkward, unpleasant…An example occurred…" *M.C.C.*

p.54 "a fourth division club…" *M.C.C.*

p.54 "Several of our players…" *M.C.C.*

p.56 "I don't think Brian…" *I Declare*

p.59 "Despite our previous success…" *Boot Boy to President*

p.59 "a personal disaster…" *Pirate and Rebel?*

p.60 "potentially the best…" *It's Knott Cricket*

p.60 "the nicest man…" *Boot Boy to President*

p.61 "His ability to communicate…" *Pirate and Rebel?*

TWO

p.66 "one of the most nervous…" *Beating the Bat*

p.66 "so distraught that…" *Boot Boy to President*

p.71 "A successful club…" *Beating the Bat*

p.71 "We realised that…" *I Declare*

p.74 "He talked of the kudos…I shall never forget…" *Pirate and Rebel?*

p.75 "tense and unfriendly…The ill-feeling…" *Pirate and Rebel?*

p.77 "I wanted another 24 hours…" *I Declare*

p.79 "sackings of successful…" *from conversation with Mike Denness*

p.81 "aloof, stand-offish…This confirmed to me…" *I Declare*

p.83 "He was the best…" *Pirate and Rebel?*

p.88 "was an all-rounder…" *Boot Boy to President*

THREE

p.88 "Everything he did…" *Pirate and Rebel?*

p.95 "They wanted…The one person… that when I signed…" *Pirate and Rebel?*

p.99 "it was a complete nonsense" *Pirate and Rebel?*

p.100 "I went off and worked…" *It's Knott Cricket*

p.103 "perverse…I found I was living…" *Deadly Down Under*

FOUR

p.108 "Butcher lunged…" *Pirate and Rebel?*

p.110 "harshly and wrongly treated" *Pirate and Rebel?*

p.112 "He had a very good cricket brain" *It's Knott Cricket*

FIVE

p.130 "I could murder…He and his moustache…" *Good Enough?*

p.131 "Having dried up ..." *Good Enough?*
p.133 "He played an unforgettable ..." *Good Enough?*
p.134 "He has kept to me ..." *Beating the Bat*

SIX

Between Peter Richardson's arrival from Worcestershire in 1959 and Dean Headley's signing for the 1993 season, the following England-qualified players left Kent to join other counties: Roger Prideaux (Northants 1962), Dave Halfyard (Notts 1968), John Dye (Northants 1972), Mike Denness (Essex 1977), Richard Elms (Hampshire 1977), James Graham-Brown (Derbyshire 1977), Grahame Clinton (Surrey 1979), Paul Downton (Middlesex 1980), Nick Kemp (Middlesex 1982), Charles Rowe (Glamorgan 1982), John Shepherd (Gloucs 1982), Laurie Potter (Leics 1986), Stuart Waterton (Northants 1986), Lindsay Wood (Derbyshire 1986), Graham Dilley (Worcs 1987), Steve Goldsmith (Derbyshire 1988), Kevin Jarvis (Gloucs 1988), Chris Tavaré (Somerset 1989), Paul Farbrace (Middlesex 1990), Chris Cowdrey (Glamorgan 1992), Mark Dobson (Glamorgan 1992), Simon Hinks (Gloucs 1992), Vince Wells (Leics 1992).

Danny Kelleher left in 1991 to join Surrey, but never played for them, and Headley's arrival coincided with Graham Kersey's departure to Surrey. NB: Dave Halfyard was out of first-class cricket for three years after leaving Kent.

NINE
p.239 "expensive circus" *On and off the Field*

Bibliography

The following books were consulted:

Arrowsmith, R. L., *A History of County Cricket: Kent*, Arthur Barker, 1971

Briggs, Paddy, *John Shepherd: The Loyal Cavalier*, ACS Publications, 2009

Cowdrey, Christopher and Smith, Jonathan, *Good Enough?*, Pelham Books, 1986

Cowdrey, Colin, *M.C.C: The Autobiography of a Cricketer*, Hodder and Stoughton, 1976

Denness, Mike; *I Declare*, Arthur Barker, 1977

Fowle, Dennis, *Kent: The Glorious Years*, Kentfern, 1979

Fulton, David, *The Captains' Tales: Battle for the Ashes*, Mainstream, 2009

Hayes, Dean, *Cricket's Golden Cup: The Finals 1972-2002*, Sutton, 2003

Hill, Alan, *Les Ames*, Christopher Helm, 1990

Knott, Alan, *It's Knott Cricket*, Macmillan, 1985

Luckhurst, Brian, *Boot Boy to President*, KOS Media, 2004

Marsh, Steve, *The Gloves are Off*, West Ridge, 2001

Moore, Dudley, *The History of Kent County Cricket Club*, Guild Publishing, 1988

Pawson, Tony, *Runs and Catches, An Autobiography*, Faber and Faber, 1980

Rayvern Allen, David, *Jim. The Life of E. W. Swanton*, Aurum Press, 2004

Robertson, David, *A Legend Dies: The Story of a Tree with a Cricketing History*, 2006

Sandford, Christopher, *Godfrey Evans, A Biography*, Simon & Schuster, 1990

Smith, Ed, *On and off the Field*, Viking, 2004

Tennant, Ivo, *The Cowdreys*, Simon & Schuster, 1990

Underwood, Derek, *Beating the Bat, An Autobiography*, Stanley Paul, 1975

Underwood, Derek, *Deadly Down Under*, Arthur Barker, 1980

Waugh, Steve, *Out of My Comfort Zone: The Autobiography*, Michael Joseph, 2006

Woolley, Frank, *The King of Games*, Stanley Paul, 1936

Woolmer, Bob, *Pirate and Rebel? An Autobiography*, Arthur Barker, 1984

Also consulted were the *Wisden Cricketers' Almanack, Playfair Cricket Annual* and Kent CCC Annuals 1990-2009.

Index